With a Flash of His Sword

With a Flash of His Sword

The Writings of Major Holman S. Melcher
20th Maine Infantry

Edited By
William B. Styple

Belle Grove Publishing Co.

Copyright ©1994 by William B. Styple

All rights reserved

For information about permission to reproduce selections from this book, write to, Belle Grove Publishing Company, P.O. Box 483, Kearny, N.J. 07032.

Library of Congress Catalog Card Number 94-70662.

ISBN 1-883926-00-9

Printed in the United States of America

Front Cover: Holman S. Melcher
Back Cover: Officer's and wives of the Twentieth Maine Vols.
Reverse image of photo in Portrait Gallery, page 2.

Table of Contents

Introduction..vii
Chapter One...Page 1
Chapter Two...Page 17
Chapter Three...Page 36
Chapter Four..Page 144
Chapter Five..Page 158
Chapter Six...Page 186
Chapter Seven...Page 245
Appendix I..Page 294
Appendix II...Page 302
Picture Credits...Page 324
Bibliography..Page 325
Index...Page 328

Acknowledgments

I want to express my gratitude to the many friends and colleagues who made contributions both during the research and writing of this book. Thanks to the following:

Bob Crickenberger, who generously provided invaluable information on the 20th Maine; Jack Fitzpatrick, Bill Dekker, Bruce Jones, Jim Nevins, Larry Sangi, and John Moroz, who made available to me their libraries and sources.

Susan Ravdin at the Hawthorne/Longfellow Library, Bowdoin College, was helpful in making available the Holman S. Melcher letters.

The Pejepscot Hist. Society of Brunswick, Me., was a great resource of material. Thanks to Curator Julia C. Oehmig; and to Micheal Winey of the Army War College, Carlisle, Pa.

At Gettysburg National Military Park, Kathleen Georg Harrison and Scott Hartwig made available to me, the park library and collection. Gary Kross provided insight about the fight on Little Round Top.

Thanks to Abbott Spear, grandson of Gen. Ellis Spear, who permitted me to use many of the magnificent photographs that appear in this volume. I am also very grateful to Mr. and Mrs. Theodore Johnson. Mr. Johnson is the grandson of Holman S. Melcher, and his kind permission allowed me to utilize his grandfathers' papers. Henry Deeks and Bedford Hayes were generous in providing images from their collections.

I extend my thanks to: Nick Noyes of the Maine Historical Society, Portland; Jeffrey Brown, Maine State Archives, Augusta.

My colleague, Brian Pohanka was a continuous source of intellectual support throughout the compilation of this book. His belief in this project is greatly appreciated.

I extend my sincere thanks to Bill and Karen Mapes for offering their technical expertise and generous hospitality. Thanks to Buddy Kruk and Sonia Krutzke, who were of great help in reviewing the manuscript. Also, to Diana Stefan and Andrea Wilkerson, who helped prepare the manuscript.

And especially to my wife Nancy, for always believing in me and my work, thank you for everything.

INTRODUCTION

Ever since man began warring with his fellow man, rarely have individual recollections of a specific engagement agreed in the detail of events. Opinions of what happened during a battle differ not only between enemies, but also among friends and comrades.

The Battle of Gettysburg, through its estimated 150,000 surviving participants and countless historians, has spawned an incalculable number of books, articles, poems, paintings, songs, speeches, film epics, and prize-winning novels. Of all these, the last is perhaps the most damaging to the truth. In the novelization of history, artistic license is used freely. Dramatic and often romanticized passages are inserted by the author, and consequently fiction may be mistaken for fact. This problem is faced when one attempts to re-examine the truth of history.

It has been long believed, (regardless of the truth) that the legendary hero Colonel Joshua Lawrence Chamberlain led the charge of the Twentieth Maine Regiment down the rocky slope of Little Round Top. It makes an inspiring story. The college-professor-turned-soldier, uses a complex military tactic to win the day and save the Union. Unfortunately, novelization of the truth has perpetuated an injustice to the other gallant soldiers who surrounded Chamberlain that day. These others, though not as charismatic as Chamberlain and lacking his talent for rhetoric, were veterans of the same fight and should not be forgotten. These men of Maine had their own experience and deserve to have their story told.

Holman Staples Melcher was one of these heroic soldiers. As a young lieutenant, barely twenty-two years old, Melcher responded to the cries of his wounded comrades and led the advance down Little Round Top, not waiting for orders from Col. Chamberlain. Melcher's decisive action at Gettysburg was ultimately eclipsed over the years by more romantic figures. When Medals of Honor were awarded in the decades following the battle, Lt. Melcher's heroics went unrecognized, and there were some veterans who believed that others had received too much credit at the cost of the brave, but silent, dead. Holman Melcher never sought the recognition or fame that accompanies heroism, and it is his deed of valor that deserves the credit which is long overdue. This book intends to reveal the truth of what occurred on July 2, 1863, on a rocky hilltop south of Gettysburg.

Holman Staples Melcher was born in the village of Topsham, Sagadahoc County, Maine, on June 30, 1841, son of James H. and Nancy (Curtis) Melcher. Holman's father was a native of Brunswick, Maine; his mother, a daughter of Captain Nehemiah Curtis of Harpswell, Maine, whose ancestors first came to New England in 1632. Young Holman was reared on the family farm with his brother Nathaniel and sister Mary, about three miles from Topsham, where they attended the small district school. At age fifteen, Holman entered the Maine State Seminary (now Bates College) at Lewiston.

In the spring of 1861, the firing on Fort Sumter in Charleston harbor inflamed Americans with patriotic fervor and plunged the nation into Civil War. Holman had nearly completed his seminary studies and was teaching school in Harpswell when the call to the colors became irresistible to him. He enlisted on August 19, 1862, as a private in Company B, Twentieth Regiment Maine Volunteer Infantry. Nathaniel, at Holman's urging, decided against enlistment and enrolled in Bowdoin College. Before parting, the brothers had promised to faithfully write each other once a week.

Ten days after enlisting, Holman was mustered into the United States service with the rank of Corporal, and from that time he was in active service for nearly three years, participating in many of the great battles of the war, including Antietam, Fredericksburg, Gettysburg, the Wilderness, Spottsylvania, and Petersburg. While in the army, Holman's morale was sustained by letters from home and his faith in God. In Holman's correspondence to Nathaniel, he reflected the horrors of battle, and urged his brother not to come into the army.

During the battle of Fredericksburg on December 13, 1862, Melcher was promoted to Sergeant-Major "for meritorious conduct" by Colonel Adelbert Ames. On April 2, 1863, he was appointed First Lieutenant of Company F. At Gettysburg, his company and regiment performed brilliant service in holding Little Round Top for the Federal army. Lieutenant Melcher's service at Gettysburg was recognized by his commanding officer, Colonel Joshua Lawrence Chamberlain, who appointed him acting Adjutant of the regiment. Melcher served in this capacity until the reorganization of the army under General Ulysses S. Grant in March, 1864.

During the Battle of the Wilderness, Lieutenant Melcher led his small company of seventeen men through the blind struggle amid the thick forest until they found themselves completely surrounded by the enemy. In a desperate effort they escaped by fighting their way to freedom in the course of which they captured 30 Confederates. Three days later, during the Battle of Laurel Hill, Melcher was severely wounded by a gunshot in the right leg. He was taken by ambulance with the other wounded to Fredericksburg, where he occupied one of the hospital rooms established in the Mary Washington house. From Fredericksburg, Holman was sent to Armory Square hospital in Washington, and then finally home to Maine for convalescence.

Upon his return to the army in the fall of 1864, Captain Melcher served on the staff of Major-General G.K. Warren, Commander of the Fifth Corps. General Warren was relieved of his command on April 1, 1865 for misconduct at the Battle of Five Forks. Captain Melcher remained on the Corps Staff under Major-General Charles Griffin until the consolidation of the army in June, when he was appointed Inspector-General on the staff of Major-General Chamberlain, in which capacity he served until the army was mustered out in July, 1865. Holman Melcher was brevetted Major for "brave and meritorious services at Five Forks and Appomattox," the honor to date from April 9, 1865.

With the end of hostilities, Holman Melcher returned to Portland uncertain of his future course in life. Several partnerships in business led eventually to a highly successful mercantile career. One friend complemented Melcher by saying that he was, "Enterprising, liberal and progressive, yet careful and conservative in all his operations, always avoiding speculative ventures." Melcher soon became one of the most respected businessmen in Portland, and politics naturally followed.

In an open letter to the Portland Daily Advertiser, Melcher's old commander Joshua Chamberlain (possibly the most respected man in the State of Maine), recommended his comrade and friend for political office.

To the Editor of the Advertiser:

I want to propose a name for the Republican nomination for mayor--a name that needs no recommendation; a man with a record of splendid courage and endurance in the late war, from the beginning to the end; since the war an honorable, high-minded citizen and energetic business man, enjoying the confidence and respect of his fellow citizens of both parties. From this man no pledges need be or would be asked. All the years of his well-regulated life are pledges for his good conduct in any station. And his name is Holman S. Melcher.

C.

Holman Melcher was twice elected mayor of Portland. A short biography of Melcher that appeared in the volume, *Men of Progress, Leaders in Business and Professional Life in and of the State of Maine*, summed up the Mayor's term: "Mayor Melcher was an able, conscientious and painstaking executive, devoting a large part of his time to public business, and his administration was a clean and progressive one."

Veterans' affairs were among Melcher's principle concerns. Along with membership in the Grand Army of the Republic and the Loyal Legion, Major Melcher founded the Twentieth Maine Regiment Association and served continuously as its only president for 30 years. That Melcher held the respect of his old comrades is clear since he was invariably reelected as their leader at the annual reunions.

On June 10, 1868, Holman married Ellen M. McLellan, the daughter of George McLellan, a well-known Portland lawyer. Within a few short years Ellen died of consumption leaving no children. In 1874, Melcher was married a second time, to Alice E. Hart, daughter of Deacon Henry B. Hart, also of Portland. A daughter, Georgina Hill Melcher was born on May 26, 1876.

Still pained by his old wound, Holman Melcher suffered ill health in his later years. He eventually succumbed to Bright's Disease (kidney failure) on June 25, 1905 at age 63. His widow Alice, survived him by eighteen years. Brother Nathaniel had died in 1902.

The letters that Holman Melcher wrote during the Civil War fortunately were saved, and carefully preserved by his brother. These letters, along with his 1865 diary, provide a rare glimpse of the experiences of a dedicated soldier in one of the most famous regiments in the Union Army. Holman and Nathaniel kept a tally of each others' letters by numbering each one, and Holman was quick to criticize Nathaniel's failure to reply promptly. Without news from his family, Holman would sink into a depression common among the soldiers, who would easily weep at thoughts of "Home Sweet Home." For the homesick, a letter from home was often more precious than gold.

As typical of a Civil War soldier writing informally under uncomfortable conditions, Melcher frequently used abbreviations and sometimes left names incomplete. The editor has expanded these identifications, which are indicated in brackets. Punctuation has been added when necessary for clarity, and paragraphs were made consistent. Editorial comments appear in italics, and at the beginning of each chapter, there appears an editorial introduction.

Holman Melcher's letters are published with the permission of Sherrie Bergman, Librarian of Bowdoin College and Theodore and Bertha Johnson, descendents of H.S.M.

William B. Styple
Kearny, N.J.
March, 1994

At last in Dixie

CHAPTER ONE
1862:
AT LAST IN DIXIE

The men of the 20th Maine Volunteer Infantry left their home state in early September, 1862 and embarked for the theater of war in Virginia. Their proud flag was defended by Corporal Holman Melcher, who had earned an honored place in the color-guard of the regiment. During the Maryland Campaign, the 20th spent several days of hard marching, but were held in reserve during the fighting at Antietam. The following months were rigorous for the men, while being trained in military drill, and learning to become soldiers.

At the Battle of Fredericksburg on December 13, 1862, Corporal Melcher carried the regimental flag forward, through the terrific enemy fire, over the dead and wounded comrades of the previously unsuccessful assaults. Promoted by Col. Adelbert Ames to Sergeant-Major for bravery at Fredericksburg, Holman Melcher rose steadily through the ranks. He earned the respect and admiration of his superiors, eventually being commissioned 1st lieutenant of Company F (the color company) on April 2, 1863. Holman's modesty for his achievments is apparent in the letters written to his brother Nathaniel.

Camp Mason, Sept. 1st 1862

Dear Brother:

As you see, we yet remain here although we expected to go at 2 o'clock this A.M. but the order was countermanded last evening as there was no steamer to connect with the train at Boston. They intending for us to go to Fortress Monroe, probably to prepare for a southern expedition. Well I would like to see the old Fortress, and would enjoy the passage, if we have good accommodations, and am not "seasick" and I think I had rather go there at any rate than to Washington.

We have received all our equipments, which make quite a load when all packed. 1 Knapsack with straps to lash the blanket on the top. 1 Haversack, a bag on the left side in which to carry food. 1 Canteen. 1 Cartridge-box. 1 Cap-pouch. 1 Bayonet sheath, and a rifle (Enfield), neat they are too, and light.

We have a dress parade every night and morning now, but I have not drilled and since you were here before today, having been writing all the while. There was a great time last Friday and Saturday. Paying off. There were three payments and we all had to be reviewed before each payment.

I shall send my money to-day, which will reach you to-morrow or Wednesday. It will come by express. I would like for you to pay for my music lessons out of it before you pass it to father. I believe I have no other bills to be paid.

I shall send $85.00 which I hope will reach you safely. We shall probably leave tonight but perhaps not till the last of the week, "large bodies, like us, move slowly." I shall write again as soon as we get settled in our new home, which I want you to answer, and write often. Excuse this writing for the wind is shaking the tent so that it is very difficult to write at all.

Hoping you will enjoy your term at Bowdoin.

H.S. Melcher

Arlington Heights, Va
Sept. 10, 1862

Dear Brother:
Here we are at last in Dixie with the rebels. We marched here from Washington yesterday, a distance of 6 miles, heavily equipped, but it would not have been very hard if it had not been for the "sacred dust" of Virginia. I am well but I did not think I should be so well and hearty after pressing through our journey. We have been three nights without tents, since we disembarked at Washington, but we have had our rubber blankets so it was not so bad.

Our passage from Boston to Washington was a prosperous one certainly. Capt. Wilson said he never saw the sea so free from swells in all his voyages at sea. We were in sight of land till after we passed Nantucket, which was in the evening of the first days steaming and I was not at all sea-sick. The third day of our voyage brought us in sight of the shores of Virginia--low and sandy, with wood forests but a short distance back from the shore. Passed Fortress Monroe in the afternoon, and from there to Washington. We were continually meeting and passing vessels of all kinds, all of which got a good cheering, that displayed the Stars and Stripes. We passed the fleet of Gen. [Ambrose] Burnside, the black gunboats looking defiantly at all rebels that might dare to make their appearance.

I did not get a good view of the Mount Vernon estate, so hidden was it among the trees, but what I did see resembled the pictures perfectly, or rather the engravings.

Continued...

Bivouac in the field
Frederic City, Md. Sept. 14, 1862

Dear Brother:
Not having an opportunity to send what I had before written, I will add another leaf.

You see by the date that we have moved our head-quarters. We received orders to march here and accordingly took up the line of march at 7 A.M., Friday. Joined [Maj.-Gen. Daniel] Butterfield's brigade at Fort Concord, two miles ahead, crossed the aqueduct at Georgetown to Washington, then direct to this city. Our march was through beautiful country and on a fine road. We marched 18 miles the first day, 24 yesterday and about 12 today. We came on a forced march in order to intercept [Confederate Gen. Thomas] Stonewall Jackson, but we arrive too late to join in the affray. We find this city evacuated by the rebels, they being driven out by Gen. Burnside's Division, Friday after a sharp conflict. The battle-ground we passed as we came in. Dead horses lie in every direction, causing an unpleasant stench and beef-cattle partly devoured, the sesech not having a chance to savor their beef-steak! We shall probably have a chance at the business before to-morrow night as the roar of the artillery about 15 miles off is incessant, jarring the air.*

* *Battle of South Mountain.*

The Aqueduct Bridge at Georgetown.

The rebels have left their mark here in the way of cut telegraphs, and a splendid iron rail-road bridge blown up.

I stood the march much better than I expected, and I have warm friends in the camp and regt., those who are ready to assist me in time of need, even Lt. Col. Chamberlain took my blankets onto his horse this forenoon. We are encamped in the midst of [Maj.-Gen. Fitz John] Porter's army corps, which presents a lively spectacle, the different kinds of troops intermingling.

I will not write more as I am very tired, but I could not refrain from letting you know where I am.

Please write soon and often,
H.S. Melcher

Banks of the Potomac near Sharpsburg
Sept. 21st 1862

My Dear Brother:

I almost have a minute to write you again till I get one from you but perhaps you did not get mine so I will write you again. I sent one to you when we halted at Frederic City enclosing 50 cents for postage stamps as we have spoiled all ours on the march.

We are encamped here near the Potomac with the rest of Porter's [5th] Corps. Encamped I say, though we have not been in a tent since we left Portland. But we substituted our rubber blankets. Two of us tie them together, they being provided with eyelet holes, then draw them over a frame, they make a tent high enough to sit up in but not to stand, and with straw on the ground, and our woolen blankets we get along very well. We shall get our tents, which are at Arlington, when we know that we are to remain any time in a place. We are liable now to move at any moment, but know not when.

    The enemy are on the opposite side of the river, and it is said they are throwing up fortifications about four miles from the river. There is a balloon a few rods from us which ascends every day, it is kept inflated all the time and tied to the ground. Gen. Porter's head-quarters are quite near us. He occupies a brick house and is a noble looking man, quite spare in the face, looking quite careworn. We traveled in beautiful country on our march here from Washington, almost all the way on a paved road. As we ascended the Blue Ridge the sight was grand on reaching the summit, the valleys on either side lay spread out before us with the farm-houses scattered here and there with frequently a village. It was a sight I should have appreciated much if I had not been so tired, but all of this was darkened by war. Dead men (mostly rebels) and horses

Federal Observation Balloon

lying here and there, broken wagons and leveled fences, destroyed cornfields and gathered orchards. How badly we should feel if this were in our own state! May it be spared.

Do not send me any luxuries till we go into camp, although I should appreciate them much, but if we receive orders to march, I should loose all, as I could not carry it. I get along well as I expected, but by all means don't you enlist. If you are drafted, well...but do not enlist.

Truly,
H.S. Melcher

Headquarters 20th Maine Vols.
Oct. 23, 1862

My Dear Brother:

I gladly improve the evening in writing you. I have almost broken my promise in not writing every week, but the days are getting short, that after doing my own, and camp duty, drilling four hours per day, and dress-parade, there is but little time remaining.

Hearing the order read at dress-parade that an "impending movement" was at hand, and that our regiment would be likely to share in it- -as we were ordered to have three days rations ready in the morning and sixty rounds of cartridges. I went to the Sutler's as soon as it was over and got a candle, (cost only .05 cts.) so that I might improve the evening in writing you.

Yours of the 8th: was received with the greatest pleasure. It was so free and natural, that I seemed to be present with you while reading it. You can't know yet, how much I appreciate such a letter; it makes me feel, on reading it, just as though I had been home visiting.

As to ourselves, we remain as where I wrote before with nothing particular for excitement. I was to the 5th Mass. battery today, which is situated on a high hill between our encampment and the river. It overlooks the river with our line of pickets and sees three miles into Virginia. Their guns are six rifled Parrotts--12 pounders.

We got our tents, parade ground, etc. in pretty good shape for a temporary encampment. We are governed now by the brigade bugle and corps of drummers. Reveille now comes at six o'clock and the guard mounting comes at 7:00 o'clock A.M. and is really grand on those fine mornings. It consists of a regiment for picket and the brigade guard: their arms and equipments are all inspected by the proper officers, and have to be in the nicest order possible, not a particle of rust or dirt being allowed upon them in or outside.

I have now got so that I can take what pleasure there is in camp life: strong and hearty, with appetite enough to eat my rations even if there is a little dirt with it. The worst place of all in the world to be sick is in camp, and I am really thankful that I am well.

Our rations are good enough in quantity. We have good fresh beef every other day, pork the same. We are now almost deprived of apples; there were enough when we came here, but there are so many to eat them that they are now a costly luxury. Butter has also got to be 40 cts. per pound, where it was only 12 before we came. Milk is 10 cts. per quart, but I have to indulge in a little once a week, even if it is costly--(never weaned you know).

Guess I have written enough for once of such stuff as this. "brain rather unproductive" this evening.

Everything now indicates a grand move of the army stationed around here. We may go to-morrow, perhaps for not several days. But I do hope when we move, we shall accomplish much towards putting down the rebellion. I am ready to do my part towards it though it may be but little, and will trust in God for his help in the hour of battle. I know that I have the prayers of you all. Write soon and often.

I am ever truly yours,
H.S. Melcher

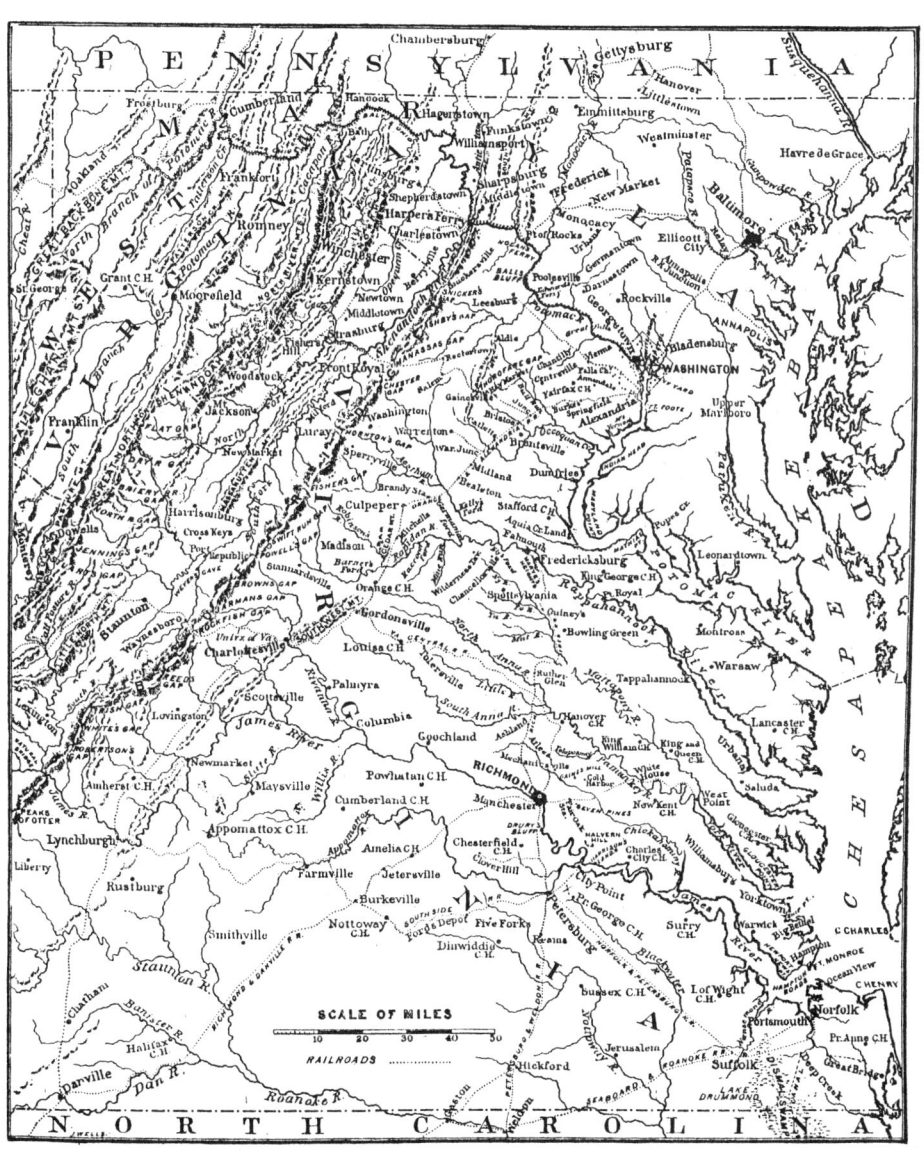

Theater of War in Virginia

Head Quarters 20th Me. Vols.
Falmouth, Va. Dec. 19th 1862

Dear Brother:

You are anxious to know if I am safe after the battle, and I will pen you these lines to let you know that I have passed through the conflict without a scratch. Although I am some tired and I should have written you the day after the battle but I was so much exhausted that I was unfitted to do it. I wrote home twice during the battle as I knew they would be anxious as to my fate when they learned that the battle was going on.

Oh! Brother: I should feel much better to write if the result of the struggle had only been different, but perhaps it might have been worse. We all feel the result and that Monday night as we evaluated our position and recrossed the river - sober faces and no others, would have been seen - (had it been light enough), although we all saw what would have to be the sacrifice necessary to take those batteries, which would have to be by storm as our batteries could find no commanding position. Thursday morning (11th) the Reveille awoke us from our slumbers at 3 1/2 o'clock which made us think that something was to be done. Which was confirmed by the booming of artillery at 5 o'clock in the direction of Fredericksburg. Which continued to increase till 9 o'clock, at which time it was almost a continual roar. From that time till night the firing was less rapid, only at short intervals when it would be very rapid.

Our brigade started for the scene of action at 5 1/2 o'clock in the morning and marched to within about 3/4 of a mile of the river. Where we were drawn up in solid columns, with the massed thousands on either hand, waiting the result of the bombardment. Thus we waited till night, when we were marched to a piece of woods, where we bivouacked for the night. The cannonading ceased about sunset. Although we had been near our batteries all day, we could see nothing of what was going on, on account of the smoke which obscured the whole scene from our view. Friday at 11 o'clock the bugle sounded the call to march; the morning was pleasant and enlivened by the massed bands of the troops who had been passing all the morning to cross the river. We marched but a short distance and halted in sight of the city, and batteries of both sides. But the smoke was so dense we could get only a slight view of them. In the afternoon a slight wind drove away the smoke and the enemy discovered our troops crossing into the city. The Rebels opened upon them with their whole line of batteries and was promptly replied to by ours on this side to the river. As I stood there and looked at those batteries through my glass as they belched forth their storm of shot and shell from their commanding position I could see in a moment what must be the sacrifice of life to take them, which must be by storm as they were too far off for our batteries on this side of the river to shell them effectually (and there was no eminence on which to plant batteries on the other side). Yet I felt ready to attempt it and I think nearly all of the 20th were also. Some did not realize how strong their position was. This kind of entertainment lasted about an hour when the rebels finding that they could not frighten our troops from crossing, and also a large number of our shells bursting in their works thought it well to stop. We again bivouacked for the night. And the next morning the battle opened in earnest. The volleys of musketry were truly terrific, (we could see from the hill on which we were) our troops charge up close to the enemies lines and pour in their volleys, and we longed to assist them in their work. This was granted us, for about noon we started for the field of strife, crossing over on the pontoon bridge. We marched through the lower end of the city on the "double quick" and formed in the line of battle just behind an old fence. But we were not sheltered from the enemy's fire for the balls and fragments of shells fell all around us and one wounded our bugler in the knee. I picked up a nice Springfield rifle and filled my pocket with caps and cartridges intending to do

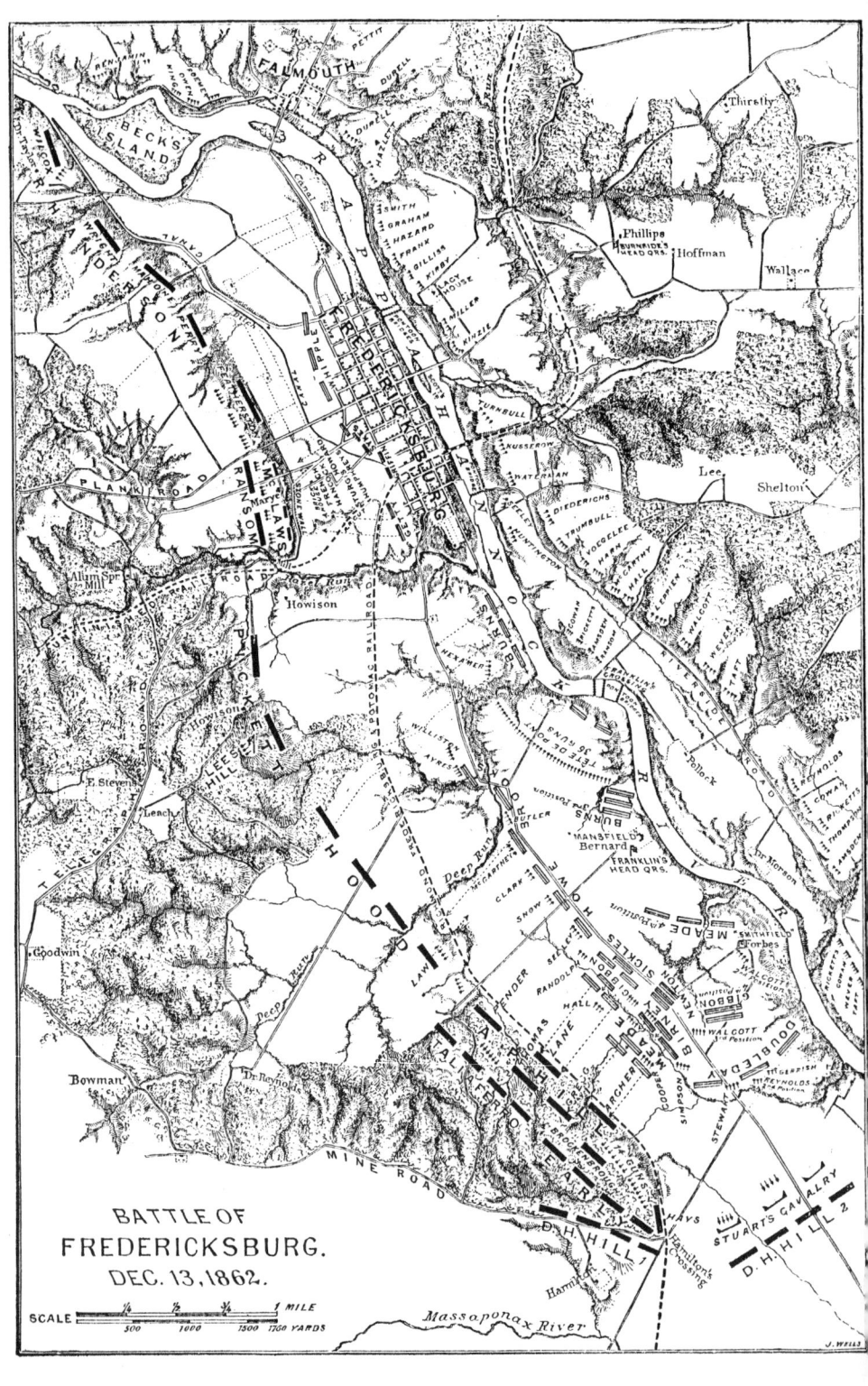

a little shooting but finding that I had enough to attend to besides. I had to leave it.

Soon the bugle sounded the advance, and our brigade moved forward with loaded rifles and fixed bayonets: our Colonel leading us on with drawn sword some twenty paces in front. For some reason the two regiments on our right did not advance with us, which left the right of our regiment exposed to a double fire from the front, and also a battery at the right, but by the prompt and efficient efforts of our brave Lieut. Col. Chamberlain, assisted by the Adjutant, the right wing advanced in good order. Our Major Gilmore, although suffering from old wounds, could be seen where his presence was most needed, cheering on the men. But it is useless to mention any one, for every officer and also the men seemed determined to do their whole duty and military men who witnessed the charge unite in saying it was the best they ever witnessed. We advanced across a level piece of ground fully exposed to the enemy's fire of artillery and musketry, of which they had yet a good range as proved by the way they burst their shells. None burst in our ranks but I looked around to see the result of some that came howling over our heads and saw three of them burst in the ranks of some troops that were advancing on our rear and left, throwing up great bodies of earth. The regiment charged to a ravine close to the rebel batteries and rifles, where it was ordered to halt and advance cautiously to the crest of the ridge, where the boys poured in their fire upon the enemy till darkness closed the scene of conflict. And after it was dark they fired, guided by the flashes of the fine musketry of the enemy. Three of our number were killed instantly being shot through the head and several wounded. After the firing had ceased, our pickets were sent out in front to keep watch while the tired men lay down upon their blankets, amongst the dead, many of which had to be moved to give the men a chance to lie down. Perhaps you think it could not have been a very sweet sleep, well perhaps not. I got some, but I must acknowledge it was far from being sweet, as some that I have had at home. But tired nature seeks the restorer.

After darkness had put a stop to the carnage, the Colonel called me to him and said, "Corporal Melcher, you are appointed Sergeant-Major on my staff, with a chance for promotion." I thanked him and returned to my post. The time, place, and by Whom, I received the appointment made it valuable to me.

Long before the light the men were up and prepared for the conflict, how severe it would be they know not. The firing commenced as soon as it was light but receiving orders from Headquarters "to hold the position and nothing more," the firing ceased; only enough to keep the rebels carefully crouched in their pits out of sight. We heard the thunder of [Maj.-Gen. William B.] Franklin's guns on our left and hoped he was flanking their position for we now saw what a sacrifice of life would be necessary to take them in front. Yet all were ready and had the order been given every man I think would have nobly advanced to the charge.

The ground over which the 20th Maine advanced at Fredericksburg.

The stone wall behind which the Confederates fought.

During the morning the enemy tried our position with one of his guns which was in position on a high hill far in the rear of the first lines. But after firing four shots which struck quite near us, ploughing great trenches in the ground. The last one only bursting, he gave it up. They were promptly replied to by our artillery in the city. One of our regiment was killed during the day: He was shot through the head standing at his post- a noble soldier of Co.B named [Seth D.] Woodard. Thus passed away the Christian Sabbath and what a way to spend this Holy day! After dark we were relieved and returned to the City- first burying our dead where we bivouacked in the street, but some of the companies occupied the vacant houses, my room was one formerly occupied by a rebel officer, every thing remaining in it. But my letter is getting too long. I will give you a description of our sojourn in the city of Fredericksburg some future time.

Monday night about 12 o'clock we were aroused and went out

to the front and relieved the troops occupying, but soon the order came to evacuate and recross the river. It was done in the best order. After coming to this side of the river we pitched our tents as it had commenced raining and rested till morning when we marched to our old campground, where we now are. How long we shall remain is to be seen, not "Winter quarters" I hope. The men following the example of their officers have logged up the sides of their tents and built fireplaces and chimneys on the end. In real southern style they made themselves quite comfortable. The weather is fine and travelling good.

Most truly yours,
H.S.Melcher

Nathaniel Melcher.
Brother of Holman S.

CHAPTER TWO
1862-63:
OVER THE NOBLE FALLEN

The beginning of the new year found Holman Melcher and the 20th Maine Volunteers in comfortable quarters in winter camp. Sickness soon would be the deadliest enemy the men would have to face.

Changes in the high command of the Army of the Potomac were frequent. In the first five months of his enlistment, Melcher would serve under three different commanding generals: George McClellen, Ambrose Burnside and Joseph Hooker. Instead of being disillusioned like some of the soldiers, Melcher became more determined to achieve victory and put his faith in God.

In camp near Falmouth, Va.
Jan. 17, 1863

My Dear Brother:

  As I have a few moments of leisure this evening, I will improve them in writing you. To-day finds us yet in our old camp, although we expected, till late last night, to be far away from here at sunrise this morning, as we had orders to march at 2 o'clock, but they were counter-manded late in the evening. I should have written you last evening, informing you of the fact, but was so busy packing up, I did not have time. We are now under orders to march to-morrow, but where we shall go, I do not know. I think we are to try and flank their position, as no wagons are to accompany us except Ambulances.* We start with four days rations in our haversacks, which makes quite a load, for anyone who is hearty as I am. Never weighed as much as I do now. (156 lbs.)

It seems almost too bad to leave our quarters just at the time for the rainy season. Yet I am ready and willing to do what I can. Oh! how much exposure I would endure if we could only do this which would bring this war to an honorable close. The army is in a good condition, and good spirits, I judge from what portions I see. But the spirits of the men would be greatly raised if we could only win a decided Victory. There are many in the army, as elsewhere, that talk as though all was lost, because we were repulsed at Fredericksburg. The people of the North, who have done so much to raise and support this army, and the world, are looking to see something done, that will fall heavily upon the head of Rebellion, by this army, and may they be satisfied. Oh! pray that the efforts about to be made may be crowned with success, if right, "God speed the right."

I dread the scenes of another bloody field. I dread the carnage that must be the result of the meeting of these two great armies, armed as they now are. I shrink from the ghastly wounds that will meet our vision as we rush on over the noble fallen. But do not think my courage has forsaken me, and I am growing faint hearted, no! no! I am firmly resolved that as long as I do stand, God help me, my whole duty as far as I know it, shall be done, and should I fall, may it be at my post, my face to the foe!

To-morrow is Sunday, but how much unlike the Sabbaths that I enjoyed at home. Pray that through all these cold and hardening scenes, which I am now passing, my heart may be kept warm with the love of Christ and the presence of the Holy Spirit.

Holman

* *This was to be know as "Burnside's Mud March."*

(No. 7)
In camp near Falmouth, Va.
Feb. 11, 1863

Dear Brother N:

The pattering of the rain upon my tent, and the quietness inside as I sit here alone is well calculated to make me thoughtful. And my imagination pictures scenes past, of home and dear friends left there. But as I cannot enjoy their society, I do the next best thing: from my bundle of precious letters, I take out your good No. 8, and again read it with much satisfaction, after many previous readings. And now I take my pen to acknowledge its receipt. I hope I have not forgotten my promise to write once a week, although I sometimes think you have; it seems so long between some of your letters.

I have not much news to chronicle as it is very quiet around here now. We have had no moves. We are stick-in-the-muds since my last. Although the troops of some of the other divisions are moving; where, you probably know better than me. We see the long trains pass our encampment--for Aquia Creek--laden with troops, and wonder how soon it will be our turn. But I infer from some orders that we have had, the 3rd & 5th army corps are to remain and hold present positions, (we are in the 5th Corps, 1st Division, 3rd Brigade), while the others go to new fields of operations. And I

Fredericksburg from the Falmouth heights.

really hope they will accomplish much; and that soon.

This army has done far too little this fall. We ought to have been in Richmond long ago. But perhaps it will bring some of the foolish politicians of the north to their senses, and make them willing to do the right thing. I am glad I am a believer in God and an Overruling Providence, for I should despair were I not.

But I believe when the people have suffered enough; have sacrificed enough of their sons and brothers upon the bloody plains of battle, to make them willing to do what is right, the war will close.

Why brother, you have no idea how much injury that ----- (can't do it justice by any adjective in our language) Herald, (N.Y.), is doing to the army. I have got so mad at it, that I won't buy or read one. Better never to see a paper. That is about all the newspapers that are sold here now. Sometimes the Baltimore Clipper and Philadelphia Inquirer are brought into camp, they are sound-hearted and patriotic.

Our regt. is having a real easy time now, for the first time since we left Portland. We have got all our tents arranged with bunks, fire-places etc., but it is very hard for us to get wood, as every stick is swept off for over a mile distant--(the country was thickly wooded when we got here). The wood is hauled for the officers and cookhouses, but the men have to carry what they consume in their tents. I get clear of backing up wood by my being in the present situation. Enjoying myself finely here, and hope I have the confidence of all the officers. Have been used first-rate by the Col. thus far, he is a very strict, stern man, but a noble officer, brave and decided. The men all having much better food now, potatoes, onions, soft-bread, flour, and tea, being issued with their other rations. The variety improving the sanitary condition of the regt. very much and improving the spirits of the soldiers as well, which is seen in their frequent games and where before they were quiet and lifeless.

I suppose you think we are a horrid dirty set of Gents. We are dirty enough, I will admit, but I would like to have you here a short time, to see the regt. now. It is surprising to see what a change has come over it since going into camp. When we first came out, say at Antietam, the men would let their hair and beard grow long. And clothes, face and hands dirty. Never think of blacking or oiling their shoes; but now, the men seem to take pride in having the brightest rifle, cleanest clothes, neatest equipments, blackest shoes, and best looking whiskers.

There are some exceptions to this. But those who have dirty faces and hands, the Col. puts under guard and has them walk before a sentry with a rail on their shoulder--a la--long shooter. It is quite amusing to see the crowd up the guard house after inspection, which occur once a week, each one armed with his rail walking the beat before the sentry of post 1. Some of them complain bitterly because they have to "lug poles" all day. But make up their minds, that it is better to wash their faces in future. It is really interesting to see the rivalry among the boys about getting onto the post at Head Quarters. They will come to the guard mounting, their boots just as highly polished as blacking and brush can make theirs. And their rifles and equipments in the best order possible. When the guard is inspected, the Adjutant orders the best looking ones to step forward one pace. Then from this number, after a careful inspection of their rifles, equipments, clothes, boots and general appearance, he selects four of the best looking for duty at H'd. Qt's. Three for guard and one for orderly--to carry orders etc. They think themselves highly honored if they can only get the situation, and they do not have to be on duty in the night either.

So much for the soldiers, the line officers go looking as they like, generally better than they would if home. The Field and staff officers wear starched or paper collars all the time, boots blacked etc. This is in camp, but on the march we have to do the best we can.

The men formerly have done their own washing of shirts etc., but one man is detailed from each company, for that purpose. Government furnishes an abundance of soap.

                Thank you for those postage stamps.
                                Holman

                                    Camp near Falmouth, Va.
                                          April 21, 1863.

Dear Brother N.

    Again with pleasure do I improve a few moments this evening in writing you, and you are probably astonished to see it dated at our old Camp. Well so am I, for I expected long before this time to be far away, but we seem to be destined to disappointment. Perhaps the future will be brighter, hope it will.

    This is the second time we have been stopped by rain. This time we had to stop for the mud to dry away, and while doing so, the enemy found what the plans were and so we must wait till new ones are made. I am not complaining of Providence, no, no!! only excusing our delay. I am aware that the world is looking to this army for deeds that will tell upon the rebellion. And the south too are gaining courage from our inactivity. But I hope the time is not far distant when this army will come forth from a contest crowned with victory in a great and glorious cause.

       But the North is expecting too much of us. They have confidence in Gen. [Joseph] Hooker and I trust it is not wrongly placed. Let them remember the material that he has to work with since [Maj.-Gen. Ambrose] Burnside fought. The 9th Corps de armie has been taken away. Many have been discharged for disability, and also are the two years and nine months men are soon to leave us. How soon a movement will be made, we do not know, but I should infer from orders read at Dress Parade to-night, that it would be soon, the men still have five days rations packed in their knapsacks. The most disagreeable of all, is we have got to remain here, and have a good time all to ourselves, having the Small Pox. There are some 80 or so cases sick now. Four have already died with it, one man from our company. You can see the impropriety of marching with other regiments, camping close to them while we are with this horrid disease, and then our men would be dropping all along the road and would certainly die for the want of care. Murder! Nothing more nor less, only a little indirectly. It is just what was intended by the villains that procured the "matter." It was probably done to cripple the army.

With our regiment in the condition that it was before this broke out, and in the hands of Col. Ames and Lt. Col. Chamberlain, we would have made a "mark" amongst the rebels. The Col. feels badly about it. It is very hard for one so ambitious to remain inactive at such a time as this. I think he will leave the regt. if he can get a position in the field. We now have four large Hospital tents filled with the sick from this disease, in the rear of our encampment, surrounded with a guard that allows no one to pass on penalty of his life. They are ordered to shoot every one that attempts to run the guard. If this had been instituted before, it would not have spread as it has.

If I should have it, I shall stop writing at the first symptoms, for fear of transmitting it to you, but don't stop yours, only write them oftener and give me that comfort during the "siege." If my letters stop, you may know the cause. I have written of the disease to no other person, and I hope you will not let them know it at home.

Lieut. [Weston H.] Keene returned today bringing the gloves, (3 pairs) and gave me a proper receipt of $9 from your hand. I am greatly obliged to you for your kindness. It is certainly a great accommodation to me, for it saved the danger of transmitting the money to me by mail, and the gloves I could not get here. I wore one pair at Dress Parade to-night. I asked if "you looked poor." He replied, "He looks like a student." So I suppose you look about "as usual." But how am I ever going to know how you do look if you don't send me your Ambrotype.

I enjoy my present situation finely. I like Capt. [Samuel F.] Keene much thus far, and find my duties lighter than when I was Sergt. Major. Although I now have to do guard and picket duty which I did not before.

[Frederick W.] Lane got his commission as 2nd Lieut. yesterday, and he is just beside himself with joy. I never saw one more pleased in my life. Well I don't wonder, for he has done everything that he could since leaving Portland, that could help him get one. We prize everything by its cost. He would have obtained it sooner

Fredericksburg from the Federal position.

if he had taken a different course. George Royal in Co. K has been promoted to a corporal. He makes a good soldier, and I have had some good talks with him about Topsham, the inhabitants, "Fair Ones" etc., etc. He is a very neat, clean soldier which is quite an item. A man that won't keep clean stands no chance at all. Now don't forget to write. If I stop write much oftener. Give my love to all the family and compliments to inquiring friends. There are no inquiring Darlings, probably, so I will not send my love to them.

Yours,
Holman

May 9, 1863

My Dear Brother:
It will be useless for me to give any description of the battle, as it would take much more time than I have, and you will have it full in the papers. You can imagine the intensity of feeling with which I have watched the progress of the battle. The smoke of the artillery, the bursting of shells, the roar of musketry, and the shouts of the victors, were all in sight and hearing of me.*

I watched all the movements through my glass, till my eyes were going dim. Had it not been for the disgraceful, cowardly, break of the 11th Corps, I might have the great pleasure of writing you of a glorious..........but it is otherwise. The nation is getting severely chastised. I trembled when, the quiet of that beautiful Sabbath morning was broken by the tremendous discharges of artillery and volleys of musketry. All the brilliant achievements of Sunday were lost. Why will not our leaders know that God reigns? When will they learn wisdom?

The forces of the 6th Corps that had crossed below the city, extended its skirmishers and occupied the city Saturday night. The storming column led by the Sixth Maine, formed in the rear of the

*Melcher witnessed the 2nd Battle of Fredericksburg on May 3, 1863.

city and under cover of our batteries, which poured in shell upon the enemy with deadly precision. They advanced upon the enemy works on the run and faltered not till the first line of batteries was carried and the Stars and Stripes planted upon the heights. Such a shout arose from the witnessing thousands, was never before heard as they saw the dear old flag unfurled where the hateful rag had waved so long.

   The enemy had to leave so suddenly that they did not have time to spike their pieces, which were turned upon them. The column was reformed and again pressed on carrying tier after tier of batteries, the rebels running like sheep before the charge. The Sixth Maine lost its Major [Joel A. Haycock], and 3 captains shot dead. Capt. [Sewell C.] Gray, (of the Seminary) was shot through the breast at the battery. Poor fellow! his military career is ended. He was a brave officer. He got married when at home last winter.

   Our victorious men pursued the enemy too far, and were overpowered by the superior numbers of the enemy. [Maj.-Gen. John] Sedgwick was too ambitious. He held his position till Monday night, but seeing that the enemy were trying to surround him, he began to fall back, recrossing the river at Bank's Ford, just above the city.

   The failure of the right is all traced to the 11th Corps. Everything was going fine, till they ran.* Gen. Hooker had to fall back a short distance. He then took a stand and the enemy never could have driven him out. Tuesday afternoon, one of the severest tornadoes came in that I ever witnessed, and it rained and hailed, filled up the rifle pits with water, and so swelled the river. The mud was deep and it was almost impossible to transport supplies to the army, so Hooker recrossed Wednesday morning unmolested, and reported back to the old camps. It was raining and cold, which made it very disagreeable to many. Added to this, the feeling of not having accomplished their object, made them pretty blue.

   The loss of officers has been heavy, as well as the men. Our

---

*Gen. O.O. Howard's 11th Corps was routed by Confederate Gen. Stonewall Jackson's flank attack near Chancellorsville.

noble Gen. [Hiram] Berry fell, shot through the breast. [Maj.-Gen. O.O.] Howard was again wounded. Gen'l. [Amiel W.] Whipple died in his country's defence.

    We are now under marching orders and perhaps before this reaches you, another struggle will have taken place. Your last letter came to hand last night and was gladly received. I could not think the reason you neglected writing me so long a time. If you knew how much I missed your weekly letters, you would not omit writing me.

    I am rejoiced to hear of the good health of you and the family, and it is my daily prayer that God will protect and bless you. It gives me much strength and courage to have you write as you do about affairs and I wish every soldier could have such letters as I receive. Your name shall never be disgraced by my sword, as long as I have my present will.

I am yours most affectionately,
Holman

Aquia Creek, Va. May 21, 1863

My Dear Brother:

    I will inform the movements in writing you, that I find not immediately occupied. I have been very busy for the past week. Col. Ames was ordered by Gen. Hooker to come here and straighten out affairs which had got into a complicated state, by the inefficiency of the commanding officer of the post. The regt. was out on Picket, and I was just going to relieve the line, when I received a note ordering me to report to Col. Ames in person, in camp, immediately. So off I went, leaving my company in charge of the sergeant. He told me I was to go with him, and to be ready for the 8 o'clock train in the morning. On arriving here we found much disorder and I have worked hard, for a soldier.

The 8th U.S. Infantry is here doing the guard duty in the place. They are much better than volunteers, for such a place as this, being more stern and decided. There is a great amount of business done here. Boats continually arriving, laden with supplies for the army. All of which have to be examined to see if there is no whiskey on board, or contraband articles. Long trains of cars are going and coming, all the time, night and day.

Much more labor is added to this place now there being so many regiments going home. It takes much care to keep some of these unprincipled fellows from getting off with them. Yesterday the old 2nd Maine went, all but a handful of them. The 2nd are noble men, men that have fought for their country's rights in every battle from the 1st Bull Run till the 2nd Fredericksburg. I was there when they embarked.

What a blunder was the raising of the 9 months men!* It looks like the greatest that the administration has committed during the war.

There are three forts in this command in the rear of the creek to resist an attack from the enemy. I went up with the Colonel yesterday to inspect them, and having a good saddle horse made it very pleasant.

I am getting many useful "ideas," for my military benefit, by going with the Colonel, who is a perfect soldier. Then having intercourse with the regular officers.

The Colonel to-day received his appointment as Brigadier General, and is to take command of a brigade in the 11th Corps. Soon I shall go back to my regiment. I am very glad he has got his "star," for I think he is in every way worthy of it. He is as "brave as a lion." He got much honor at the last battle, being where he could show his steel. Gen. Howard is doing all he can to get him into his corps.(11th) He will probably succeed, but I wish we could have him in our corps. I was to go to Washington to-day with the Colonel in the Mail Steamer, but he gave it up on the receipt of his

*Term of enlistment.

appointment.

    We are having beautiful weather now, quite warm but not oppressive. Oh! what a pity it is that we could not be improving this splendid weather; but here we are, weakened so much by the leaving of the 2 years and 9 months men. That to move upon the enemy would be perfect folly, unless they should withdraw some of their forces from Fredericksburg.

    I thank you for your kind invitation to me to visit "home." If I am with the regt. and the army does not move, perhaps I can make a visit to Maine. It would certainly be a happy time to me, but I don't feel as though I had any right to be at home when my regt. is in the field, even if the commander of the army will grant me a leave of absence.

    Pray for me, Brother, that I may have grace to overcome all the temptations by which I am surrounded. I thank God that I have been able to overcome the temptations thus far.

Affectionately yours,
Holman

Camp 20th Maine Vols.
Ellis's Ford
June 6, 1863

Dear Brother N.

    We are having a taste of a soldier's life just now. We were at U.S. Ford when I last wrote you if I remember correctly.

    We have had so much changing about of late, that I have almost lost my reckoning of letters and time. We remained at the ford doing picket duty till Thursday the 4th, and then received orders to march, and down came the tents which we had got so nicely arranged and off we started up the river on the Warrenton road, bivouacked for the night in a beautiful grass field, and early in the morning came to our present camp distant from U.S. Ford about 14 miles. Are now encamped in a beautiful oak woods on dry ground and good water near, about a quarter of a mile from the river. One other regt. in our brigade is with us, while the other two are back about a mile to render any assistance we may need.

We relieved the 2nd Brigade who had dug all the rifle pits needed, so that we have nothing to do but picket along the river. There is no body of the enemy to be seen from here. Their picket line extends along the other bank of the river--their old gray clothes giving them as much the appearance of an old sand bag as anything. They have not offered to fire upon us, but they let fly a volley of musketry and a round of canister at the 2nd Brigade when they saw them throwing up entrenchments, but immediately a battery of our Parrots showed themselves looking over the crest of the hill behind which they had been concealed and on seeing this the enemy stopped their nonsense promptly.

This is a pretty tract of country where we are now, although quite sparsely inhabited. There has never been any body of soldiers here any length of time before, so that it does not have that look of desolation that about all the rest of Virginia does, over which I have been. The grain is now in bloom but all the I have seen is very thin and short, what we should call in Maine a poor piece of grain. I have never asked the inhabitants what they call it here. I have not seen any corn yet over two inches tall, but I don't wonder for their manner of cultivation is ruinous in the extreme. There is a gold mine near this ford and quite extensive works for the operation of the mines. There are three mines in this vicinity. I think two of which we have passed, the Eagle mines at U.S. Ford, this one here, and I am told there is another just above here.

The movements of both armies are very perplexing now. I suppose Gen. Hooker knows what he is about and where all the army is going, but all I know about is what our regt. is doing. All matters of rumors reach our ears--a telegraph announces the fall of Vicksburg, another that we are falling back upon Alexandria via the Alexandria and Orange R.R., and another that we are to advance on Richmond via Culpepper-Gordonsville etc. But there is one rumor we distinctly hear, and it is the thunder of cannon at Fredericksburg below, and Beal's Station above us, fighting on both sides of us, and we are under marching orders, but do not know which way we shall go yet. We are expecting to march to-night. We have it reported to us that the 6th Corps has again taken possession of Fredericksburg, and the heights, but as no papers have reached us since we began to move, we cannot learn anything definite.

I received your kind but very short letter by the due course of the mail, and also the $10 from Father, for which I have receipted to him. I guess you think at home that I am very extravagant. It does cost much more to live here than in Maine, for we have to buy all of our butter, eggs, cheese, and all the luxuries from the sutler who charges a large price for his goods. Butter 60 cts., cheese 40 cts., eggs 50 cts. per doz. All our provisions, such as flour, pork, beef, sugar, tea etc., we get at the commissary of the brigade, and have to pay a fair price.

While at the Creek with Gen. Ames, I dined with him and shared the expenses, which were much more than in camp. My board there was over $1.00 per day, but being on the Gen's staff, I had to pay all of his expenses also. He has not paid me yet and I do not know how soon he will, but I think I shall get along well enough.

Perhaps you think it takes much money for whiskey. It does with many of the officers, who drink because they like it and also popularity--Those without the courage to decline an invitation to drink. Fools. When I can't have a decent standing without any whiskey, I should then come home.

Pray brother that strength be given me to triumph over all temptations.

Affectionately,
H.S. Melcher

(No. 21)
Camp at Ellis Ford, Va.
June 12, 1863

My Dear Brother:

After having my letter (No. 20) that was written in such a fright, you may think that there was some cause for fearing the Rebel bullets: and so to allay any such, I will write you this evening. You have heard of all the news that has taken place at Fredericksburg, Bealton, Kelly's Ford, etc. so that it will be of no interest for me to repeat them...The firing at both places, we could plainly hear, but at the time knew nothing of what was going on, only by rumors of which we have had "any gravity" of late, but no hopes till last evening.

You probably thought by the tone of my last letter that I was just on the point of expiring from fear of the rebel guns behind the entrenchments on the other side of the river---yet I have survived. The enemy probably mistrusted something and hastily left, this saving the trouble of attacking them. So the next morning Col. [Strong] Vincent, our Brigade commander crossed with two companies of skirmishers from the 16th Mich., but could find no enemy and so returned. And as Gen. [Alfred] Pleasonton did not advance after the battle of Kelly's Ford, we did not here and so remain on this side of the river as before. The enemy make their appearance in small bodies now & then. Our duty here is very light, but it is rather dull, as we have no drills, no dress parades, no drum, no bugles, no "nothing hardly" that is military anymore. And I have no letters! Not one from home since I have been here, and only one from you! What do you mean? We have been under marching orders for a week past, but to-day are under special orders to be ready to march at a moments notice with only what we cannot get along without. I understand that all of the army, except the 2nd Corps, has gone up the river passing yesterday and to-day, and are massing near Warrenton, which would indicate another movement, some think we are to advance towards Gordonsville. At any rate, a few days will decide.

You see Gen. Ames mentioned in the last battle, in command of two brigades. He is a man that is to make his mark, if his life is spared. I would for many reasons like to be on his staff. 1st, I would like to learn his promptness and decision of character, and 2nd, it is rather more honor to be on a staff than equal rank in the regt.

Affectionately,
H.S. Melcher

On the march from
Edward's Ferry
June 27, 1863

Dear Brother:

   I have long neglected writing you, but for two weeks we have been where no mail came to or left us, so that it was of no use to write. Now that we are coming into the Free States--Oh, how Shameful! I will write hoping to get an opportunity of sending it. I wrote you last when at Manassas Junction, and I will give you a hasty sketch of our movements since. The 5th Corps came first to Gum Springs, 22 miles which we marched in one day, resting two days we went to Aldie 4 miles Sunday 21st. The 1st Div. started from camp at 3 o'clock in the morning in light marching order and passing through the Kittoctan [Catoctin] mountains at Aldie. March to Middleburg 6 miles and one mile beyond. Encountered the enemy behind a branch of Goose Creek, with their skirmishers advanced this side. Our batteries opened on them at 8 o'clock and immediately our brigade advanced in line, our skirmishers in front who kept up an incessant fire on the enemy. As soon as we came in sight the rebel batteries opened upon us with shell and more particularly on our Regt., it being the largest in the brigade. Most of the shelling went too high and burst in our rear, as we advanced so rapidly that they could not get the precise range. A shell burst directly over the heads of our company, knocking down one Corp. by the explosion, and severely wounding a Sergt. and Private in Lieut. [James H.] Nichol's company, the next to the right of us. A piece of the shell struck me on the leg above the knee, but it was not permitted to wound me for its force was taken away so that it did not cut through my pants, although it bruised my leg quite badly. I thought at the time that my leg was broken, but I soon was able to go ahead. Had it been going with a little more force I should have lost my leg. How thankful I am that it was not.

Our brigade advanced with such coolness and rapidity that it frightened the enemy and away they went before our lines got within rifle range. They made several stands but would not remain long enough to allow us to get near enough to open upon them with rifles. All this time our skirmishers ahead were bringing them down with precision of fire, and as we came along, here would be a private stretched dead upon the field or severely wounded, and there would be an officer suffering the penalty of fighting against a good government. At one place were five horses in a pile, the result of a shell. Our artillery did nobly, firing with the most precise precision. Thus we drove them back 6 miles till we got them beyond the many stone walls, and then Gen. [Alfred] Pleasonton took them in hand with his cavalry, where till this time had kept in our rear, and skirmishing on our flanks, and charging them. Driving them 6 miles farther through Upperville and up Ashby's Gap. I did not see the cavalry charge as our Regt. was behind the woods at the time. Those that witnessed it represented it as grand. We stopped here all night and the next morning returned to camp. I have not time to give you more than this hasty sketch of the battle now. It is called all a cavalry fight, as we were under the direction of Gen. Pleasonton. The 25th we were on picket and our company did duty on the estate of Ex Pres. Monroe, now owned by Maj. Fairfax, Inspector-Gen. on [Lt. Gen. James] Longstreet's staff. The mansion is beautiful, but shows neglect, and is in a state of decay. Yesterday we resumed the march from Aldie, first to Leesburg thence to Edward's Ferry, where we crossed the Potomac on pontoons. There are two bridges across at that place. Bivouaced last night about two miles this side. This morning we again started and have crossed the Monocacy where we are halting for some of the 12th Corps trains to pass over. We were to go to Frederick, but any movement will be wholly governed by those of the enemy.

We are now "In the Field" in the complete sense of the phrase. March all day, sleep on the ground without shelter for the night. A shelter tent is now quite a luxury. We have had no mail for over two weeks, no newspapers, nothing but rumor lets us know that the world is yet alive, except our immediate corps.

We can bear it all very well, for it is what we expected when we came with the army. But to be deprived of the mail, of letters from home, and Dear Ones, is almost more than a soldier can endure. Why I have not had a letter from home since May 26, and from you since the 1st of June--unendurable.

As to the present state of affairs I will not write my feelings, for you can imagine the disgust at the bungling blunders that have transferred the seat of war to our borders, that is now destroying the property of good citizens and that have caused these tedious marches that kill more men than the battle-field of the Rappahannock. Brother pray for me. Hoping for better days, I close asking you to write.

Sincerely,
H.

P.S.
Our beloved Col. Chamberlain is not able to command us owning to sickness, but he is on the recovery and we all hail the day he is able to resume his command of the regiment.

CHAPTER THREE
GETTYSBURG:
ONE WILD RUSH

The courage and discipline of the officers and men of the 20th Maine would be put to the supreme test on July 2, 1863. Their battle was waged on the sector of Little Round Top known as Vincent's Spur, near the town of Gettysburg, Pennsylvania. Though the regiment had been in service for ten months, this was their first experience in fighting the enemy at close quarters. Their conduct in that struggle would immortalize the 20th Maine, and their commander.

In a desperate moment during the battle, Lt. Melcher's courage prevailed. With his Captain disabled and fifty percent of his company killed or wounded, Melcher impetuously, and without orders, led the survivors of Company F forward to save their wounded comrades. This action would spur the entire regiment forward in an unstoppable charge that saved the fortunes of the Army of the Potomac. Holman Melcher sought no glory or laurels for his actions at Gettysburg. He considered what he did simply his duty.

More than 130 years have passed since Melcher's gallant act, and the historical record has become clouded. The participants who chronicled their experiences soon after the battle generally agreed in their recollections, but in the years following the war, the accounts naturally became more varied and contradictory. Personal memoirs are usually written near the end of one's life, and faded memories add to the fog of war. Official reports submitted immediately after the battle conflict with accounts written twenty years later, and differ still more from memoirs written at the turn of the century. As the years passed, it seemed no two veterans could agree upon what actually happened. Sadly, in some instances, life-long friendships ended over the controversy.

Col. William C. Oates, the commander of the 15th Alabama (the regiment that opposed the 20th Maine), would in later years write: "The truth of history can be vindicated only by bringing all the testimony before the impartial reader." This chapter brings together the written evidence that resulted from the fight for Little Round Top/Vincent's Spur. The accounts of over a dozen witnesses have been collected which form a different perspective of what took place on the afternoon of July 2nd. Also included in this chapter are the orations that were given at the dedication ceremony of the Twentieth Maine monument in 1889. When one re-examines the speeches and testimony, minus the colorful rhetoric of the 19th Century, a clearer picture emerges. Unfortunately, any letters written by Melcher during the first two weeks of July, have been lost.

Some years after the war, Melcher spoke to an assembly at which he discussed the battle of Gettysburg. A reporter who was present commented on Melcher's lecture, "With the modesty of a true soldier as to personal service rendered, his remarks were a tribute, feelingly expressed, to the valor of all who were in that great contest."

It was Gen. Joshua Lawrence Chamberlain, with his typical grace, who settled any difference of opinion that existed amongst his men when he spoke the words: "They are all right; no one of them is wrong." As far as Chamberlain was concerned, anyone who survived that awful battle was an honored veteran, entitled to his opinion.

PART I
Official Report of Col. Joshua Lawrence Chamberlain.

FIELD NEAR EMMITSBURG, July 6, 1863.

Sir: In compliance with the request of the colonel commanding the brigade, I have the honor to submit a somewhat detailed report of the operations of the Twentieth Regiment Maine Volunteers in the battle of Gettysburg, on the 2nd and 3rd instant.

Having acted as the advance guard, made necessary by the proximity of the enemy's cavalry, on the march of the day before, my command on reaching Hanover, Pa., just before sunset on that day, were much worn, and lost no time in getting ready for an expected bivouac. Rations were scarcely issued, and the men about preparing supper, when rumors that the enemy had been encountered that day near Gettysburg absorbed every other interest, and very soon orders came to march forthwith to Gettysburg.

My men moved out with a promptitude and spirit extraordinary, the cheers and welcome they received on the road adding to their enthusiasm. After an hour or two of sleep by the roadside just before daybreak, we reached the heights southeasterly of Gettysburg at about 7 a.m., July 2.

Massed at first with the rest of the division on the right of the road, we were moved several times farther toward the left. Although expecting every moment to be put into action and held strictly in line of battle, yet the men were able to take some rest and make the most of their rations.

Somewhere near 4 p.m. a sharp cannonade, at some distance to our left and front, was the signal for a sudden and rapid movement of our whole division in the direction of this firing, which grew warmer as we approached. Passing an open field in the hollow ground in which some of our batteries were going into position, our brigade reached the skirt of a piece of woods, in the farther edge of which there was a heavy musketry fire, and when about to go forward into line we received from Colonel Vincent, commanding the brigade, orders to move to the left at the double-quick, when we took a farm road crossing Plum Run in order to gain a rugged mountain spur called Granite Spur, or Little Round Top.

The enemy's artillery got range of our column as we were climbing the spur, and the crashing of the shells among the rocks and the tree tops made us move lively along the crest. One or two shells burst in our ranks. Passing to the southern slope of Little Round Top, Colonel Vincent indicated to me the ground my regiment was to occupy, informing me that this was the extreme left of our general line, and that a desperate attack was expected in order to turn that position, concluding by telling me I was to "hold that ground at all hazards." This was the last word I heard from him.

In order to commence by making my right firm, I formed my regiment on the right into line, giving such direction to the line as should best secure the advantage of the rough, rocky, and stragglingly wooded ground.

The line faced generally toward a more conspicuous eminence southwest of ours, which is known as Sugar Loaf, or Round Top. Between this and my position intervened a smooth and thinly wooded hollow. My line formed, I immediately detached Company B, Captain Morrill commanding, to extend from my left flank across this hollow as a line of skirmishers, with directions to act as occasion might dictate, to prevent a surprise on my exposed flank and rear.

The artillery fire on our position had meanwhile been

constant and heavy, but my formation was scarcely complete when the artillery was replaced by a vigorous infantry assault upon the center of our brigade to my right, but it very soon involved the right of my regiment and gradually extended along my entire front. The action was quite sharp and at close quarters.

In the midst of this, an officer from my center informed me that some important movement of the enemy was going on in his front, beyond that of the line with which we were engaged. Mounting a large rock, I was able to see a considerable body of the enemy moving by the flank in rear of their line engaged, and passing from the direction of the foot of Great Round Top through the valley toward the front of my left. The close engagement not allowing any change of front, I immediately stretched my regiment to the left, by taking intervals by the left flank, and at the same time "refusing" my left wing, so that is was nearly at right angles with my right, thus occupying about twice the extent of our ordinary front, some of the companies being brought into single rank when the nature of the ground gave sufficient strength or shelter. My officers and men understood my wishes so well that this movement was executed under fire, the right wing keeping up fire, without giving the enemy any occasion to seize or even to suspect their advantage. But we were not a moment too soon; the enemy's flanking column having gained their desired direction, burst upon my left, where they evidently had expected an unguarded flank, with great demonstration.

We opened a brisk fire at close range, which was so sudden and effective that they soon fell back among the rocks and low trees in the valley, only to burst forth again with a shout, and rapidly advanced, firing as they came. They pushed up to within a dozen yards of us before the terrible effectiveness of our fire compelled them to break and take shelter.

They renewed the assault on our whole front, and for an hour the fighting was severe. Squads of the enemy broke through our line in several places, and the fight was literally hand to hand. The edge of the fight rolled backward and forward like a wave. The dead and wounded were now in our front and then in our rear. Forced from our position, we desperately recovered it, and pushed the enemy down to the foot of the slope. The intervals of the struggle were seized to remove our wounded (and those of the enemy also), to gather ammunition from the cartridge-boxes of disabled friend or foe on the field, and even to secure better muskets than the Enfields, which we found did not stand service well. Rude shelters were thrown up of the loose rocks that covered the ground.

Captain Woodward, commanding the Eighty-third Pennsylvania Volunteers, on my right, gallantly maintaining his fight, judiciously and with hearty co-operation made his movements conform to my necessities, so that my right was at no time exposed to a flank attack.

The enemy seemed to have gathered all their energies for their final assault. We had gotten our thin line into as good a shape as possible, when a strong force emerged from the scrub wood in the valley, as well as I could judge, in two lines in *echelon* by the right, and, opening a heavy fire, the first line came on as if they meant to sweep everything before them. We opened on them as well as we could with our scanty ammunition snatched from the field.

It did not seem possible to withstand another shock like this now coming on. Our loss had been severe. One-half of my left wing had fallen, and a third of my regiment lay just behind us, dead or badly wounded. At this moment my anxiety was increased by a great roar of musketry in my rear, on the farther or northerly slope of Little Round Top, apparently on the flank of the regular brigade, which was in support of Hazlett's battery on the crest behind us. The bullets from this attack struck into my left rear, and I feared that the enemy might have nearly surrounded the Little Round Top, and only a desperate chance was left for us. My ammunition was soon exhausted. My men were firing their last shot and getting ready to "club" their muskets.

It was imperative to strike before we were struck by this overwhelming force in a hand-to-hand fight, which we could not probably have withstood or survived. At that crisis, I ordered the bayonet. The word was enough. It ran like fire along the line, from man to man, and rose into a shout, with which they sprang forward upon the enemy, now not 30 yards away. The effect was surprising; many of the enemy's first line threw down their arms and surrendered. An officer fired his pistol at my head with one hand, while he handed me his sword with the other. Holding fast by our right, and swinging forward our left, we made an extended "right wheel," before which the enemy's second line broke and fell back, fighting from tree to tree, many being captured, until we had swept the valley and cleared the front of nearly our entire brigade.

Meantime Captain Morrill with his skirmishers (sent out from my left flank, with some dozen or fifteen of the U. S. Sharpshooters who had put themselves under his direction, fell upon the enemy as they were breaking, and by his demonstrations, as well as his well-directed fire, added much to the effect of the charge.

Having thus cleared the valley and driven the enemy up the western slope of the Great Round Top, not wishing to press so far out as to hazard the ground I was to hold by

Col. Joshua Chamberlain, as depicted in Deeds of Valor, see Appendix I, page 294.

leaving it exposed to a sudden rush of the enemy, I succeeded (although with some effort to stop my men, who declared they were "on the road to Richmond") in getting the regiment into good order and resuming our original position.

Four hundred prisoners, including two field and several line officers, were sent to the rear. These were mainly from the Fifteenth and Forty-seventh Alabama Regiments, with some of the Fourth and Fifth Texas. One hundred and fifty of the enemy were found killed and wounded in our front.

At dusk, Colonel Rice informed me of the fall of Colonel Vincent, which had devolved the command of the brigade on him, and that Colonel Fisher had come up with a brigade to our support. These troops were massed in our rear. It was the understanding, as Colonel Rice informed me, that Colonel Fisher's brigade was to advance and seize the western slope of Great Round Top, where the enemy had shortly before been driven. But, after considerable delay, this intention for some reason was not carried into execution.

We were apprehensive that if the enemy were allowed to strengthen himself in that position, he would have a great advantage in renewing the attack on us at daylight or before. Colonel Rice then directed me to make the movement to seize that crest.

It was now 9 p.m. Without waiting to get ammunition, but trusting in part to the very circumstance of not exposing our movement or our small front by firing, and with bayonets fixed, the little handful of 200 men pressed up the mountain side in very extended order, as the steep and jagged surface of the ground compelled. We heard squads of the enemy falling back before us, and, when near the crest, we met a scattering and uncertain fire, which caused us the great loss of the gallant Lieutenant Linscott, who fell, mortally wounded. In the silent advance in the darkness we laid hold of 25 prisoners, among them a staff officer of General [E.M.] Law, commanding the brigade immediately opposed to us during the fight. Reaching the crest, and reconnoitering the ground, I placed the men in a strong position among the rocks, and informed Colonel Rice, requesting also ammunition and some support to our right, which was very near the enemy, their movements and words even being now distinctly heard by us.

Some confusion soon after resulted from the attempt of some regiment of Colonel Fisher's brigade to come to our support. They had found a wood road up the mountain, which brought them on my right flank, and also in proximity to the enemy, massed a little below. Hearing their approach, and thinking a movement from that quarter could only be from the enemy, I made disposition to receive them as such. In the confusion which attended the attempt to form them in support of my right, the enemy opened a brisk fire, which disconcerted my efforts to form them and disheartened the supports themselves, so that I saw no more of them that night.

Feeling somewhat insecure in this isolated position, I sent in for the Eighty-third Pennsylvania, which came speedily, followed by the Forty-fourth New York, and, having seen these well posted, I sent a strong picket to the front, with instructions to report to me every half hour during the night, and allowed the rest of my men to sleep on their arms.

At some time about midnight, two regiments of Colonel Fisher's brigade came up the mountain beyond my left, and took position near the summit; but as the enemy did not threaten from that direction, I made no effort to connect with them.

We went into the fight with 386, all told—358 guns.

Every pioneer and musician who could carry a musket went into the ranks. Even the sick and foot-sore, who could not keep up in the march, came up as soon as they could find their regiments, and took their places in line of battle, while it was battle, indeed. Some prisoners I had under guard, under sentence of court-martial, I was obliged to put into the fight, and they bore their part well, for which I shall recommend a commutation of their sentence.

The loss, so far as I can ascertain it, is 136—30 of whom were killed, and among the wounded are many mortally.

Captain Billings, Lieutenant Kendall, and Lieutenant Linscott are officers whose loss we deeply mourn—efficient soldiers, and pure and high-minded men.

In such an engagement there were many incidents of heroism and noble characters which should have place even in an official report; but, under present circumstances, I am unable to do justice to them. I will say of that regiment that the resolution, courage, and heroic fortitude which enabled us to withstand so formidable an attack have happily led to so conspicuous a result that they may safely trust to history to record their merits.

About noon on the 3rd of July, we were withdrawn, and formed on the right of the brigade, in the front edge of a piece of woods near the left center of our main line of battle, where we were held in readiness to support our troops, then receiving the severe attack of the afternoon of that day.

On the 4th, we made a reconnaissance to the front, to ascertain the movements of the enemy, but finding that they had retired, at least beyond Willoughby's Run, we returned to Little Round Top, where we buried our dead in the place where we had laid them during the fight, marking each grave by a head-board made of ammunition boxes, with each dead soldier's name cut upon it. We also buried 50 of the enemy's dead in front of our position of July 2. We then looked after our wounded, whom I had taken the responsibility of putting into the houses of citizens in the vicinity of Little Round Top, and, on the morning of the 5th, took up our march on the Emmitsburg road.

   I have the honor to be, your obedient servant,
   JOSHUA L. CHAMBERLAIN,
   Colonel, Commanding Twentieth Maine Volunteers.

Joshua Lawrence Chamberlain

PART II
Official Report of Capt. Walter G. Morrill.

Dear Colonel:

In compliance with orders from you to take my Co. "B," and cover your front and left flank at the time your Regiment went into position, I immediately deployed my men as skirmishers and moved to the front and left, ordering my men to connect on the right with the 16th Mich. Regt. Skirmishers.

Having advanced across the flat and just commenced to ascend Big Round Top, was somewhat surprised to hear heavy volleys of musketry in our rear, where we had just left the regiment.

The enemy having come in on our right and attacked the 20th Maine. I at once ordered my Co. to march by the left flank so as to uncover the enemy, and at the same time to guard against flank movement on the left. Having arrived on the field at the left of the woods, I found some twelve or fifteen [2nd] U.S. Sharpshooters under the command of a non-commissioned officer, and he asked leave to remain under my command during the battle. We took position behind a stone wall there. In the mean time, I sent some men to the left of us as flankers to guard against any attack in that quarter from the enemy. We remained in that position until the enemy made its appearance to the right of us and at the edge of the woods, and about the time your regiment charged them, at which time we opened fire on them, at the same time giving loud commands to charge, in order to have them think I had a large body of troops there. At which time they broke and run, going in the direction of Big Round Top. We immediately followed them part way up the hill until they began to stop and fire at us and having two men wounded and knowing my command could not expect to make much of a fight with them, I ordered my men to cover themselves the best they could. In which position we remained until nine o'clock P.M. at which time you ordered me to report to you with my Co. for duty with the Regt., which I did, having performed my duty to the best of my ability, and hoping the same was satisfactory to you.

>I am yours respectfully:
>Walter G. Morrill
>Capt. Co. "B" 20th Maine Vols.
>Keedysville, Md. July 8th, 1863.

Marker locating the position of Captain Morrill's Company B.

PART III
Gettysburg, The Battle on the Right.
by Col. William C. Oates.
Southern Historical Society Papers.

I have read with deep interest the historical articles contributed to the press within the last twelve months from different sections of the Union, but none of them have interested me so much as those on the Pennsylvania campaign and the battle of Gettysburg, because I have always regarded the battle as the turning point in the great struggle, "the war between the States" which culminated in the overthrow of the Confederacy. I am not a fatalist, nor a believer in destiny, and hence cannot say of Gettysburg, as Victor Hugo did of Waterloo, "that God passed over the battle field." I believe in responsibility for human conduct, and although the Federals greatly outnumbered the Confederates, yet the disparity was not so great as on many fields where the latter had been completely victorious. The army under Lee was never much stronger numerically, nor its condition better than at Gettysburg. The rank and file was never more confident of success.

I commanded one of the five Alabama infantry regiments of Brigadier-General [Evander] Law's brigade of [Maj.Gen. John B.] Hood's division, Longstreet's corps. As to when the division left Chambersburg, I don't pretend to know, for Law's brigade was on picket some three of four miles southeast of that town on the 1st day of July, when, in the afternoon, the cannonading of the engagement between portions of [Lieut.-Gen. Richard S.] Ewell's and [Lieut.-Gen. Ambrose P.] Hill's corps and the Federals under [Maj.-Gen. John F.] Reynolds, [Maj.-Gen. Oliver O.] Howard and [Maj.-Gen. Abner] Doubleday, near Gettysburg, was distinctly heard by us. About dark we received an order to be ready to move at any moment. Subsequently, we were ordered to cook rations and be ready to move at 4 o'clock A.M. When that hour came, the brigade was put in motion, and after a rapid and fatiguing march, it arrived on the field within sight of Gettysburg at about 2 o'clock P.M., having marched, as I now recollect, between twenty and twenty-five miles.

When we arrived, Generals Lee and Longstreet were together on an eminence in our front, and appeared to be inspecting, with field glasses, the positions of the Federals. We were allowed but a few minutes' rest, when the divisions of [Maj.-Gen. Lafayette] McLaws and Hood were moved in line by the right flank around to the south of the Federal position. There was a good deal of delay on the march, which was quite circuitous; I suppose, for the purpose of covering the movement from the enemy.

Finally, Hood marched across the rear of McLaws and went into line on the crest of a little ridge, with [Brig-Gen. Henry L.] Benning's brigade in rear of his center, constituting a second line --his battalion of artillery, sixteen pieces, in position on his left. McLaws then formed his division of four brigades in two lines of battle on Hood's left, and with sixteen pieces of artillery in position on McLaws' left.

This line was in the general direction of the Emmittsburg road and nearly parallel with it --the extreme right of Hood's line being directly opposite to the centre of the Round Top mountain. Law's brigade constituted the right of Hood's line, and was formed in single line as follows my regiment, the Fifteenth Alabama, in the centre; the Forty-fourth and Forty-eighth Alabama regiments to my right, and the Forty-seventh and Fourth Alabama regiments to my left. Thus formed, between three and four o'clock P.M., both battalions of artillery opened fire; the Federals replied. Then our whole line advanced in quick time, under the fire of our guns, through the valley which lay spread out before us at the foot of the range of mountains or hills, with a small muddy, meandering stream running through it near midway. The reports of some of the Federal and newspaper correspondents claim that our advance was in two lines or a double line of battle. I presume this was true as to McLaws' division and a portion of Hood's; but there was no line in rear of Law's brigade. There were no reliefs in its rear; if there were any, I never saw them at any time, and I am confident there were none. When crossing the little run we received the first fire from the Federal infantry, posted behind a stone fence near the foot of Round Top mountain. Our line did not halt, but pressing forward drove our enemy from the fence and up the side of the mountain.

Account of Wm. Ripley, 2nd U.S. Sharpshooters:

"That [Gen. Evander] Law's advance upon Round Top was so slow was in large part due to the sharpshooters, who fell back slowly from rock to rock, while the enemy to his surprise found his numbers diminishing steadily before an almost invisible skirmish line. But in time the riflemen were forced back to the northerly border of the defile, and were barely holding their own, when a Union regiment appeared on the eastern slope of the ridge and drove back the foremost of the intruders."*

*Taken from Vermont Riflemen in the War for the Union.

Just at this point General Law marched the Forty-fourth and Forty-eighth regiments by the left flank across my rear to the support of [Brig.-Gen. J.B.] Robertson's Texas brigade, which was said to have been hard pressed at that time and unable to advance further without reinforcements. This left my regiment on the extreme right flank of Lee's army, and as I advanced up the mountain side, my right was soon exposed to a flank fire from Federal skirmishers,

[2nd U.S. Sharpshooters] which I promptly met by deploying my right company at short distance. I continued to advance straight up the southern face of Round Top. My men had to climb up, catching to the bushes and crawling over the immense boulders, in the face of an incessant fire of their enemy, who kept falling back, taking shelter and firing down on us from behind the rocks and crags that covered the mountain side thicker than grave stones in a city cemetery. My men could not see their foe, and did not fire, except as one was seen here and there, running back from one boulder to another. In this manner I pressed forward until I reached the top and the highest point on top of Round Top. Just before reaching this point, the Federals in my front as suddenly disappeared from my sight as though commanded by a magician. From the top of the mountain a Federal soldier could not be seen, except a few wounded and dead ones on the ground over which we had advanced. Here I halted and permitted my men to lie down and rest. The Forty-seventh Alabama regiment was on my immediate left-- had kept in line with me during the ascent and halted in line with my regiment on Round Top. The Fourth Alabama was to the left of the Forty-seventh, and was not on the top, but on the side of Round Top, towards and perhaps as far as Vincent's Spur. During my halt, which continued less than ten minutes, from about Vincent Spur along the left and about the southern face of Little Round Top, the battle was raging furiously. I think not more than five minutes after I halted, Captain Terrell, A.A.G. to General Law, rode up and inquired why I had halted. I told him that the position I then occupied was, in my opinion, a very important one, and should be held by us. He informed me that the order was to press forward. I replied that some of my men, from heat and exhaustion, were fainting, and could fight a great deal better after a few minutes rest, and inquired for General Law. He then informed me that General Hood was wounded and that Law, who was the senior brigadier, was in command of the division, and was along the line somewhere to the left, and said that General Law's order was for me and Colonel Bulger to lose no time, but to press forward and drive the enemy before us as far as possible. To move then was against my judgment. I felt confident that General Law did not know my position, or he would not order me from it, and this was my reason for inquiring for him. I had not seen him nor any general officers after crossing the branch at the foot of the mountain, and am confident that no Confederate general nor staff officer, other than Captain Terrell, ascended Round Top at any time during the engagement. In fact, I saw no general officer until the morning of the 3d of July. But notwithstanding my conviction of the importance of holding Round Top and occupying it with artillery, which I endeavored to communicate to General Law through Captain Terrell, I considered it to be my duty to obey the order communicated to me by the latter, who was a trustworthy and gallant officer. I ordered my line forward, and passed to the left oblique entirely down the northern or northeastern side of Round Top without encountering any opposition whatever. After I had reached the level ground in rear of Vincent's Spur, in plain view of the Federal wagon trains, and within two hundred yards of an extensive park of Federal ordnance wagons, which satisfied me that I was then in the Federal rear, advancing rapidly, without any skirmishers in front, I saw no enemy until within forty or fifty steps of an irregular ledge of rocks--a splendid line of breastworks formed by nature, running about parallel with the front of the Forty-seventh Alabama and my two left companies, and then sloping back in front of my centre and right at an angle of about thirty-five degrees. Our foes, who had so suddenly and mysteriously disappeared from Round Top, had evidently fallen back to a second line behind this ledge, and now, unexpectedly to us, this double line poured into us the most destructive fire I ever saw. Our line halted, but did not break. As men fell their comrades closed the gap, returning the fire most spiritedly. I soon discovered that the left of the Forty-seventh

Alabama was disconnected--I do not know how far--from the right of the Fourth Alabama, and consequently the Forty-seventh was outflanked on its left, and its men were being mowed down like grain before the scythe. Just at this time Lieutenant-Colonel [Michael J.] Bulger, a most gallant old gentleman over sixty years of age, commanding the Forty-seventh Alabama, fell severely wounded, and soon afterwards his regiment, after behaving most gallantly and sustaining heavy losses, broke and in confusion retreated back up the mountain.

Just as the left of the Forty-seventh regiment was being driven back, I ordered my regiment to change direction to the left, swing around and drive the Federals from the ledge of rocks, partly for the purpose of enfilading their line and relieving the Forty-seventh. My men obeyed, and advanced about half way to the enemy position, but the fire was so destructive that my line wavered like man trying to walk against a strong wind, and then, slowly, doggedly, gave back a little. Then, with no one upon the right or left of me, my regiment exposed, while the enemy was still under cover to stand there and die was sheer folly; either to retreat or advance became a necessity. My Lieutenant-Colonel, J.B. Feagin, had lost his leg; the heroic Captain Ellison had fallen, while Captain Brainard, one of the bravest and best officers in the regiment leading his company forward, fell, exclaiming: "Oh God! that I could see my mother," and instantly expired. Lieutenant John A. Oates, my beloved brother was pierced through by eight bullets, and fell mortally wounded. Lieutenants Cody, Hill and Scoggin were killed, and Captain Bethune and several other officers were seriously wounded, while the hemorrhage of the ranks was appalling. I again ordered the advance, and knowing the officers and men of that gallant old regiment, I felt sure that they would follow their commander anywhere in the line of duty, though he led them to certain destruction. I passed through the column waving my sword, rushed forward to the ledge, and was promptly followed by my entire command in splendid style. We drove the Federals from their strong defensive position; five times they rallied and charged us-twice coming so near that some of my men had to use the bayonet- but vain was their effort. It was our time now to deal death and destruction to a gallant foe, and the account was speedily settled with a large balance in our favor; but this state of things was not long to continue. The long blue lines of Federal infantry were coming down on my right and closing in on my rear, while some dismounted cavalry were closing the only avenue of escape on my left, and had driven in my skirmishers. I sent my Sergeant-major with a message to Colonel Bowles, of the Fourth Alabama, to come to my relief. He returned and reported the enemy to be between us and the Fourth Alabama, and swarming up the mountain side. By this time, Federal reinforcements had completely enveloped my right. The lamented Captain Frank Park (who was afterwards killed at Knoxville) came and informed me that the Federals were closing in on our rear. I sent him to ascertain their numbers, and he soon returned, accompanied by Captain Hill (subsequently killed in front of Richmond), and reported that two regiments were coming up behind us, and just then I saw them halt behind a fence, from which they opened fire on us. At Balaklava, Captain Nolan's six hundred had "cannon to right of them, cannon to left of them, cannon in front of them that volleyed and thundered"; but at this moment the Fifteenth Alabama had infantry to the right of them, dismounted cavalry to the left of them, infantry in front of them and infantry in the rear of them. With a withering and deadly fire pouring in upon us from every direction, it seemed that the entire command was doomed to destruction. While one man was shot in the face, his right hand or left hand comrade was shot in the side or back. Some were struck simulta- neously with two or three balls from different directions. Captains Hill and Park suggested that I should order a retreat; but this seemed impracticable. My dead and wounded were then greater in number than those still on duty. Of 644 men and 42 officers, I had lost 343 and 19 officers. The dead literally covered the ground. The blood stood in puddles on the rocks. The ground was soaked with the blood of as brave men as ever fell on the red field of battle. I still hoped for reinforcements. It seemed impossible to retreat; I therefore replied to my captains: "Return to your companies; we will sell out as dearly as possible." Hill made no reply, but Park smiled pleasantly, gave me the military salute, and replied: "All right, sir." On reflection, however, a few moments later, I did order a retreat, but did not undertake to retire in order. I had the officers and men advised that when the signal was given every one should run in the direction from whence we came, and halt on the top of the mountain.

When the signal was given, we ran like a herd of wild cattle right through the line of dismounted cavalrymen. Some of my men as they ran through, seized three or four of the cavalrymen by the collar and carried them out prisoners. On the top of the mountain I made an attempt to halt and reform the regiment, but the men were helping wounded and disabled comrades, and scattered in the woods and amongst the rocks, so that it could not be done. This was just about sunset, and the fighting all along our line had pretty well ceased. At this time their were no Federals on Round Top. They never occupied the top of it until near dark. I was on foot, and in my exertions to reform my regiment on the top of the mountain I was so overcome with the heat and fatigue that I fainted, and was carried near to the point from which our advance commenced. It was now dark, and here we bivouacked for the night. After all had got up, I ordered the rolls of the companies to be called. When the battle commenced four hours previously, I had the strongest and finest regiment in Hood's division. Its effectives numbered nearly 700 hundred officers and men. Now 225 answered at roll call, and more than one-half of my officers had been left on the field. Some of my men that night voluntarily went back across the mountain, and in the darkness penetrated the Federal line for the purpose of removing some of our wounded. They reached the scene, and started out with some of the wounded officers, but were discovered and shot at by the Federal pickets, and had, in consequence, to leave the wounded, but succeeded in getting back to the regiment. These men reported to me that Round Top was even at that late hour, only occupied by a skirmish line.

By a survey of the field, made since the war by United States engineers, it has been demonstrated that Round Top is 116 feet higher than Little Round Top--the latter being 548 feet and the former 664 feet high, and only about 1000 yards distant from the latter, which is almost in a direct line from the summit of Round Top with Cemetery Ridge, which was occupied by the Federal line of battle: so that it is manifest that if General Longstreet had crowned Round Top with his artillery any time that afternoon, even though it had only been supported by the two Alabama regiments, who had possession of it until sunset, he would have won the battle.

Col. William C. Oates

Gettysburg

PART IV
The Left at Gettysburg by Gen. Ellis Spear.
From the National Tribune, June 12, 1913.

I think I may also mention without impropriety, as illustrating this point, the men of my own regiment, the 20th Me., with whom I had the honor to serve as Major in that battle. We came on the field in the afternoon of the second day, being in the Third Brigade of the First Division, Fifth Corps. The brigade, then under command of Strong Vincent, of glorious memory, Colonel of the 83d Pa., had been ordered into the Wheat Field and has passed the north end of Little Round Top, when a staff officer from [Gen. G.K.]Warren, then Cheif Engineer, brought [Col. Strong] Vincent word of the critical position at that point, where the right of [Gen. James] Longstreet had been discovered sweeping around and threatening to envelop that undefended hill, the key of the left.

There was no time to consult with the division commander, but Vincent, the true hero of Little Round Top (if any officer is to have that honor), then a young man of 27 years, took the responsibility and turned his brigade to the left and rear and formed it in Little Round Top. As first formed the line extended along the crest of the rocky ridge and the left was refused and faced the valley between the Tops and the northern slope of Big Round Top beyond. The 16th Mich. was at first on the extreme left and the 20th Me. next, but the 16th was taken away to fill a gap on the right, which gave the 20th Me. the extreme left. We had been in position perhaps not more than 20 minutes when the right of Longstreet appeared, advancing from the bushes at the foot of the woodcovered slope of the hill, extending, apparently, past our left. It seemed to have cut off our Company B (Capt. Morrill), which had been put out as skirmishers into the woods on the left, and had not made connections on its right.

Our refused line, bent further back from the center, occupied the rock slope, perhaps 20 feet higher than the thinly-wooded valley between the

Tops into which the solid line of the enemy was advancing upon us. On our right and beyond, the wood was thicker and extended to the left, so that the view on our left was quite cut off. Thus our line was approximately hook-shaped and faced to the left in part rearward, in relation to the main line on the ridge of Little Round Top, and the line of the enemy conformed thereto. They were lower down, among the trees and boulders, with the woody background of the hill behind them and the woods on their right and rear. Our line of colors, to the left especially, was among large boulders, heaviest near the center. I decribe the position thus particularly in order that the action of the regiment may be clear.

The fire on both sides was soon hot and men were falling. I walked to the center after a little. The color company and colorguard had suffered severely, and the men on the left of the colors had readjusted themselves among the rocks about the salient of the line, shortening and withdrawing a few feet rearward, but were holding firmly and firing rapidly.

I returned immediately to my place on the left, and almost immediately thereafter I heard a shout of "Forward!" on the right and progressing to the left, and, looking saw the center advancing. Wondering for an instant what this might mean (as I received no orders), the next impulse was that if any part of the regiment was charging all must, we all shouted "Forward!" and plunged down the hill into the enemy. Some of them, nearer, crouching behind the boulders, threw down their guns and we ran over them. The main body yeilding easily, as it seemed, ran among the trees behind them.

Then we discovered Morrill and Co. B. They had been behind a stone wall in rear of the enemy, and had been paying their respects to him in true backwoods fashion. They were all sharpshooters, Captain and all, and loved a gun.

The fight was over and we gathered the enemy in. Col. Oates, who commanded the Confederate regiment (afterwards a member of Congress from Alabama, a most delightful gentleman after the fighting was over), many years afterward told Capt. [Howard L.] Prince and myself that he became aware during the severity of the fight that he was fired on from the woods in his rear, thought himself surrounded, very naturally, and gave orders to his men to take care of themselves. They did the best they could, but we got the larger part.

But how did we happen to charge? I give the story as told by the men at the time and on the spot. It appeared that on the left of the colors there were men wounded by the earlier fire and left in front as the line readjusted itself among the rocks. They were calling upon their comrades to get them back out of the fire. Comrades will understand that that involved cessation of fire on the part of the men attempting it, and danger and disturbance to the line at a critical moment. But some enterprising and unduanted fellow said, "It's a damned shame to leave the boys there; let's advance and cover them." And those in the immediate vicinity joined the cry of "Forward!" Then the wounded would be in the rear and in reach of the stretch-bearers.

The shout was heard and the movement seen to right and left further than the explanation of the original purpose of the movement, and every comrade also will understand that those were good men who made that proposition and carried it out. To use the expressive slang of the present day, they were "on the job." They repected their officers, and they also had confidence in themselves and an interest in the business. They were of the kind of men whose temper hardens under blows. They had stood till their ranks were thinned 40 per cent (the color company lost over 50 per cent) and comrades lay dead at their feet, and they were mad and ready to strike hard.

It was rash, of course, thus to take the bits in their teeth and leave the line, but it turned out excellently, and helps to illustrate the common saying that "the battle of Gettysburg was fought by the men."

I do not mean to disparage the officers, high or low. They shared in the battle fully and honorably, regimental, brigade and division officers; some of them nobly led with success, due more largely than usual to the spirit of the enlisted men. Of course, also, the spirit and firmness and effectiveness of these men were based to a greater or less degree on their regiment specified had been fortunate in this respect. Its first Colonel, Adelbert Ames, though young, was a trained soldier, with the original instincts of a soldier, and his firm and made skillful discipine and instruction had made out of the original town-meeting enlisted men of the 20th Me. a regiment which was always ready to charge, and whose line, in three years of active service, from Antietam to Appomattox, never was broken. Ellis Spear, Colonel, 20th Me., and Brevet Brigadier-General, Washington, D.C.

Gettysburg 63

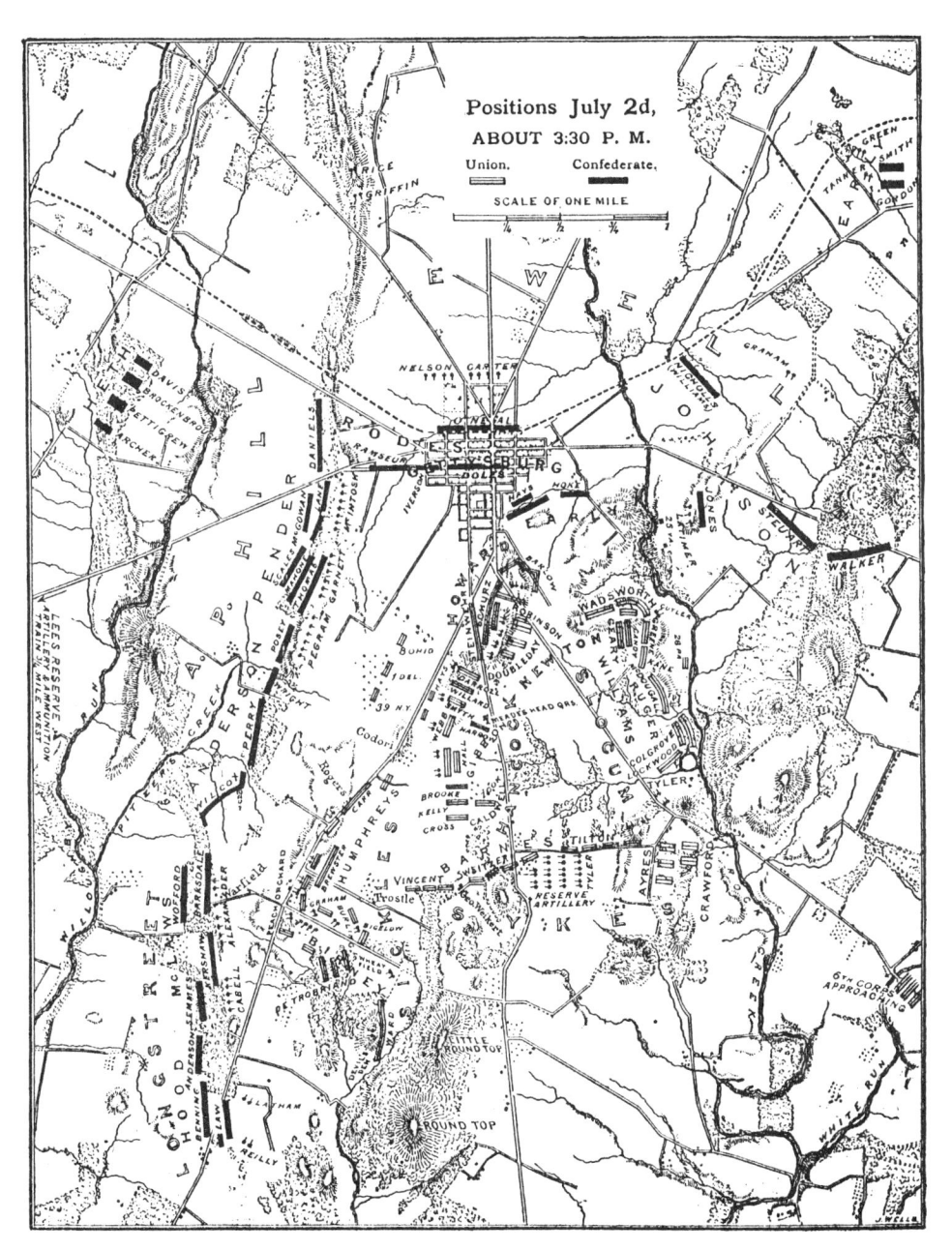

Gettysburg, July 2nd.

PART V

Account of Theodore Gerrish, Co. H, 20th Maine,
From the Portland Advertiser, March 13, 1882
and reponse of Capt. James Nichols.
From the Lincoln County News, April, 1882

The Twentieth Maine at Gettysburg
Lieutenant Melcher's Gallant Conduct.

At daylight on the morning of July 2nd we resumed our march, and in a few hours halted within supporting distance of the flank of our army, about a mile to the right of Little Round Top. The long forenoon passed away and to our surprise the enemy made no attack. This was very fortunate for our army, as it enabled our men to strengthen our lines of fortifications, and they also obtained a little rest, of which they were in great need. The rebels were also engaged in throwing up rude lines of defense, hurrying up reinforcements, and in discussing the line of action they should pursue—for, to use General Lee's own words in his report of the battle, they "unexpectedly found themselves confronted by the Federal army."

The hour of noon passed and the sun had measured nearly one-half the distance across the western sky before the assault was made. Then as suddenly as a bolt of fire flies from the storm cloud, a hundred pieces of rebel artillery open on our left flank—and under the thick canopy of screaming, hissing, bursting shells, Longstreet's corps was hurled upon the troops of General Sickles.

Instantly our commanders discerned the intention of General Lee. It was to turn and crush our left flank, as he had done at Chancellorsville. It was a terrible onslaught. The brave sons of the South never displayed more gallant courage than on that fatal afternoon of July 2nd. But brave Dan Sickles and the old third corps were equal to the emergency, and stood as immovable against the surging tides as blocks of granite.

But a new and appalling danger suddenly threatened the Union army. Little Round Top was the key to the entire position. Rebel batteries planted on that rocky bluff could shell any portion of our line at their pleasure. For some reason I know not why, no infantry had been placed to hold that all important position. A few batteries were there, but they had no support. Lee saw at a glance that Little Round Top was the prize for which the two armies were contending, and with skillful audacity he determined to wrest it from his opponent. And while the terrible charge was being made upon the line of General Sickles, Longstreet threw out a whole division, by extending his line to his right for the purpose of seizing the coveted prize.

The danger was at once seen by our officers, and our brigade was ordered forward to hold the hill against the assault of the enemy. In a moment all was excitement. Every soldier seemed to understand the situation, and to be inspired by its danger, "Fall in! Fall in! By the right flank! Double quick! March!" and away we went, under the terrible artillery fire.

It was a moment of thrilling interest. Shells were exploding on every side. Sickles's corps was enveloped in sheets of flame and looked like a vast window of fire. But so intense was the excitement that we hardly noticed these surroundings. Up the steep hillside we ran and reached the crest. "On the right, by file into line," was the command, and our regiment had assumed the position to which it had been assigned.

We were on the left of our brigade, and consequently on the extreme left of all our line of battle. The ground sloped to our front and left, and was sparsely covered with a growth of oak trees, which were too small to afford us any protection. Shells were crashing through the air above our heads, making so much noise that we could hardly hear the commands of our officers. The air was filled with fragments of exploding shells and splinters torn from mangled trees. But our men appeared to be as cool and deliberate in their movements as if they had been forming a line upon the parade ground in camp. Our regiment mustered about three hundred and fifty men.

Company B from Piscataquis county, commanded by the gallant Captain Morrill, was ordered to deploy in our front as skirmishers. They boldly advanced down the slope and disappeared from our view. Ten minutes have passed since we formed the line. The skirmishers must have advanced some thirty or forty rods through the rocks and trees, but we have seen no indications of the enemy. "But look! Look! Look!" exclaimed half a hundred men in our regiment at the same moment. And no wonder, for right in our front between us and our skirmishers, whom they must have captured, we see the lines of the enemy.

They have paid no attention to the rest of the brigade stationed on our right, but they are rushing on, determined to turn and crush the left of our line. Colonel Chamberlain with rare sagacity understood the movement they were making and bent back the left flank of our regiment until the line faced almost a right angle with the colors at the point, all these movements requiring a much less space of time than it requires for me to write of them.

How can I describe the scenes that followed? Imagine

if you can nine small companies of infantry numbering perhaps three hundred men, in the form of a right angle, on the extreme flank of an army of eighty thousand, against a force at least ten times their number, and who are desperately determined to succeed in the mission upon which they came. Stand firm ye boys from Maine, for not once in a century are men permitted to bear such responsibilities for freedom and justice, for God and humanity, as are now placed upon you!

The conflict opens. I know not who gave the first fire or which line received the first lead. I only know that the carnage began. Our regiment was mantled in fire and smoke. I wish that I could picture with my pen the awful details of that hour. How rapidly the cartridges were torn from the boxes and stuffed in the smoking muzzles of the guns. How the steel rammers clashed and clanged in the heated barrels. How the men's hands and faces grew grim and black with burning powder. How our little line baptized with fire, reeled to and fro as it advanced or was pressed back. How our officers bravely encouraged the men to hold on and recklessly exposed themselves to the enemy's fire. A terrible medley of cries, shouts, groans, cheers, prayers, curses, bursting shells, whizzing rifle bullets and clanging steel. And if that was all, my heart would not be so sad and heavy as I write. But the enemy was pouring a terrible fire upon us, his superior forces giving him a great advantage. Ten to one are fearful odds where men are contending for so great a prize. The air seemed to be alive with lead. The lines at times were so near each other that the hostile gun barrels almost touched each other. As the contest continued the rebels grew desperate that so insignificant a force should so long hold them in check.

At one time there was a brief lull in the carnage and our shattered line was closed up. But soon the contest raged again with renewed fierceness. The rebels had been reinforced and were now determined to sweep our regiment from the crest of Little Round Top.

Many of our companies have suffered fearfully. Look at company H for a moment. Charley my old tent mate, with a fatal wound in his breast staggered up to Captain [Joseph F.] Land. "My God, Sergeant Steele!" ejaculated the agonized captain as he saw the fate of his beloved sergeant. "I am going, captain," cried the noble fellow, and fell dead, weltering in his blood. Sergeant Lathrop, with his brave heart and gigantic frame, fell dying with a frightful wound. Sergeant Buck, reduced to the ranks at Stoneman's Switch, laid down to die and was promoted as his life ebbed away. Adams, Ireland, and Lamson, all heroes, are all lying dead at the feet of their comrades. Libby, French, Clifford, Hilt, Ham, Chesly, Morrison, West and Walker—are all severely wounded and nearly all disabled.

But there is no relief and the carnage goes on. Our line is pressed back so far that our dead are within the lines of the enemy. The pressure made by the superior weight of the enemy's line is severely felt. Our ammunition is nearly all gone. We are now using the cartridges from the boxes of our wounded comrades. A critical moment has arrived. We can remain as we are no longer.

We must advance or retreat. It must not be the latter, but how can it be the former? Colonel Chamberlain understands how it can be done. The order is given "Fix bayonets!" And the steel shanks of the bayonets rattle upon the rifle barrels—"Charge bayonet, charge!" Every man understood in a moment that the movement was our only salvation, but there is a limit to human endurance, and I do not dishonor those brave men when I write that for a brief moment the order was not obeyed, and the little line seemed to quail under the fearful fire that was being poured upon them. Oh, for some man reckless of life and all save his country's honor and safety, who would rush far out to the front, lead the way, and inspire the hearts of his exhausted comrades.

In that moment of supreme need the want was supplied. Lieutenant H. S. Melcher, an officer who had worked his way up from the ranks and was then in command of Company F, at that time the color company, saw the situation and did not hesitate, and for his gallant act deserves as much as any other man the honor of the victory on Round Top. With a cheer and a flash of his sword that sent an inspiration along the line, full ten paces to the front he sprang—ten paces—more than half the distance between the hostile lines. "Come on! Come on! Come on boys!" he shouts. The color sergeant and the brave color guard follow, and with one wild yell of anguish wrung from its tortured heart the regiment charged.

The rebels were confounded at the movement. We struck them with a fearful shock. They recoil, stagger, break and run, and like avenging demons our men pursue. The rebels rush toward a stone wall, but to our mutual surprise two scores of rifle barrels gleam over the rocks, and a murderous volley was poured in upon them at close quarters. A band of men leap over the wall and capture at least a hundred prisoners. Piscataquis has been heard from, and as usual it is a good report. This unlooked for reinforcement was company B, whom we supposed were all captured.

Our Colonel's commands were simply to hold the hill, and we did not follow the retreating rebels but a short distance. After dark an order came to advance and capture a hill in our front. Through the trees, among the rocks up the steep hillside we made our way, captured the position, and also a number of prisoners.

On the morning of July 3rd we were relieved by the Pennsylvania Reserves, and went back to the rear. Of our three hundred and fifty men, one hundred and thirty-five had been killed and wounded. We captured over three hundred prisoners, and a detachment sent out to bury the dead, found fifty dead rebels upon the ground where we had fought. Our regiment had won imperishable honor, and our gallant Colonel was to be known in history as the hero of "Little Round Top". We cared for our wounded as well as we could. There was but little we could do for them. Our dead were buried and their graves marked by the loving hands of their comrades. I supposed that their remains have since been removed to the national cemetery at Gettysburg. But somehow I wish they had been left where they fell, on the rugged brow of Round Top, amid the battle-scarred rocks which they baptized with their blood as they died.

> An Old Private.
> [Thoedore Gerrish]
> The Twentieth Maine Volunteers

An Officer of the Regiment criticizes the Rev. Mr. Gerrish's History as unjust to Company K. The following letter was written to the Lincoln County News.

Rev. Mr. Gerrish:

> Dear Sir:
> Having with considerable care read what you claim to

be a complete history of the 20th Regiment Maine Volunteers in the war of the Rebellion, I feel compelled as one of the thousand or more men comprising that regiment to enter my protest against your book being accepted as such.

As a work of fiction, or as a history of perhaps one or two companies, with the usual quota of officers, I have no particular fault to find, but as to its being considered a history of the regiment, I have very decided objections.

In writing this communication I want it to be distinctly understood that I disclaim any intention of detracting from the record of any company, or disparaging the individual efforts of any man or of any officer.

Without entering into any detailed statement of the many errors, more perhaps of omission than of commission, I propose to confine my objections to the important omissions relative to the history of Company K, with which I was connected, and because in the line of my duty with that company I was enabled better to judge of its operations than of those of any other company. Take as the first illustration the battlefield of Gettysburg, where the general good conduct of Company K should have entitled them to some kind of recognition in the book purporting to be a history of the regiment. When by the mistake, or misapprehension, of an order given by one of our acting field officers, the companies on our right wavered and broke to the rear, Company K held its ground, firm as the rocks on which it stood; not one foot or inch, or for one moment, did they waver or yield, but held their position, thereby rendering some considerable aid to the commanding officer who so gallantly rushed up and rallied them into line, and connected them with us.

Now you state in your history that when the order to

charge was given, there was a disposition on the part of the regiment to hesitate, and a reluctance to obey. This is an imputation of cowardice which I respectfully deny. It may have been true of that part of the line where you were, and of this I will admit you are better informed. If so, your company was not the first to advance, nor could your officers be the first to be in front in that portion of the line occupied by us. Your statement so far as it relates to Company K, is decidedly inaccurate. I say, and I know what I say to be true, that instead of any hesitation on the part of Co. K, and before the completion of the order, it was anticipated by them, and when the command "Charge" was given they were already on the move, and that with such a rush that the officer who could get in front of them must have been exceedingly alert in his movements.

Now, Reverend Sir, you may think this criticism severe, but when you consider that said company was raised largely by me, my townsmen and my neighbors, every one of them my friends--as brave a set of men as have ever been permitted to meet an enemy, manly, young and ardent in the cause, whose mothers, wives and sisters I promised should be protected as far as I was able to--you will see it was impossible to let this pass without a contradiction. It seems to me that I should be recreant to the promises made, and that my duty to the memory of those brave men who fell on that day, and those who survived, both demand that justice should be done to them.

      Respectfully yours,
      J.H. Nichols
      Capt. Co. K, 20th Maine Vols.

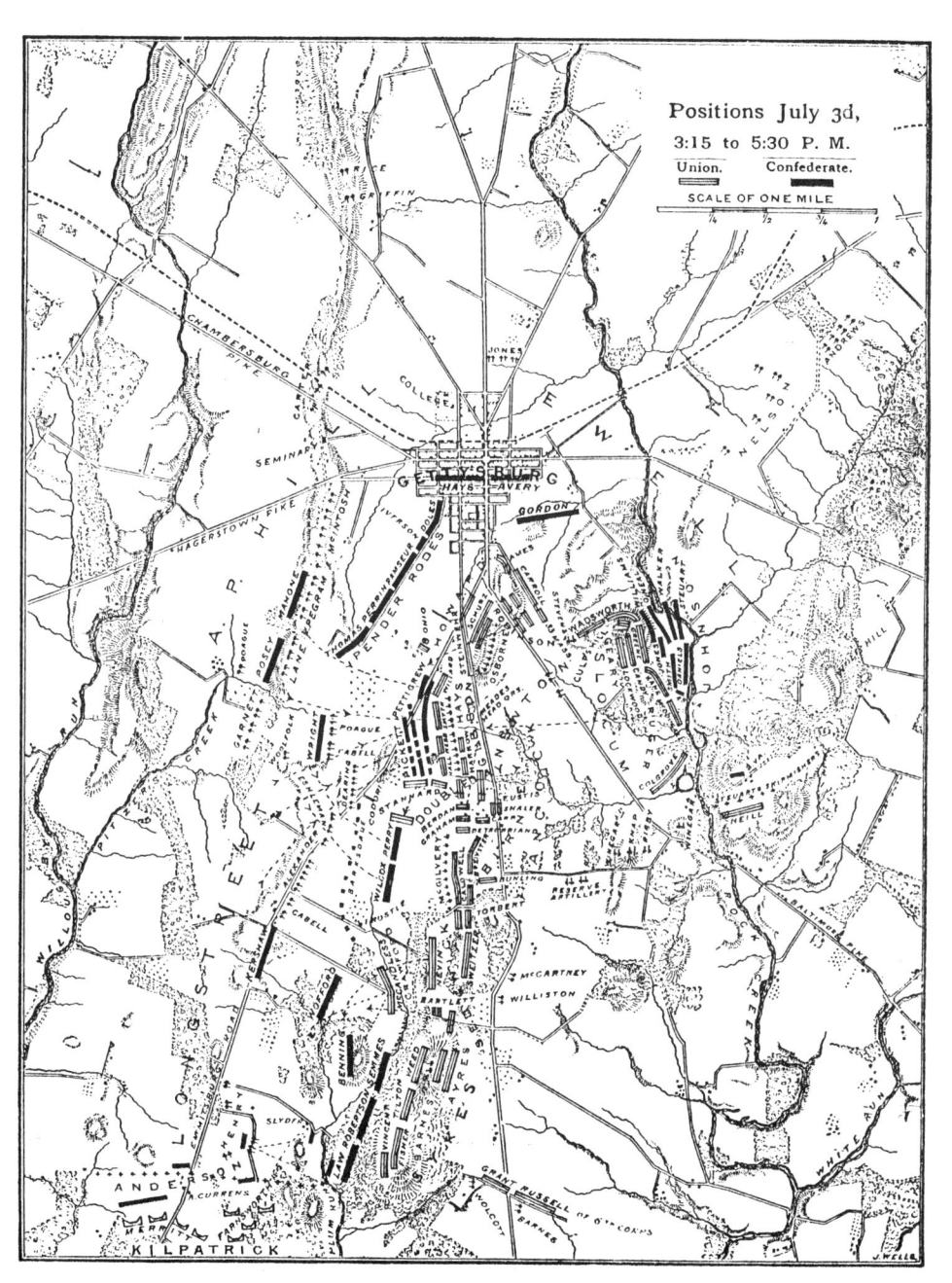

Gettysburg, July 3rd.

Chamberlain Avenue is clearly shown in this photograph of the Twentieth Maine monument upon Little Round Top. The road was constructed in the 1890's and removed in the 1930's.

The remains of Chamberlain Avenue can be seen in this current view taken in 1993. The topography of the area where the 20th Maine and 15th Alabama fought was forever altered by this road, making an accurate understanding of the fight impossible.

PART VI
Diary of William Livermore, Color Guard, 20th Maine.
From the Lincoln County News, June 1883.

In 1883, members of the Twentieth Maine Veteran Association began to openly debate the Little Round Top fight, through letters to local Maine newspapers. Veterans of that fight were asked to come forward with their accounts. Sergt. William T. Livermore of Company B, who was detailed to serve in the color guard, faithfully kept a diary throughout the war. Twenty years after Gettysburg, his comrades called publicly for the diary to be published. In a letter to the Lincoln County News, dated May 7, 1883, Holman Melcher wrote, "W.T. Livermore says: 'Accounts of the battle on Little Round Top do not exactly agree with his diary and recollection.' Why can he not be induced to give us the benefit of that diary and his recollections? His prominent position in the centre of the regiment, by the colors, enabled him to see and know more of that fierce fight than most members of the Twentieth." Livermore relented and the diary appeared some weeks later.

Extracts from a Veterans Diary.

Bivouac near Hanover, Pennsylvania, July 1st, 1863. Marched at 10 A.M. We crossed the line into Pennsylvania at 1 o'clock P.M. As we crossed the line we unfurled our colors and gave three cheers for Pennsylvania. The ladies were at every gate and supplied us with water. We marched through Hanover and halted until sunset, then we fell in and marched ten miles, halting at 12 o'clock at night. We marched through Macherrisville which is quite a place. The troops felt nicely and I never heard such cheering. Cheer after cheer ran along our line of march. Every man, woman and child was out to see us as we passed. The rebels had just gone through the town and the people gave us a hearty welcome.

July 2nd. Weather warm and misty. Marched at 4 o'clock A.M., three miles from Gettysburg. There is a large force here and the 6th Corps is coming in at 10 A.M. Our Corps rested until 3:30 P.M. Drew twenty rounds of cartridges in addition to the forty which we had. All quiet until 3 o'clock P.M. when the artillery became engaged. Our corps immediately fell in and marched rapidly to the front, and left, passing in rear of our own batteries, which were hotly engaged. The rebel shells came over among us thick and fast, but on we marched at a step between quick and doublequick until some fell exhausted. Our brigade marched into the woods to the left of our batteries. We took our position on the extreme left of our line of battle, our Regiment on the left of the Brigade, to protect our batteries. Our line is formed on the crest of a rocky ridge. Company "B." under Capt. Morrill, was deployed as skirmishers and pushed forward. By this time we heard terrible musketry on our right which rolled along, coming nearer and nearer. We were ordered to come to a ready and take good aim, when the enemy appeared; soon scattering bullets came singing through the trees. Then I saw a rebel and fired at him. The same instant a sheet of fire and smoke belched forth from our line   Col. Chamberlain says, "Boys, hold this hill!" The enemy's object was to turn our flank and capture our artillery, as the prisoners said they thought we had only a skirmish line there. They came to within four or five rods, covering themselves behind big rocks and trees, and kept up a murderous fire, which was returned by us. Soon we found the enemy flanking us, had got behind a row of rocks under our left wing and were making fearful havoc in our ranks as every one who dared raise his head was sure of his man, and many lost their brains in the attempt. We stood until our center had lost half our men, and we knew we could not stand longer. We were ordered to charge them when there were two to our one. With fixed bayonets and a yell we rushed on them, which so frightened them, that not another shot was fired on us. Some threw down their arms and ran, but many rose up, begging to be spared. We did not stop but told them to go to the rear, and on we went after the whipped and frightened rebels, taking them by scores and giving those too far away to be captured deadly shots in the back. After chasing them as far as prudent, we "rallied around the colors" and gave three hearty cheers, then went back to our old position, with our prisoners. Two of our boys guarded 81 in one squad to the rear. We, in this charge, took about two hundred prisoners, and behind the rocks where they fought, they lay in a windrow.

Company F, the color company had seven killed on the spot and fourteen wounded, Company A, joining the colors on the left, had two killed and sixteen wounded, some mortally. Our color guard was composed of four men, three besides myself, [Melville C.] Day, my file leader was killed; [Charles H.] Reed was wounded; E.S. Coan and myself only, remained with the colors. We had twenty-one killed on the field. Our whole loss in killed, wounded and missing is 144. Our wounded were carried to the rear by our prisoners and we brought in the rebel wounded. At sunset the firing had ceased, save that of the sharpshooters who were busily engaged.

Col. Chamberlain says: "Boys, I am asked if I can carry that hill in front." We all say, "Yes." Our little regiment fell in (only 8 in Company A.) and marched over rocks and through brush to [Big Round Top] without meeting any foe. We halted and sent skirmishers out, who encountered the rebel pickets and by strategy captured twenty-five of the 4th Texas. We lay on our arms with equipments and everything ready for any emergency. The Regiment we fought and captured was the 15th Alabama. They fought like demons and said they never were whipped before and never wanted to meet the 20th Maine again. Our victory seems complete, and while we mourn the loss of our brave comrades that have fallen, we rejoice over our victory. Ours was an important position and had we been driven from it, the tide of battle would have been turned against us and what the result might have been we cannot tell.

July 3d. Near Gettysburg. Weather cloudy. At daylight we heard the enemy in front, throwing down a stone wall or building up breastworks. We were ordered to build breastworks in our front, which we did of small stones that covered the hill. After finishing it we were ordered to advance which we promptly did. Our pickets and the rebel skirmishers were exchanging shots. Lieut. [Arad H.] Linscott took one of the boy's muskets and went in advance of the pickets to get a shot at them, but received a severe if not mortal wound in the thigh. [First Lieut. Linscott died from his wound on July 27th.] At 10 A.M. we were relieved by some of the Pennsylvania Reserves. We marched back over the ground where we fought the night before seeing the dead rebels just where we lay them. Our boys had been buried and nothing but the blood was to be seen. Twenty-one were buried in one grave. We marched back near the centre in rear of two lines of battle, and threw up two lines of stonewall in rear of the first, expecting an attack. In the afternoon the enemy massed their artillery, estimated at 150 guns, on our left and centre. There was the most terrific cannonading for three or four hours I ever heard. There was fighting all day in our front, with favorable results. Gen. Ames was here to-day; said he was proud of the 20th. Gen. Meade passed us and received tremendous cheers. Afternoon rainy. I went out to the front in the evening where they were burying some of our dead, twenty-eight lay side by side. The scene is revolting. We saw [Brig.-Gen. Judson] Kilpatrick make a charge on the enemy, and it is said he captured 2,000 prisoners. Some that were wounded have since died. The night sets in rainy and muddy.

July 4th. Weather cloudy. We went out and picked up Springfields and left our Enfields. Nearly every one did so. It seems quiet today, except some picket firing. I think they are withdrawing. In the fight of the 2nd, there was but one man wounded in Company "B", E. Morrill; three missing Leach, Stone and Sanders. In the fight of the 2nd, the enemy came inbetween Company "B" who were sent out as skirmishers, so they were cut off from the Regiment while we were fighting, but they were brought in all right, under the command of our worthy Captain. Thus passes a 4th of July to be remembered. Our troops are in the best of spirits.

On the battlefield near Gettysburg, July 5, 1863. Weather cloudy. Our brigade fell in at 6 o'clock, A.M., and advanced through the belt of wood our men occupied yesterday. Then we formed a line of battle and advanced nearly across the large field where some of the most desperate fighting took place July 2nd. We halted in line, the centre of the Regiment on the ruins of a barn that was burned by our shells. In the fight the rebel wounded took shelter in the barn and when it burned many were burned in it. We were ordered to build breastworks which we did, of the underpinning of the barn. The field was about a half mile wide and a mile long. In the fight July 2nd, our men attempted to cross this field and after advancing about half way were met by the enemy where some of the most desperate fighting took place. I followed the rebel line where they threw down their knapsacks, blankets and tents and nearly everything but muskets and equipments before making the charge that drove our men from the field. I am not competent to describe the awful scene. The field is covered with dead men and horses, cannon and caissons, muskets, sabres and everything usual in battle. The feet of our dead are all stripped as the enemy held the field until this morning. Details from our brigade are burying the dead and picking up the muskets. Men killed on the 2nd, lying in the burning sun present an awful spectacle. Swollen to double their natural size they cannot be moved but are buried as well as possible where they fell. Men cannot be recognized. The stench

Gettysburg 81

is sickening. I never saw anything like this. The rebels are retreating and the 6th Corps has passed us in pursuit. At 4 o'clock P.M. we fell in and marched back across the field and continued our march until 12 o'clock at night. It is raining and the mud is from two to sixteen inches deep. The night was so dark we could not see our file leaders. We halted, pitched tents with our muskets and lay down tired but in good spirits.

Union dead near the Emmitsburg Rd. This photograph was taken on July 5th, and these could be the very same bodies that Livermore viewed.

PART VII
Memoirs of Corporal Elisha Coan, Color Guard, 20th Maine.

Our regt. was formed in an open level space comparatively free from rocks and bushes but in our front was a slight descent fringed by ledges of rock & our side of the hill was covered with boulders. Beyond this line of ledge and other rocks at that time the eye could not penetrate on account of the dense foliage of bushes. Hardly had our line been formed when we heard a yelling in the distance.

We did not know whether it was by our own men in another part of the line making a charge or whether it was the enemy. Meantime Co. B. under Capt. Morrill had deployed as skirmishers and disappeared in the foliage in our front. We had not long to wait before we found that the sound of yelling came nearer and we knew that it was the "rebel yell" once heard it is never to be forgotten. We braced up for the shock. Soon scattering musketry was heard in our front. Then bullets began to clip twigs and cut branches over our heads and leaves began to fall actively at our feet. Every moment the bullets struck lower and lower until they began to take effect in our ranks. Then our line burst into flames, and the crash of musketry became constant. My place in the line was on the color guard, to which place I had been detached by John Marshall Brown while Adjutant of the 20th Me. I was in the rear rank, and as we were somewhat crowed I could not see to fire over the shoulders of the front rank so I had a chance to observe what was going on. Col. Chamberlain was standing upon a rock about 15 ft. in rear of the colors. I noticed that some of the bullets came from our front and soon some officers came from our left lengthwise of the regt. line, I said to my comrade on my right they are getting on our flank. Just then an officer from the left of our line came up to Col. Chamberlain and reported that the enemy was flanking us and getting in our rear. Col. C. met this new movement by ordering a left backward wheel of the left wing of the regt. with the colors for a pivot. This movement was quickly made. Then our left wing faced nearly at a right angle with the original line and with the right wing which retained its original position. This left the colors in the salient formed by these two facings. By this time many of the men had fallen killed or wounded but our men kept up a rapid effective fire. The backward movement of the left wing uncovered many of our men that had fallen killed or wounded. The latter of which were before our eyes writhing in the agonies of their fallen killed or wounded. Over them flew the leaden spray from the two lines, for the storm was raging furiously. The calm of the early afternoon had been succeeded by a cyclone.

    Major & Ex-Mayor Melcher was then a Lieutenant in command of Color Co. F. as Capt. Keene was assisting Col. Chamberlain in the capacity of Major. Lt. Melcher conceived the idea of advancing the colors so that our line would cover our wounded & dead so that they could be removed to the rear and he asked Col. C. for the privilege of advancing his Company for that purpose. Col. C. hesitated for the step would be a hazardous one, for the enemy had a strong position behind the rocks 3 rods in front of us. But our line was melting away like ice before the sun, and something must soon be done or all would be lost. On that mornings roll call we numbered 358 officers and men. Capt. Morrill's Co. of 50 men had been sent on the skirmish line, and was supposed had been captured for they had not fallen back on the approach of the enemy line. As a matter of fact they had been detached from all skirmishers of the rest of the brigade, the enemy had passed through the gap thus formed, and Capt. now Col. Morrill tells me that the first he knew of the proximity of the rebels was the firing in his rear when they struck our line and that he did not see our enemy until they retreated. Of the 308 men & officers, only one hundred and fifty were now left for duty. Other officers joined Melcher in urging a forward movement and

Col. C. gave his consent. Immediately Melcher passed to the front of his company & placing himself in front of the colors ordered his men forward. Other officers followed his example. The men not knowing that the movement was sanctioned by the Col. hesitated, realizing the hazardous risk and what the result would be if unsuccessful. Then Col. C. gave the order "forward." This was heard by but a few but it spread along our lines and the regt. with a yell equal to a thousand men sprang forward in a wild mad charge. The result was like magic. The rebel front line, amazed at the sudden movement, thinking we had been reinforced, and which they declare to this day was the case, throw down their arms & cry out "don't fire! we surrender." The rest fled in wild confusion back to their starting point a mile away, and the battle on Little Round Top was ended. For about that time the fighting ceased along the whole left front of the army.

Illustration of the fight on Vincent's Spur.

The rocky slope of Little Round Top with the heavily wooded Big Round Top at right. This photograph was taken on July 15, 1863.

Gathering of the Twentieth Maine Regiment Association on October 2, 1889 at the dedication of their monument upon Little Round Top. Holman S. Melcher and his wife Alice are seated in the center of the group. To the right, near the colors, is Gen. Chamberlain.

PART VIII
Orations at the dedication of the 20th Maine monument, Oct. 3, 1889.

DEDICATION

OF THE

TWENTIETH MAINE

Monuments

AT

GETTYSBURG,

OCT. 3, 1889.

WITH REPORT OF

ANNUAL REUNION, OCT. 2d, 1889.

ANNUAL REUNION

The annual reunion of the Twentieth Maine Regiment Association was held at the Springs Hotel, Gettysburg, Pa., Wednesday evening, October 2, 1889. The following were present:

J. L. Chamberlain, New York
J. F. Land and wife, New York
H. L. Prince, wife and two ladies, Washington, D.C.
F. M. Rogers, Melrose, Mass.
J. E. DeWitt and wife, Natick, Mass.
Arthur M. Bean, East Bethel
J. F. Safford and wife, Farmington, N.H.
H.S. Melcher, Portland
S. L. Miller, Waldoboro
W. K. Bickford, Thomaston
J. B. Wescott, Bath
Joseph Tyler, Merrimac, Mass.
Reuel Thomas, North Cambridge, Mass.
E. S. Coan, Auburn
H. A. Swett, Gloucester, Mass.
L. B. Heald, East Sumner
G. W. Reynolds and wife, Waterville
A. B. Latham, West Auburn
W. H. True, Portland
J. L. Bradford, Union
W. B. Bradford, Cushing
Edwin Keating, Warren
John M. Kennedy, Warren
Theodore Gerrish and wife, Portland
O. P. Tucker, Mexico
B.F. French, Linneus
Benj. R. Fields, Rockport
A. E. Fernald and son, (Roy Fernald), Winterport
C. S. Cook and wife, Portland
Ira R. Sylvester, Washington
S. A. Bennett, New Portland
J. B. Bachelder, (Honorary Member), Hyde Park, Mass.

The Association was called to order by President Melcher. The report of the Secretary and Treasurer was read and accepted.

The President read a letter from Maj. P. M. Fogler, regretting his inability to be present. The President gave an outline of the program of exercises for the next day, followed by remarks on the same subject by Gen. Chamberlain, Col. Bachelder and Capt. Prince.

Comrades J. E. DeWitt, W. K. Bickford and J. L. Bradford were made a committee to nominate a board of officers. The committee subsequently reported the following:

>For President, H. S. Melcher.
>Vice President, F. M. Rogers.
>Secretary and Treasurer, S. L. Miller.

Dr. Wescott was authorized to cast the vote of the Association for the above.

Voted that a committee on necrology be appointed. The chair appointed the following; E. S. Coan, A. E. Fernald, Reuel Thomas.

Voted that a reunion of the Association be held next year at such time and place as the Executive Committee may designate. (The President, Vice President and Secretary constitute the Executive Committee).

Remarks by Maj. F. Land.

Voted to lay upon the table the question of the sons of members, which had been called up.

Voted that a committee of three be appointed to prepare resolutions of sympathy to Mrs. Gen. Warren and have them published in the press. The following comrades were constituted that committee: T. Gerrish, J. F. Land, E. S. Coan.

The meeting closed with the reading by the secretary of a poem entitled, "The Maltese Cross," followed by benediction by Comrade Gerrish.

DEDICATION OF MONUMENTS

Thursday afternoon, Oct. 3. 1889, after the general exercises on the battlefield, the members of the Twentieth Maine Regiment Association, with their ladies and many other excursionists, assembled on Little Round Top, where the exercises, dedicatory of the monument erected by the survivors of the regiment, were held. (A cut of the monument appears on the opposite page.)

President Melcher, having called the assembly to order, made the following remarks:

Ladies and Comrades:

It is an occasion of great interest to us all, that after these twenty-six years so many of the survivors of the Twentieth Regiment, Maine Volunteer Infantry, are permitted to meet and stand on this historic ground, made sacred by the blood of our comrades who fell here in the defense of this vital position of the great battlefield of the war of the rebellion.

We are assembled here today to dedicate this monument, erected by the survivors of the regiment and

Twentieth Maine Monument, Little Round Top. According to Chamberlain this does not mark the spot where the colors stood during the battle.

their friends, to commemorate the important fight at this point on the great battlefield of Gettysburg, and also as a memorial of the thirty-eight brave men who gave their lives that this position might be held and defended.

Seven years ago, this month, a company of the survivors of our regiment made a pilgrimage to this place to select and dedicate the site on which this monument should be erected.

Appropriate exercises were held here at that time, consisting of prayer by Rev. T. Gerrish , oration by General Chamberlain, singing of America by the company and benediction by Rev. C. A. Southard.

At a meeting of the Association in the parlors of the Eagle Hotel, in town, a monument committee was appointed, Gen. Ellis Spear and Capt. Howard L. Prince, of Washington, Maj. J. F. Land, of New York, and Capt. A. E. Fernald and Rev. T. Gerrish, of Maine, constituting that committee.

The Executive Committee of the Association was authorized to raise the necessary funds. The work has been completed and paid for.

It is built of granite from the hills of our own State, and will stand as long as these hills and mountains endure—to forever witness to what the brave sons of Maine did here to save the Nation and defend the flag in the day of peril.

We stand here, today, under the same battle-torn and blood-stained flag that was carried to victory in the struggle for this key-point, to dedicate this monument. Our comrades, Capt. Howard L. Prince is the Historian and General J. L. Chamberlain, who led us in this battle, will deliver an Address, after which "Joe" Tyler, the bugler of the Regiment during the war, will sound "Lights Out", in memory of our brave comrades, who gave their lives in defense of this position, whose names are not only engraved in the monument but in our hearts and in history—while they are gently sleeping in the National Cemetery yonder, awaiting the bugle-call of the resurrection day.

After the exercises here, we shall proceed to the position held by Capt. Morrill's Co. B. on the flank, and direct the placing of the tablet to mark his line, and thence to the summit of Round Top, where we shall dedicate the monument, erected there by the State, to mark the position captured by the Regiment after the fight here and held by it until relieved at 10 o'clock a.m., July 3. The exercises there will be: historical address by our Comrade S. L. Miller, address by General Chamberlain, singing of America by the company and prayer and benediction by Rev. T. Gerrish.

The historian of the occasion, Capt. Howard L. Prince, was then introduced.

Capt. Howard L. Prince's Address.

Comrades:

Your historian has evidently been selected on the same plan as the contributors of war articles for the magazines. He acknowledges, with perhaps a pardonable pride, that he was within hearing of the guns of Gettysburg, and asserts that circumstances beyond his control detained him at a distance, which at that time would doubtless have been gladly shared by many, to whom their part in this great battle is now their most cherished recollection. The most intimate connection he had with battle, was to conduct a train-load of shoes for the gallant but foot-sore survivors thereof, over the stony roads of South Mountain at midnight. On this expedition he painfully and laboriously directed the movements of a small white mule, an animal possessed of most astonishing military accomplishments. He habitually advanced by company front, while his head as persistently pointed to the flank, came to a halt every third corner of the prevalent worm fence, and threw out an active skirmish line to the rear.

It is needless to further state to his audience that the shoes were the usual admirable collection of misfits, that none of them were large enough for Co. B., and if adjectives had been bullets the Quartermaster Sergeant would have been better off in front of the 15th Alabama. That is the usual reward of a Quartermaster and a historian. What can the combination of the two expect? It is with surprise therefore at my own temerity, that I dare to speak of great deeds in the presence of the actors themselves, and to air my feeble periods in the face of one whose eloquence has made the "20th Maine at Gettysburg" a classic scarcely less renowned than his own brilliant career. I can only hope to set forth in plain and simple phrase, the things done here a quarter century ago, to tell with such accuracy as I may, the story of those few hours, big with such great consequence to country and humanity, and ask your kindly charity on the effort, which, however feeble, will, I trust, be found faithful and just to comrades living and dead.

In the afternoon of July first, the Fifth Corps, forming the right of the wide-spread fan of the Union army, after marching for days through the green lanes and over the blooming hills of Maryland, crowned with generous fruitage and promise of corn and wine, on which liberal levies were made by the dusty and hungry boys in blue, had crossed, with gladsome shouts and waving banners, amid strains of exultant music, the line which separated Dixie's Land from "God's country" and sweeping down the broad pike, had halted near the town of Hanover. But little time was given to enjoy the novel sensations of a camp in a friendly land, where the red-cheeked maidens leaned over rose-bordered hedges to exchange smiles and admiring glances with the bold-eyed lads, who were only too ready to take snap-shots at flirtation, and put in practice arts almost forgotten amid the sour faces and averted heads of a hostile population. The echoes of Lee's cannon far away to the left had sent the orders flying from corps to corps for a speedy concentration at the little village, destined to become famous as the Waterloo of the Western Continent, and as the evening shadows gathered, the merry corporal snatched his last mouthful of fried hardtack, the gay staff officer waved a farewell kiss to the fair acquaintance of an hour, and the men of the Maltese cross streamed away along the roads that led to battle, to fame, and death. None who made that night's march will ever forget it. The crowded roads, the ever-present sense that great necessities waited on the presence of the corps, at the earliest possible moment on the field in front, the variations of hearty welcome and churlish inhospitality that, in some cases, weighed the use of pump or a drink of milk against the deliverance from hostile invasion, filled that night with memories, whose recital enlivened many a picket reserve among the pines of Virginia, and have furnished stock in trade for volumes of "swapped lies" at Grand Army campfires in these latter days of peace. Till midnight the march continued, and then arrived within supporting distance of our friends in arms, the wearied ranks threw themselves down for a sleep till daylight, when a march of some three miles brought the corps in touch with the right of the Twelfth, Williams' Division, which was then east of Rock Creek on the slopes of Wolf Hill, to the south-east of the village between the Hanover and Baltimore Pikes. This position was reached and the command massed between 6 and 7 a.m. At eight o'clock, Geary's troops having been relieved from the left, and regained their corps, Gen. Slocum moved the division of Williams to the West side of Rock Creek, and as that was withdrawn, the Fifth Corps was massed by division at the crossing of Rock Creek, near a mill. This was some distance to the left and rear of the position first occupied. At this time Gen. Meade, struck by the inactivity of the enemy, whose only sign of life was a somewhat lively reception of a skirmish line sent out by the Third Corps from the Peach Orchard to the Warfield ridge, had become impressed with the idea that Lee had not finished the concentration of his forces. He then formed the plan of assuming the offensive and attacking Lee's left on Benner's Hill with the Twelfth Corps, supported by the Fifth Corps as soon as the Sixth should arrive. A dispatch making these dispositions was sent to Gen. Slocum at 9:30 a.m., but both Gen. Slocum and Gen. Warren advised against it on account of the difficult character of the ground, Slocum's answer and adverse report being made at 10:30 a.m. But a small portion of the Sixth Corps was then within reach, and the Fifth had by no means recovered from its exhausting march of the preceding night, and the command can count it among their bits of good luck that they were thus reserved for a defensive battle rather than an attack against Jackson's veterans on the slopes of Rock Creek. The corps was then moved across Rock Creek by the narrow bridge at the mill and massed in column to the left of the Baltimore Pike and of a cross road, connecting the Pike with the Taneytown road, the reserve artillery being parked on the same cross road a short distance in advance, the First Division occupying a peach orchard. The corps was therefore in a position to reinforce the front line either to the right, left or center, and these operations being completed soon after midday the troops were enabled to obtain some needed rest and food in preparation for the mighty struggle so near at hand; while at this point twenty rounds of cartridges were issued to each man in addition to those already in the boxes, making a total of sixty rounds.

As we are concerned with the movements of one regiment only, out of the vast array which lined these hills on that July day, we need only touch upon the wider tactical movements sufficiently to show why and when our regiment reached the point which was to be the scene of its sorest struggle and greatest triumph. The movements of the enemy having indicated with sufficient clearness that he intended to attack the left, and Gen. Meade having satisfied himself that the position taken up by the Third Corps could not withstand the onset of the foe, with the numbers then in line between the Peach Orchard and the Devil's Den, had given directions to Gen. Sykes to bring forward his corps. Consequently as stated in Gen. Barnes' official report, the corps was started from its position, near Rock Creek, about four o'clock and moved rapidly by the cross road, which debouches into the Taneytown road just east of Gen. Weikert's house. Nothing is harder than to make a successful reconciliation of the hours named in different reports and histories when certain events took place. And the battle of Gettysburg is peculiarly confusing in this respect. While the writers substantially agree in opening the artillery fire at about 3:30, the time of the successive attacks of Hood and McLaws varies both in Union and Confederate authorities from 4 to 5:30 p.m. The Confederate attack was to commence at the right and be taken up towards the left, and the brigade commander on the right (Law) claims to have gone into action at five, carried the crest of the Devil's Den, and then gone to find out why McLaws did not support his left, while the latter says he opened at four! Our own authorities are no better. I mention this because Gen. Doubleday charges the Fifth Corps with delay in coming to the support of the Third Corps. I am certain, however, that the advance of the Fifth Corps was at the Wheat Field before the troops of Birney's Division were seriously engaged at all, and certainly long before any troops of McLaws had attacked the Peach Orchard on the right of De Trobriand. And this is proved by the incident which caused our brigade, the head of the corps, to be deflected from its march to the Wheat Field and carried to Round Top. Gen. Warren left Meade and Sickles at the Peach Orchard, "just before the action began in earnest" says Warren—at a quarter of four o'clock" says the Comte de Paris—and, under Gen. Meade's directions, proceeded to the extreme left; he found Little Round Top bare of troops and used only as a signal station. No enemy was then in sight, and he directed Smith, whose battery of rifle guns was on the hill above Devil's Den, to send a shot over the thick woods beyond the Emmittsburg road, a mile away, where he thought their lines were concealed. As the shot screamed through the tree tops the Confederate soldiers instinctively glanced up, their arms moving at the same time, and the sun sent a flash of light reflecting from their polished guns, that ran through the edge of the forest like a gleam of lightning, revealing the extent of the line that far outflanked the Union position, and would easily overlap this hill, which Warren recognized at once as the key to the position. Communicating at once with Gen. Sykes, who was with Gen. Barnes just completing his reconnaissance at the Wheat Field, the brigade of Vincent, leading the division, was ordered to Round Top. As this brigade reached the Spur before Hood's advance had fairly swung its right wing into contact, it follows that not only was Warren's precaution successful, but also that our two brigades, following in our rear, were at the Wheat Field before McLaws' attacked, and the Comte de Paris asserts that these two brigades, which had halted near the field, while Birney was rectifying his alignment, were pushed into a front line by half past four. Thus, disregarding the inaccuracies and inconsistencies of the time reports, the sequence of events fully exonerates the whole of the first division from the charge of tardiness. The Third Brigade, pursuing its march towards the Third Corps' line, had passed Weikert's house and reached the strip of woods running down from the Trostle's house, coming, as it passed down the slope toward the woods, within sight of the position at the Orchard, and of our batteries on the cross road, now hotly engaged with the rebel guns on the Emmittsburg road and the Warfield Ridge, the shells from which fell beyond our batteries and several burst near the column before it turned. Several accounts have spoken of the Third Corps being then engaged at the Peach Orchard, but this is clearly erroneous. There was no infantry engaged there for at least an hour later, and any musketry heard in that direction must have been from the pressing skirmish lines. Just as the edge of the forest was reached, Col. Vincent, answering the call of Warren, under the orders of Gen. Sykes, turned the head of column sharply to the left, and striking the Millerstown road, it was hurried at the double quick up the northern slope of Round Top, thence passing under the shoulder of the hill on its eastern side, until reaching the point where Col. Vincent had directed it to form in order to hold the spur on its southern and western faces, against the onset of Hood's division, so soon to burst upon it. The 44th N. Y. was placed on the right of the line, then the 16th Mich., the 83rd Pa. and the 20th Me. on the left, that being the order of march for the day, but for some reason, the 16th was shifted to the right of the brigade. The historian of the 83rd Pa., Capt. Judson, is authority for the statement that this change was made at the request of Col. Rice of the 44th, who said to Col. Vincent, that "the 83rd and 44th had hitherto fought side by side in every battle and he wished they might do the same today." The two right regiments were placed somewhat below the brow of the hill on its western slope, facing the Devil's Den and the gorge of Plum Run, while the 83rd filled the semi-circular bend of the escarpment as it doubles back to face the loftier summit of Round Top, and the 20th prolonged this line, facing generally toward the higher mountain, and looking down into the comparatively open and smooth depression between the summits, filled with scattering trees and sparse underbrush, through which to the left could be seen the glint of the sunshine upon open fields beyond the mountain slope. Still farther to the left and rear of the general line of the 83rd and 20th prolonged, the ground falls off more sharply and is filled with huge boulders. On this line Col. Chamberlain brings the regiment into place "on the right by file into line," that the flank nearest the enemy may be first firmly planted, and receives from Col. Vincent his last orders, "to hold this ground at all hazards" and then that gallant soldier, without fear or reproach, departs forever from the sight of his soldiers of the 20th Maine, to fall within a short hour at the very moment of victory. Each regiment threw out skirmishers, Co. B., Capt. Morrill, being ordered to extend the left flank of the 20th across the low ground, and cover the front and exposed flank against attack, it being known that the command at that time held the extreme left of the Union line. As the regiment stands there in the terrible hush that precedes the actual clash of arms, the few minutes that try men's souls more than the charge or the retreat, as each man tightens his belt, prepares his cartridges for most rapid use, and gives a last hurried thought to home and friends, then shuts his teeth and glances with firm lips and set eyes through the forest for signs of the approaching enemy, let us for a moment consider the dispositions of our adversary and learn, what we could not then know, of the direction and weight of his advance.

The right division of Longstreet's Corps, which was to open the battle and by whose movements the others were to be guided, was composed of the brigades of Law, Robertson, Benning and Anderson, formed in two lines, the two first named brigades leading. These were massed in the woods beyond the Emmittsburg road, and the order of advance was to make a half wheel to the left in order to attack the left of Sickle's line, stationed at the Devil's Den, roll it up, and by the successive attacks of the other divisions to the right, sweep away the whole corps and crush that wing of our army. Before the advance was made, however, Gen. Law, commanding the right brigade, had sent Sergt. McMiller in command of a scouting party to ascertain in what force the Federals were posted on the heights of Round Top. His report sent back and received before the advance, showed that the position could be easily carried from the rear, and commanded the whole Federal line. Gen. Law thereupon remonstrated with Hood against a front attack, and advised the turning of Round Top. Hood was impressed with the idea sufficiently to send a staff officer to Longstreet with the protest and his endorsement, but the corps commander dispatched one of his own aides with order's "to begin the attack at once." Longstreet had already been over-ruled in his proposition to Gen. Lee, to maneuver Meade out of his position, and the attack having been delayed till Lee was becoming impatient, he doubtless thought it futile to suggest any further modification. The discussion had, however, this effect, which bore directly on our part in the battle. The importance of Round Top was so deeply felt that the right of the attacking division was so far directed to the right, as to pass over the mountain instead of bearing to the left to the stony hill, occupied by Ward. Gen. Law says that he did this to protect his right, and as Gen. Hood was wounded soon after the advance commenced, Law succeeded to the command of the division, and his dispositions were not set aside. The regiments of Law's Brigade, beginning at its right, were the 44th, 48th, 15th, 47th and 4th Ala., and Robertson's, the 4th, 5th and 1st Texas and 3rd Ark. The result of the changed direction was to expose the flank of Robertson's men to the fire of Ward's brigade, and the rebel advance became separated, the 4th and 5th Texas keeping touch with Law's men, and the 1st Texas and 3rd Ark. charging the stony hill to the left. The brigades of Anderson and Benning adhered to their original order of the half wheel and become engaged as a front line with Birney's division, as soon as unmasked by the movement of the leading brigades to the right. In order to fill the gap in Robertson's brigade, Gen. Law, just as the line reached the base of the mountain, detached the 44th and 48th Ala. from the extreme right and, marching them in rear of the line, connected them with the left of the 4th Texas, and in that line they afterwards came to attack the western slope of

Round Top in front of the 16th Mich. and Ward's brigade. This movement left the 15th Ala. on the rebel right, and in line with the 47th it advanced straight up the southern face of the mountain, pushing back the skirmishers of the Second U.S. Sharpshooters, who had been met in the open fields this side of the Emmittsburg road, and who from their vantage ground among the rocks and their accurate fire, gave the 15th so much trouble that Col. Oates believed he had driven a line of battle and thought he had found it again when he met the first fire of the 20th Me. The rebel troops had made a march of twenty-four miles since three o'clock that morning, and the climb up the hill found them pretty well exhausted, made as it was in the face of an annoying fire and clinging to bushes and over huge boulders. Arriving at the top Col. Oates gave his men ten minutes' rest, during which time the remainder of his brigade and Robertson's had gone forward by smoother routes and become engaged with the troops of Ward and Vincent on both sides of Plum Run. Maj. Melcher has elsewhere stated that this delay was a fatal one, as it enabled Vincent's brigade to become established on the Spur. I do not think this is correct, for the 4th Ala. and the Texas men, who moved straight on found Vincent's 83rd and 44th ready for them, and as the 20th was formed at the same time, allowing only for the time in coming from the rear of the brigade, the Maine men would have given the Alabamians an equally warm reception ten minutes earlier. Its only possible effect was to put our enemies in a little better fighting trim, and so make their attack more rapid and vigorous. It should be remembered also that the skirmishers of the 44th had been out ten minutes before driven in by Robertson's advance, so that the hill was occupied at least twenty minutes before Oates descended the hither slope. Col. Oates was convinced at once that the summit of Round

Top was an important position to hold, and that it should be occupied with artillery, and endeavored to communicate his views to Gen. Law, through the latter's chief of staff, who had ridden upon the hill to inquire the cause of the delay; but that officer insisted that the orders were imperative for an advance until the infantry were engaged and Col. Oates obeyed, moving down the northern face of the mountain and bearing somewhat to the left to regain touch with the remainder of the command.

Let us glance for moment at the adversaries who are about to measure strength amid these woods and gloomy rocks, and to fill this hollow with such carnage that it has been called the Valley of Death. The 20th is entirely enveloped in woods, and awaits its enemy in silence and ignorance of his force; but on the sight of the other regiments of the brigade, a grand but fearful spectacle is spread. The troops of Robertson are already out of sight. They have entered the woods at the base of the mountain, their eyes fixed on its frowning heights, brushing with almost contemptuous haste past the flanks of the Third Corps, and disdaining to notice even by a skirmish line, say the men of the 4th Me. at the Devil's Den, the fire which they poured into them at a short range. But beyond down the sunny slopes of Rose's farm, in double battle lines, come their supports of Anderson and Benning, the incomparable infantry of the Army of Northern Virginia. The rugged rocks above the gorge are blazing with the musketry of Ward, while Smith's rifled guns on the hill and in the gorge below, and a little later Hazlitt's Parrott's on Round Top, smoke and thunder, tearing great gaps in the advancing lines. Far off to the right, the road up to the Peach Orchard is crowded with the guns of the Third Corps and the Reserve, and the heights beyond tremble with the answer of all Longstreet's artillery. Their shells search all points of our lines, and scream over the heads of the 20th until the advancing infantry compels them to withhold their fire. These men, who are descending the slopes of Round Top and climbing the sides of the Death Valley, are no strangers to the Army of the Potomac. They have met at Antietam and watched our lines dash in useless valor against the bloody hills of Fredericksburg. These very divisions swept amid the shadows of evening, down from the Douglass heights, in just such an attack against the left of Pope at the Second Manassas, and drove it from the field. The memories of Chancellorsville are fresh in their minds. Is it any wonder that they are confident of victory? But now they must attack and we defend, and these hills and rocks will today repeat to them the lesson of Malvern Hill, and the flower of Longstreet's Corps, ere to-morrow's sun goes down, will be stretched in death before the lines of Hancock and is these hollows at our feet. Our brethren at the right, like us awaiting the crash of battle, are veterans of the Peninsular and of Pope's campaign, were decimated at Gaines's Mill, and covered the fatal hillside at Groveton, with their slain, up to the muzzles of Jackson's guns. But for the men of the 20th this was the first real stand up fight. They were under fire to be sure at Shepherdstown; they made a gallant advance at Fredericksburg, showing the stuff that was in them, but their losses were light in spite of their hazardous position; and the running fight at Aldie was more trying to the legs and wind than the courage. But here is to be the crucial test of temper, discipline and nerve, and who are the men to undergo it? Scarce ten months before nearly a thousand men had followed the standards of the Third Brigade into Maryland, under the gallant Ames. But exposure and disease have made fearful inroads in their ranks. Three hundred passed through the dreary portals of the hospital, from the wind and rain-swept camp of Antietam. Many found a grave in the little cemetery at Stoneman's, whence lack of proper knowledge of housing and feeding sent many more to recruit the increasing list of absent sick, till on this ground are found in line, three hundred and fifty-eight rank and file, out of almost thrice that number who gaily marched away from the Pine Tree State less than a year before. But the weak, the weary, the fearful, the shirkers have been dropped; the chaff is sifted from the wheat; these men who are left can fight all day and march all night, and have been welded by discipline into a tempered weapon of steel that will never fail its master's hand in the time of need, never to be more highly tried, more triumphantly vindicated than in the fateful moments of the next hour. Morrill and his skirmishers are already deploying on the side of Round Top, taking nearly fifty men from the line, already short, that is to meet the onset of three times its number of the best troops of Longstreet's Corps.

Let us glance down the line from the right. "Pap" Clark is acting as field officer, and E is commanded by Sidelinger, then comes Fogler, always cheerful, with his sturdy men of the coast, then the irrepressible Jim Nichols, who always had trouble to make "K" wheel, but not the least in keeping himself and "K" up to the front in a fight, then the two companies at the bloody angle, under the beloved Keene and quiet Lewis, the farmer boys of A and F., half of who are soon to fall in death and wounds. Next Aroostook's hardy sons, giant in form and stout of heart, and behind them Joe Land, who won't stop cracking his jokes till the Johnnies strike his front. Here come the "Oxford bears," with Billings, calm, modest, but true as steel, his moments of life already numbered, and D with jolly Fitch, and last old reliable G, over which Spear, never wanting in the hour of need, still keeps a fatherly eye, and how many other names these familiar letters recall to us, good boys and true, who did their duty here beneath these waving boughs, and have gone to their reward, or live to receive the plaudits of a grateful country, and to tell the deeds of their gallant dead; and up and down the line, with a last word of encouragement or caution, walks the quiet man, whose calm exterior concealed the fire of the warrior and the heart of steel, whose careful dispositions and ready resource, whose unswerving courage and audacious nerve in the last, desperate crisis, are to crown himself and his faithful soldiers with victory and fadeless laurels.

Already the regiments on our right are feeling the presence of the enemy, the musketry draws nearer, and eyes peering under the foliage see the gray lines coming down the opposite slope. They are coming on in a solid front, with no skirmishers, and it is seen almost instantly that their line extends far beyond our flank and will soon envelope and overwhelm it. In an instant a sheet of flame bursts from our front, described by Col. Oates as the most destructive fire he ever met, and it brought his advance to a stand-still at once. He states in his official report that his right exactly engaged our left, but that after two or three rounds he observed the enemy giving way in his front, except that portion confronting his two left companies and the 47th Ala. As his companies were at least twice the front of ours, his regiment having nearly six hundred and fifty men in line, that statement would include the whole right wing of our regiment. This movement which Col. Oates describes as a flight was, I believe, the refusal of the left wing of 20th to prevent its envelopment by the largely superior force opposed to it, and this hypothesis will assist in setting the time when this refusal took place, about which there is considerable difference of opinion in the regiment, some maintaining that it was done as soon as the enemy appeared and his strength was disclosed, and others that it was made under fire and after he had commenced to extend his line to the left. It is probable that both statements are correct from different points of view. It is not believed to be possible to reconcile all the theories and beliefs of the actors, even in so small a space as the front of a regiment, and when we fail, as sometimes we must, we must conclude, that as there is substantial agreement on the main features of the action, these disputed details were seen from different points, or were viewed at different stages as parts of a whole. Now it is well known that our gallant Lieut. Nichols always maintained that he first made known the extent of the Confederate line to Col. Chamberlain, and the Colonel in his official report says that his attention was called to it by an officer from the center, which was about Nichol's position, and that then mounting upon a rock he was able to discern it for himself, and took the action already described. Major Spear is equally sure that he called Col. Chamberlain's attention to it before the regiment was fairly under fire, and that the new disposition was then made. Now as the Confederate line came down the mountain, inclining to the left, in order to regain connection with the 4th Ala., (and which according to Col. Oates it never did make), it is probable that the right became engaged an appreciable space of time before the left, as the latter wing was somewhat swung back in the beginning, to conform to the ground, else it would have fallen below the crest, and this is borne out by a passage in Col. Chamberlain's report, which says the action "gradually extended along my entire front." This very nearly harmonizes all the divergent views, and also accounts for the apparent retreat noticed by Oates, of which he confesses he was unable at the time to take advantage, having plenty to do in holding his line up "under a most galling fire."

The statements of all the Union officers made at the time of the battle, including Col. Chamberlain's report and those of Col. Rice, Gen. Barnes and Gen. Sykes and Capt. Judson of the 83rd, speak of the troops assailing the 20th as moving by flank for the purpose, and with the exception of Col. Chamberlain, it is definitely stated by all, that these troops were the same who had attacked in front of the hill. The statements and publications since the war by Col. Oates, show that theory to be erroneous, and that the troops attacking us fought in no other place but came directly over Round Top, and that the flanking movement as first seen was more apparent than real, and caused by the more tardy appearance of the right wing of the attacking force. It is a high compliment to the spirit and vigor of both sides, that each commander believed disparity of force against us afforded by far the best foundation for the belief.

While still holding his command on our original front, Col. Oates says he was informed that the gap between the 47th Ala. and the 4th had not been filled, and that the first names was in consequence receiving a flank fire, presumably from the left of the 83rd, that was fast destroying its morale. Only seven companies of this regiment were in the battle, three having been left in the rear to guard a road, and in addition it was badly officered, its official report made by the Major, stating that the Colonel, while retaining nominal command, remained so far in the rear that he was worse than useless, and the Lieut. Col., Bulger, designated by Oates as a "gallant old gentleman of sixty," was dangerously wounded and fell into our hands, and soon after the regiment, having lost one-third of its number, retreated in confusion up the mountain. Whether, however, any more than the left of this regiment retreated before the final repulse, we have no certain information. Its report is short and deals only in generalities. Certain it is however, that there was no cessation of the deadly fire on our front, and it is hardly probable that the commander of the 15th would have continued to bear to his right, if he knew that his left flank was also in the air. He declared, at any rate, that, just at the moment when the 47th showed signs of distress, pivoting on his left which was then at a large rock, he made a left wheel of his regiment in order to take advantage of the more broken ground in our left front, and also hoping thereby to enfilade our line and thus relieve his distressed neighbor. Whatever the result on the 47th Ala., there is no question of its effect on the 20th Me. His great superiority in number, enabled him easily, although in the concave order, to cover our entire front, and to bring a most deadly cross fire on the salient at our color company. He made his first advance from this new direction with great vigor and weight, hoping to drive us from our position, but was met by a fire from the left companies that surpassed in its deadly effects that already experienced on the right, which had caused him severe losses. He says that his line wavered before it like men trying to walk against a strong wind, and it was compelled to give way. Again and again was this mad rush repeated, each time to be beaten off by the ever thinning line that desperately clung to its ledge of rock, refusing to yield except as it involuntarily shrunk for a pace or two at a time for the storm of lead which swept its front. Col. Oates himself advanced, as he tells us, close to our lines at the head of his men, and at times the hostile force were actually at hand to hand distance. Twice the rebels were followed down the slope so sharply that they were obliged to use the bayonet, and in places small squads of their men in their charges reached our actual front. The reports of both commanders are authority for these statements. The front surged backward and forward like a wave. At times our dead and wounded were in front of our line, and then by a superhuman effort our gallant lads would carry the combat forward beyond their prostrate forms. Continually the gray lines crept up by squads under protecting trees and boulders, and the firing became at closer and closer range. And even the enemy's line essayed to reach around the then front of blue that, stretched out in places to single rank, could not go much farther without breaking. So far had they extended, that their bullets passed beyond and into the ranks of the other ranks of the other regiments further up the hill, and Capt. Woodward, commanding the 83rd, sent his adjutant to ask if the 20th had been turned. Col. Chamberlain assured him that he was holding his ground, but would like a company, if possible, to extend his line. Capt. Woodward was unable to do this, but by shortening his line somewhat, he was able to cover the right of the 20th and enable it to take a little more ground to the left. Meanwhile the brigade in front of the hill was hard pushed to hold its own, and the heavy roar of musketry in the fitful lulls of our own guns, came to the anxious ears of our commander and told only too plainly, what would be the result if our line gave away. Not a man in that devoted band but knew that the safety of the brigade, and perhaps of the army, depended on the steadfastness with which that point was held, and so fought on and on, with no hope of assistance, but not a thought of giving up. Already nearly half of the little force is prostrate. The dead and wounded clog the footsteps of the living. Capt. Billings of C., the gallant and devoted soldier, has fallen with a mortal wound. Young Kendall is just breathing his last sighs. Great-hearted Charley Steele of Co. H., beloved by all the regiment, pours out his life-blood at the feet of his Captain. Lathrop of the same company, a giant in stature, lies cold in death, and beside him Buck, promoted and vindicated from a cruel injustice, wears a smile of content upon his bloodless lips. Two heroes are gone whom Nichols can illy spare from the rolls of K, Buxton, a mere boy, my school-mate in a quiet country town, true patriot and gentle spirit, only a few days before declaring his readiness to give his life for country, has received his death wound and seals his devotion with calm fortitude; and tall, grave, silent George Noyes, first Sergeant, an ever sure reliance of his officers in camp and field, sleeps in peace amid the horrid crash of battle. Tozier still bears the colors aloft, and of the guard Livermore and Coan will live to tell their children of the day of Round Top, but Day has answered his last roll-call and Reed lies helpless among the rocks. The two companies at the colors, receiving a fire from three sides, are swept like trees by a whirlwind. Keene has been temporarily disabled and twenty-one of forty of his men are out of the battle, seven killed on the spot, and out of the twenty-six in A, only eight still grimly face the enemy and swear to avenge their fallen comrades, while to the right and left in less proportion but in fearful totals the loss foots up; a few names among which I have recalled, but all of whom in grateful remembrance are borne on yonder sculptured stone, where in far distant summers that we shall not see, future generations will read of the valor and devotion of these heroes of the 20th Maine.

    The punishment inflicted upon the more crowded ranks of the enemy had not been less severe. These lives of ours had not been cheaply sold, but a fearful price had been exacted for each drop of loyal blood. The eyes that glanced along the rifles had been keen and true and shots not idly wasted. His officers had freely exposed themselves in leading the successive charges and the mortality among them was great. The Lieut. Co. had lost his leg, two Captains and four Lieutenants had been instantly killed, John Oates, the Colonel's brother, struck by eight bullets, and in all nineteen out of forty were disabled. With all the advantage of his heavy line, he had not been able to gain a single foot of permanent advance, and the prospects of success were not brightening, except as he must have been able to discern from his near approach that our lines were thinning. He was also becoming solicitous about his right flank, being in a hostile and unknown country and aware that he was on the extreme right of his army, and had been moreover for some time experiencing the effects of a fitful and mysterious fire, which came apparently from his rear, and at times his men had been struck by bullets from front and rear at the same time.

To understand this assistance to our fire, then unknown and unsuspected by us, we must go back to Capt. Morrill and his men, who had scarcely commenced to deploy on the sides of Round Top when the roar of battle in his rear, told him that the enemy in force had interposed between him and his regiment. He at once moved his company to uncover the enemy and at the same time to discover and guard against a flank movement on the left. Arriving on the open field at the left of the woods, he found twelve or fifteen of the Sharpshooters, under command of a non-commissioned officer, who had been driven in by Hood's advance over Round Top, and who asked leave to remain under the Captain's orders during the battle. Morrill, who generally went into action with a musket, and was, I think, the coolest man we had in the regiment in an emergency, and had no superior on the skirmish line, placed his men behind the stone wall, which crosses the depression between the mountains just at the edge of the field, and therefore exactly on the flank of the 15th Ala. before the movement to the left was made, and in its rear during the greater part of the action. This position he maintained during the battle undiscovered by the rebels, and for prudential reasons not disclosing his whereabouts by any steady fire, but none who know Co. B. will doubt that the temptation of an occasional shot through the loop-holes of that stone wall was too strong to be resisted, and these shots did excellent service in awakening uneasiness in the Confederate ranks.

Whatever misgivings the rebel commander may have had as to his position, he ordered his officers to sell out as dearly as possible, and the attack was pushed with no cessation perceptible on our side. Gen. Grant has said that in every battle there comes a time when both sides being nearly exhausted, the combatant who can make a final effort, or hold his own a moment longer by sheer force of will, is to be winner. That moment was rapidly approaching to these two wrestlers, foemen worthy of each other, but so unequally matched in numbers, for which the slight advantage of position made little amends, that the issue seemed almost certain against the weaker party. The pressure is growing harder and harder. Every advance seems more difficult to resist. How long can flesh and blood endure it? As the line surges back from the determined rushes of the enemy and from the fire which scorches their very faces, the officers on the left, Spear, Land and others, are holding the flat of their swords against the line to assist in maintaining its place. Ammunition is rapidly exhausting. Many men have replenished their stock from the boxes of their fallen comrades, but that resource cannot last long and then what? Death is easy but defeat is worse, and there is but one last expedient, the cold steal, truly a forlorn hope when the force of the enemy is at least two to one. Lieut. Melcher, in command of Co. F., has suggested to Col. Chamberlain an advance of his company, in order to cover the line of wounded, exposed by the retirement of the left wing, but such a movement if unsuccessful, might give the enemy opportunity for a counter charge which would sweep us from the hill. Yet matters are now at such a crisis that boldness, even of that of desperation, may be the truest safety, and the Colonel has decided to take the offensive with the whole regiment. The die is thrown, and the one word "bayonets" rings from Chamberlain's lips like a bugle note, and down that worn and weary line the word and the action go, like a flash of lightning through the powder-smoke. To the anxious, frenzied heart of every man in that battle-torn array, it came as the chance of life to the drowning, and as his hand drew the shining weapon his foot was advanced to carry it toward the bosom of his foe. The lines were in motion before the word of command was completed, and Col. Chamberlain does not know whether he ever finished that order. In an instant, less time than has been required to tell it, Melcher has sprung ahead of the line, the colors are advancing, and with one wild rush the devoted regiment hurls itself down the ledge into the midst of the gray lines, not thirty paces distant. Officers and men are striving for the lead. Spear and Land leap down from a broad rock into the midst of a knot of Confederates, huddled behind it for safety. Some have greater opportunities for individual deeds than others, but every man does his duty. For one instant the battle wavers in the balance. Pistols are leveled, swords flash in the air and bayonets clash. An officer fires in Col.

Chamberlain's face, and then, seeing the line upon him, surrenders his sword with the other. Which wins the day, Union or rebel? Will our little line be swallowed up in the gray ranks? No! No! They turn, they fly! and from yonder wall, as it by magic, rises a blue line and pour a deadly volley into the discomfited foe. Thank God! The victory is ours! and glory to the God of Hosts from whom all blessings are. The Stars and Bars are flying in defeat, and the flag of Freedom and Union waves in triumph over this stricken hillside, where dying eyes look up through happy tears, as the shouts of victory float back through the rattle of pursuing musketry, and death is sweetened by the knowledge that life has not been lost in vain.

Col. Oates has said that he passed the order among his men to retreat without regard to order and reform on the top of the mountain, but it is a remarkable fact that the execution of that order should have been coincident with the charge of the 20th. The extent to which his line had enveloped the Union forces, now became nearly the destruction of his command, for the advance of the right of our regiment was nearly at right angles to his line of retreat, cutting off his right wing, that bewildered dashed in all directions seeking for safety, many rushing towards a lane in the direction of the rear of our army and, throwing down their arms, are captured by scores. The biting shots of Co. B., as they pour in volley after volley from their wall, add speed to the flying feet of those who are able to pass the fast converging lines of the pursuit. The 83rd dashes out from its position, picking up those who cross its front, Morrill launches his fresh men after them, and far up the mountain side the fugitives are pressed, the list of captures still growing, till prudence compels a recall, and with lightened hearts, the regiment is reformed on the old line, and addresses itself to the task of caring for its dead and wounded and gathering in the fruits of its hard won victory. Capt. Morrill threw out his skirmish line on the left of Round Top and remained there till 9 p.m., when he rejoined the regiment.

Four hundred prisoners, mostly from the 15th and 47th Ala., were sent to the rear. These included the wounded Lieut. Col. of the 47th and several line officers. Fifty dead of the 15th were buried in our front, and about one hundred of their badly wounded were also left behind to become prisoners. Col. Oates went into the action with one of the strongest and finest regiments in Hood's Division, its effectives (and this in the Confederate army meant the men on the battle line) numbered six hundred and eighty-six officers and men. When the roll was called that night in the bivouac at the Emmittsburg road, but two hundred and twenty-five answered, and less than half the officers. Our own loss, as now reported in the rebellion records, was twenty-nine men killed on the field, six officers and eighty-five men wounded, and five men missing; the latter were captured on Round Top in the night, and three officers and six men died of their wounds, making thirty-eight whose names are borne on the tablets of the monument.

The attack of Law and Robertson on the front, though bitter and persistent, had been repulsed by the rest of our brigade and that of Gen. Weed, at the expense of the lives of many brave men and those gallant officers, Vincent, Med. O'Rorke and Hazlitt, before the final charge of the 20th, and no further attempt was made against this vital point of the line. The troops of Hood were thoroughly exhausted and the advance of McCandlers across Plum Run, and the massing of the Sixth Corps on its northern slope, deterred any movement of fresh troops.

A word may be said as to the belief of Col. Oates that his right was menaced by "long lines of Union infantry." He states that two of his Captains of the 25th reported a command with flags moving from the right. Unless this was purely imaginary, it must have been a distant view of the advance of the reserves, who were so far away that they did not reach the ground till the action was fully over. It is not impossible that a sentinel on the extreme edge of the wood might have descried them, but no one on the battle line knew of them; Capt. Morrill did not see them, and they gave no aid or comfort, physical or moral, to the imperiled battalions of the 20th. An obscurely worded passage in Gen. Doubleday's account of the battle lends some weight to the theory of the arrival of Fisher's Brigade, but as the next sentence gives the 20th Maine the credit of clearing the ground by their final charge, it may be dismissed. The regiment having fought concealed by woods, its action, unlike that of most troops at Gettysburg, was not overlooked by superior officers, but full credit was given to its services by brigade, division and corps commanders. The later publications by the Confederates who opposed us more than sustain all that our most ardent champions ever asserted, for while they show a loss in the 15th Ala. almost unprecedented, they also show, by the known positions of other troops, that this heavy punishment and complete overthrow was effected solely by the one regiment, with half the number of men, which contended also, for at least a portion of the battle, with the 44th Ala. It was the great, good fortune of Vincent's Brigade and the 20th Me. that they were taken from the vortex of the wheat field that swallowed up brigades and divisions and, subjecting them to continual enfilading fires, quenched their valor in blood and rendered their sacrifices nugatory. The men of Tilton and Sweitzer, of

Zook, and Cross and De Trobriand were no less brave than those who stood on Round Top, but victory was denied them through no fault of theirs. Ours would have been the same fate, but the fortunes of war, or let us rather say the hand of Him who doth His will among the armies of Heaven, placed our beloved regiment where it had the opportunity to render a signal service to the army and the country. If I have been able, in even so humble a degree, to show how well that duty was performed, I am more than content.

No man who wore the uniform of the 20th Me., or who followed where the bugles sang "Dan Butterfield," but may claim a part of the glories of Gettysburg. "No man who carried arms in this greatest of our country's battles but may tell the tale with glowing pride," and transmit its memory as a priceless heritage to his children's children; "no scar here won but yields its meed of honor; no life laid down upon this hard-fought field but inscribes his name who bravely gave it up upon the roll of imperishable renown."

GENERAL CHAMBERLAIN'S ADDRESS

Capt. Prince was followed by Gen. J. L. Chamberlain, who commanded the regiment during the battle. He spoke as follows:

A quarter of a century ago on this rugged crest you were doing what you deemed your duty. Today you come with modest mein, with care more for the truth than for praise, to retrace and record the simple facts—the outward form—of your movements and action. But far more than this entered into your thought and motive, and far greater was the result of the action taken than any statistical description of it could import.

You were making history. The world has recorded for you more than you have written. The centuries to come will share and recognize the victory won here, with growing gratitude. The country has acknowledged your service. Your State is proud of it. This well-earned and unsought fame has moved you already to acknowledge your deserts. Your own loyal and loving zeal for justice has indeed anticipated the State's recognition. At your own cost you set your monument here to mark the ground where faithful service and devotion wrought a result so momentous.

Today your historians have recalled the facts. On that line which has been so patiently and candidly investigated and as far as possible freed from doubt and unclearness, your admirable record leaves little to be desired. But as this is a suitable, if not final, opportunity for accurate and complete statement of these facts, I may be indulged in a remark or two germane to this matter, which recent visits and this occasion itself suggests.

I am certain that the position of this monument is quite to the left of the center of our regimental line when the final charge was ordered. Our original left did not extend quite to the great rock which now supports this memorial of honor. When we changed front with our left wing and extended it by the flank and rear, the color was brought to mark the new center, which was to become the salient of our formation; and it was placed, I was sorry to do it, on the smooth and open slope, and in a position completely exposed. Beyond this the left was refused and extended in single rank. When the charge was made I was beside the color-bearer, and I know well that we struck the enemy where their line was open to view, and the ground comparatively unobstructed. The color advanced in the direction of the proper front of the right wing, and passed the rock altogether to our left. I am not at all criticizing the judgement of our comrades who selected the great boulder for the base of the monument. It was entirely fitting to mark it with that honor, as it became so conspicuous an object during the terrible struggle—the center and pivot of the whirlpool that raged around.

I take note also of the surprise of several officers to hear that it was some other than a single one of them who came to me in the course of the fight with information of the enemy's extended movements to envelop our left. Now, as might well be believed of such gentlemen and soldiers, they are all right; no one of them is wrong.

It was quite early in the action, and while as yet only our right wing was hotly engaged, that an officer from the center reported to me that a large body of the enemy could be seen in his front, moving along the bottom of the valley below us, deliberately towards our extreme left and rear. I sprang upon a rock in our line, which allowed me to see over the heads of those with whom we were then engaged, and the movement and intent of the enemy was plain to be seen. It was this timely knowledge that enabled me to plan the prompt movement which you so admirably executed—that rapid change of front, doubling back upon ourselves, and the single rank formation, which proved so effectual for our stubborn resistance.

Sometime after this, and while we were hard pressed upon all sides, an officer from the extreme left reported to me, with great anxiety, that the enemy were outflanking our left, thrown back as it was. I found the situation critical, and immediately ordered the right company to repair to the extreme left in support, and sent to the commanding officer of the 83rd Penn. regiment, asking him to extend his left to cover the ground vacated on our right. But as I found this movement produced much confusion and this withdrawal was likely to be misconstrued into a retreat, I was obliged to countermand the order, and let the left wing hold on as best it could, and as best it did.

One more matter. In the third fierce onset of the enemy, through a rift in the rolling smoke I saw with consternation that our center was nearly shot away, and the color guarded only by a little group, who seemed to be checking the enemy by their heroic bearing and not by numbers, and I sent the adjutant to the commanding officer of the color company, to ask him to hold on if he possibly could, till I could reinforce him from some other regiment. So little expectation had I that the adjutant could live to reach the spot, I pressed into my service a trusted sergeant and despatched him with the same message. Meantime the crash had come, and out of the flame and smoke emerged that center, bearing the color still aloft, forced back, pressed in upon itself, but solid and firm, and impregnable front, face to the foe. The enemy on their part had also recoiled, and were gathering in the low shrubbery for a new assault. Our ammunition was gone. It was manifest that we could not stand before the wave that was ready to roll upon us. Knowing all this I resolved upon the desperate chances of a counter-charge with the bayonet. I at once sent to the left wing to give them notice and time for the required change of front. Just then the brave and thoughtful young Lieutenant, commanding the color company, came up to me and said, I think I could press forward with my company, if you will permit me; and cover the ground where our dead and wounded are." "You shall have the chance," was my answer, "I am about to order a charge. We are to make a great right wheel." What he did, you who know him know.

What you did, the world knows.

I am sorry to have heard it intimated that any hesitated when that order was given. That was not so. No man hesitated. There might be an appearance of it to those who did not understand the whole situation. The left wing went back like an ox-bow, or sharp lunette, had to take some little time to come up into the line of our general front, so as to form the close, continuous edge which was to strike like a sword-cut upon the enemy's ranks. By the time they had got up and straightened the line, the center and salient, you may be sure, was already in motion. Nobody hesitated to obey the order. In fact, to tell the truth, the order was never given, or but imperfectly. The enemy were already pressing up the slope. There was only time or need for the words, "Bayonet! Forward to the right!" The quick witted and tense-nerved men caught the words out of my lips and almost the action out of my hands.

So much in elucidation of facts. You see there may be stories apparently not consistent with each other, yet all of them true in their time and place, and so far as each actor is concerned.

And while every one here, officer and soldier, did more than his duty, and acted with utmost intelligence and spirit, you must permit me to add the remark that I commanded my regiment that day.

Words elsewhere spoken by me today in our State's behalf strive to express the motive and purpose of this great struggle, and the character and consequence of the victory vouchsafed us. It is there I speak of country; here it needs only that I speak of you, and of ground made glorious by you and yours.

The lesson impressed on me as I stand here and my heart and mind traverse your faces, and the years that are gone, is that in a great, momentous struggle like this commemorated here, it is character that tells. I do not mean simply nor chiefly bravery. Many a man has that, who may become surprised or disconcerted at a sudden change in the posture of affairs. What I mean by character is a firm and seasoned substance of soul. I mean such qualities or acquirements as intelligence, thoughtfulness, conscientiousness, right-mindedness, patience, fortitude, long-suffering and unconquerable resolve.

I could see all this on your faces when you were coming into position here for the desperate encounter; man by man, file by file, on the right into line. I knew that you all knew that was staked on your endurance and heroism. Some of you heard Vincent say to me, with such earnest and prophetic eyes, pointing to the right of our position and the front of the oncoming attack, "You understand, Colonel, this ground must be held at all costs!" I did understand; with a heavy weight on my mind and spirit. You understood; and it was done, Held, and at what cost! Held, and for what effect!

There is no need that I should recount to the friends who stand around us here, what would have happened had this little line—this thin, keen edge of Damascus steel—been broken down from its guard. All can see what would have become of our Brigade swallowed up; of Weed's, struck in the rear; of Hazlitt's guns, taken in the flank and turned to launch their thunder-bolts upon our troops, already sore pressed in the gorge at our feet, and the fields upon the great front and right. Round Top lost—the day lost—Gettysburg lost-who can tell or dream what for loss thence would follow!

I do not know whether any friends who now stand here in this calm and sunny day comprehend how the weight of such a responsibility presses upon the spirit. We were young then. We do not count ourselves old yet; and these things were done more than twenty-six years ago. We believe we could do them now; but we wonder how we could have done them then. Doubtless the spring and elasticity of youth helped us to bear the burden and recover from the shock. But something more than youthful ardor and dash was demanded for such a test. And that was yours. In thought, in habit, in experience, in discipline, you were veterans. It was a matter, as I have said of character. It was the soul of youth suddenly springing into the flush and flower of manhood. It was the force of the characters you had formed in the silent and peaceful years by the mother's knee and by the father's side, which stood you in such stead in the day of trial. And so it is. We know not of the future, and cannot plan for it much. But we can hold our spirits and our bodies so pure and high, we may cherish such thoughts and such ideals, and dream such dreams of lofty purpose, that we can determine and know what manner of men we will be whenever and wherever the hour strikes, that calls to noble action. This predestination God has given us in charge. No man becomes suddenly different from his habit and cherished thought. We carry our accustomed manners with us. And it was the boyhood you brought from your homes which made you men; which braced your hearts, which shone upon your foreheads, which held you steadfast in mind and body, and lifted these heights of Gettysburg to immortal glory.

This Round Top spur, as it is easy to see today, was a commanding position in that battle, and confessedly the key of the field for that day's fight. It is deliberately so pronounced in official papers by the leaders on both sides. I stood on the summit not long ago with Longstreet and officers of our own army, not so much disposed as he by the events of that day's fighting, to praise the Fifth Corps, and they one and all acknowledged that this was by nature and in fact the supreme position. One of the ablest of the southern historians, describing in his impassioned style the fight which circled and flamed around this crest, says, "That was the glittering coronet we longed to clutch." The glittering coronet was won, but not by them. All honor to those who seeing it, seized it in thought; who gained it, who held it, who glorified it. All honor to Warren, first and last, and now forever, of the Fifth Corps; to Vincent, to Rice, to Hazlitt, to Weed, to Ayres,—chief commanders here. Peace to be their spirits where they have gone. Honor and sacred remembrance to those who fell here, and buried part of our hearts with them. Honor to the memory of those who fought here with us and for us, and who fell elsewhere, or have died since, heartbroken at the harshness or injustice of a political government. Honor to you, who have wrought and endured so much and so well. After life's fitful fever, may you also, sleep well. And so, farewell.

The service on Little Round Top was appropriately closed by Joseph Tyler sounding the bugle call of "Taps," which brought tears to the eyes of many a listener.

The Association then climbed the heights of Round Top proper, where the State of Maine has erected a solid granite monument, and where the assembled veterans listened to

LIEUT. SAMUEL L. MILLER'S ADDRESS.

Mr. President:—We read upon the monument erected by our

state to commemorate the valor of her sons upon the field of battle, the following inscription:—"The 20th Me. Regt., 3rd Brigade, 1st Division, 5th Corps, Joshua L. Chamberlain, captured and held this position on the evening of July 2nd, 1863, pursuing the enemy from its front on the line marked by its monument below."

"This modest legend will not fully convey to the minds of the thousands who in coming years visit this historic ground, the dangerous character of the movement it is designed to make memorable. The magnificent defense of the extreme left of Little Round Top by the Twentieth Maine on the afternoon of July 2nd, 1863, graphicly described by Capt. Prince, so overshadowed all subsequent movements of the regiment at Gettysburg, that the importance of the occupation of Round Top proper has not been fully estimated, even by the officers and men who climbed its precipitous and rocky side the early part of the night following that eventful day. The dearly bought victory of the afternoon was insecure while the enemy was permitted to occupy Round Top, which reared its wooded crest 564 feet above the plain but a few rods from the position held by the 3rd Brigade.

It was some time after the Twentieth returned from the bayonet charge and pursuit of the enemy, and the shades of night were falling, when the 2nd Brigade, 3rd Division, 5th Corps, commanded by Col. Joseph W. Fisher, arrived in the rear of Little Round Top. Col. Rice, who had assumed command of our Brigade when Col. Vincent was wounded, asked Fisher to advance with his brigade and seize the crest of Round Top. This movement Col. Fisher hesitated to make, giving as a reason that, on account of the darkness and the nature of the ground, and his men newly arrived, being ignorant of the situation, the attempt was extremely difficult and dangerous. Col. Rice then asked Col. Chamberlain if he would take the heights, and our commander replied: "Yes, the 20th Maine will take them!" Col. Fisher then agreed to support the Twentieth in this movement.

The casualties of battle, together with the details to bury the dead and bring up ammunition, had reduced the ranks of the Twentieth to 200 muskets. The men had just passed through such an ordeal as only those who have experienced the horrors of war can comprehend; one man in every three had been shot down; they were exhausted, hungry and thirsty; but they received the command with enthusiasm. Leaving their dead comrades, who lay so thickly about them, to be buried by the detail, the regiment advanced in line of battle across the vale, and were soon struggling over the boulders which obstructed the ascent of the steep sides of Round Top. This advance was made just to the left of the present path up the mountain. When the summit was reached it was intensely dark in the woods, although the open ground was flooded with the light of a full moon.

The Twentieth was now occupying an extremely dangerous position, entirely isolated from the main line and exposed to attack from the enemy, or to be cut off altogether from the brigade on Little Round Top. This was a period of such anxiety. While strengthening his position Col. Chamberlain heard troops advancing on his right. Being challenged, they replied that they were sent to support the 20th Maine which they were trying to find. These were the 5th and 12th Penn. Reserves. They were conducted to the proper position, but as they were marching by the "right flank", in fronting, of course, they faced to the rear. The confusion and noise attending the efforts to have them "face by the rear rank," drew the attention of the enemy, who fired a sharp volley in our direction. The Reserves had been floundering around in the darkness for some time and it is not strange that they began to think they had marched

> "Into the jaws of death,
> Into the mouth of hell."

Instead of facing by their rear rank our supports moved off in a direction opposite from the enemy and disappeared.

Apprehending that the rebels might seize this opportunity to envelope our right, Col. Chamberlain hastily detailed a picket line on the front and right, and retired the main body to the lower ground near the foot of the ascent. He then dispatched a request to Col. Rice for the 83rd Penn. and afterwards for the 44th N.Y. to support the 20th on the right echelon. In this formation, being partially supplied with ammunition, the line again advanced considerably beyond its former position where the men lay on their arms till morning, expecting an attack at any moment.

I have mentioned the detail of a picket line in the early part of the night. These pickets advanced down the side of the hill in our front until they could see the enemy by the light of campfires and hear conversation, when they retired part way up to the crest. The Confederates had evidently heard their movements for they soon sent a squad to ascertain whether they were friends or foes. Being hailed by our picket they answered, "Friends," and were told to come right along. This strategy was continued till twenty-five of the 4th Texas Regiment had been captured by company E on the right of the line. At this time some officer farther to the left gave an order to fire and no more prisoners were taken that night. These prisoners were sent to the rear under the escort of John Bradford and Eugene Kelleran of company I, who tramped around in the darkness a long time trying to find the Provost Guard. Coming out into an open space they decided to bivouac till morning when the prisoners were turned over to the proper officers.

The only casualty to the Twentieth during this movement occurred in the morning when Lieut. Arad Linscott took a musket and going out in advance of the picket line to get a shot at the enemy, who were firing in among our men, was mortally wounded in the thigh by a sharpshooter.

At ten o'clock on the morning of the 3rd the regiment was relieved by other troops and marched back over the ground where it had fought the day before and, having received sixty rounds of ammunition, took position with the brigade behind a stone wall at the right of Little Round Top where it remained during the terrible connonade preceding Picket's charge.

The quiet of an October day now reigns on Round Top and it is difficult to realize the terrors of that July night twenty-six years ago. Here are the steep ascents, the huge boulders and the sturdy oaks, but the darkness of night, the presence of a brave and vigilant foe, the crack of the rifle and the singing bullet are missing. Unquestionably the movement was made under great apprehension and nervousness. One comrade, whose courage has been tested on many battlefields, says he does not know what time the advance was made; he was too excited to look at his watch as he would have done had he understood what kind of history we were making then. Another comrade, who has brevets and medals to prove his bravery, owns that he never was so scared in his life. And even our valiant Colonel confesses that he was "not a little nervous and apprehensive."

Under cover of darkness, however, the position was carried and held by our troops during the remainder of the battle. The neglect of Hood's Division which was massed in close proximity, to hold it when occupied, or attempt its subsequent capture, is one of the many mistakes which have been apparent in all great military operations. Col. William C. Oates, who commanded the 15th Alabama in the attack on the Twentieth at Little Round Top, in his account of the battle, claims that Round Top, which is 166 feet higher and only 1,000 yards distant from Little Round Top, was the more important of the two; that if Gen. Longstreet has crowned Round Top with his artillery any time on the afternoon of the 2nd, even though it had been only supported by the two Alabama regiments, who had possession of it till sunset, he would have won the battle.

This address was followed by brief remarks from Gen. Chamberlain and the exercises were closed with prayer and benediction by Rev. Theodore Gerrish.

During these ceremonies what remains of the old regimental battle flag was unfurled by Comrade E. S. Coan, one of the color guards in battle.

PART IX
Account of Holman S. Melcher, Co. F 20th Maine Vols.
Taken from the Lincoln County News, March 13, 1885.

The Confederate force designated to take possession of Little Round Top appears to have been [Brig.-Gen. Jerome B.] Robertson's Brigade, consisting of the 1st, 4th and 5th Texas, and 3rd Arkansas, and [Brig.-Gen. Evander M.]Law's Brigade, consisting of the 4th, 44th, 47th, 48th, and 15th Alabama,--both of [Maj.-Gen. John B.] Hood's Division. The former was to assault in front, while Law's Brigade was to attack the rear of the hill; but Robertson finding he could not cover the entire front with his brigade, the 44th, 48th and 4th Alabama were detached from Law's Brigade about the time they arrived at the foot of Round Top in their advance and connected with Robertson's line, then well in front of Little Round Top, leaving the 47th and 15th Alabama to carry out the flanking movement alone which they did, passing up the southern side of Round Top, and halting some ten minutes on the crest for rest. This halt proved fatal to the success of their undertaking, as it enabled our brigade (Col. Strong Vincent's) to reach Little Round Top in time to resist their advance.

Resuming their march, these two regiments passed down the northeasterly side of Round Top, and advanced across the wooded depression between the hills, to charge up the rear of Little Round Top and sweep off Vincent's brigade, then fiercely engaged with Robertson's Texans and the three regiments of Law's brigade that had been assigned to his command, who were trying to get possession from the front. But just here these two Alabama regiments met the 20th Maine, which was the left regiment of Vincent's brigade, and also the left of the whole Army of the Potomac, and to conform to the crest of the hill, was bent back at about right angles with the line of the rest of the brigade, fortunately; for in their advance the 47th Alabama, commanded by Lt. Col. M.J.

Bulger, struck our regiment squarely in front and opened a murderous fire on our unprotected line, as we had just got into position, and had no time to throw up breastworks. At the same time the 15th Alabama, commanded by Col. William C. Oates, numbering 644 men and 42 officers, moved around to attack us in the flank and rear. Col. Chamberlain met this movement by putting the right wing of the regiment into single rank to resist the 47th, and bent back the five left companies of the regiment at right angles with the right wing, the colors at the angle.

Our regiment numbered 358 men, but as Company B, numbering 50 men, had been sent out to "protect our flank," we had 308 men in line to resist the furious assault of these two strong regiments, outnumbering us more than three to one. The conflict was fierce, but necessarily brief, as it was a question of only a short time when every man must fall before the superior fire of our enemy, so greatly outnumbering us. When 136 of our brave officers and men had been shot down where they stood, and only 172 remained, hardly more than a strong skirmish line, and the 60 rounds of cartridges each man carried into the fight had been fired, and the survivors were using the cartridge-boxes of their fallen comrades, the time had come when it must be decided whether we should fall back and give up this key to the whole field of Gettysburg, or charge and try to throw off this foe, that were rapidly drawing the life-blood of our regiment by their deadly fire. It must not be the former; how can it be the latter? Col. Chamberlain decides it can be only the latter and gives the order to "fix bayonets," and almost before he can say "Charge"! the regiment, with a shout of desperation, leaps down the hill and close in with the foe, which we find behind every rock and tree. Surprised and overwhelmed by this sudden and unexpected movement, the most of them throw down their arms and surrender. Some fight till they are slain; the others "run like a herd of wild cattle," as Col. Oates himself expressed it. In their flight they were met by Capt. Morrill's company (B), which we supposed had been captured, but which, cut off from the regiment before they could deploy, so soon was the advance made on us when we went into position, had taken refuge behind a stone wall till the time arrived when they could render assistance, which they now did by such well-directed volleys that it compelled over 100 of the fugitives to surrender to them.

Lieut.-Col. Bulger, commanding the 47th, was wounded, and fell into our hands, with over 300 prisoners and all the wounded. We buried 50 of their dead left on the field. Col. Oates, in his official report, says: "After all had got up, I ordered the rolls of the companies to be called. When the battle commenced, four hours previously, I had the strongest and finest regiment in Hood's Division. Its effectives numbered nearly 700 officers and men. Now 225 answered at roll-call, and more than one-half of my officers had been left on the field."

The charging of one regiment of a brigade alone, and without orders from the brigade commander, was exceptional in the usual tactics of a battle; but it was the only way Col. Chamberlain could carry out the orders he received - to "hold the position," for there would have been none remaining for that duty in a very short time had the enemy not been routed by the charge.

The final formation of the regiment was such, that when the charge was made it was in a direction directly to the rear from the way the rest of the regiments of the brigade were facing and fighting; and the enemy, or the most of them, were driven in their flight, at first, directly to the rear of the line of battle of our army, and accounts in part for so few of them escaping.

After pursuing as far as seemed proper, the 20th Maine returned, with its prisoners, to occupy our original position, and stayed there until ordered forward, in the early evening, to occupy Round Top, which we did, supported by the 5th and 12th Pennsylvania Reserves, of [Col. Joseph W.] Fisher's Brigade, which reported to Col. Chamberlain for that duty. We were relieved from this advanced position on Round Top on the morning of July 3, and assigned to the second line of the left center, where we were on duty till the close of the battle.

Dead Confederates somewhere near Big Round Top. This photograph was taken on July 6, 1863.

This woodcut first appeared in 1882, on the stationary used by the Executive Committee of the Twentieth Maine Regiment Association. It illustrates the committee choosing the location for their monument. Chamberlain later disputed that the monument did not accurately mark the position of the colors during the battle.

PART X
Conclusion

"So much in elucidation of facts." JLC

THE CHARGE OF THE TWENTIETH MAINE
THE FIGHT FOR VINCENT'S SPUR

The following quotations were taken from the preceding accounts. When chronologically placed, a simple description of the fight is easily understood. Emphasis is italicized by the editor.

"The line faced generally toward a more conspicuous eminence southwest of ours, which is known as Sugar Loaf, or Round Top. Between this and my position intervened a smooth and thinly wooded hollow. My line formed, I immediately detached Company B, Captain Morrill commanding, to extend from my left flank across this hollow as a line of skirmishers." JLC

"I immediately deployed my men as skirmishers and moved to the front and left. Having advanced across the flat and just commenced to ascend Big Round Top, was somewhat surprised to hear heavy volleys of musketry in our rear, where we just left the regiment." WGM

"We had been in position perhaps not more than 20 minutes when the [enemy] appeared, advancing from the bushes at the foot of the wooded covered slope of the hill, extending, apparently, past our left. It seemed to have cut off our Company B." ES

"In the midst of this, an officer from my center informed me that some important movement of the enemy was going on in his front. Mounting a large rock, I was able to see a considerable body of the enemy moving by flank in rear of their line engaged toward the front of my left. I immediately stretched my regiment to the left, by taking intervals by the left flank, and at the same time refusing my left wing, so that it was nearly at right angles with my right, thus occupying about twice the extent of our ordinary front, *some* of the companies being brought into single rank when the nature of the ground gave sufficient strength or shelter." JLC

"Very quickly after this was done the enemy struck us, and mainly on our left." ES

"We were ordered to come to a ready and take good aim, when the enemy appeared. They came within four or six rods, covering themselves behind big rocks or trees, and kept up a murderous fire, which was returned by us." WTL

"Squads of the enemy broke through our line in several places, and the fight was literally hand to hand. The edge of the fight rolled backward and forward like a wave. Forced from our position, we desperately recovered it, and pushed the enemy down to the foot of the slope." JLC

"In closing up, and partly by reason of the pressure upon the left, the left was swayed back somewhat so that the line extended down to the centre about at the colors and thus the full left was somewhat bent to the rear, leaving the colors at the apex." ES

"Our line is pressed back so far that our dead are within the lines of the enemy. Our ammunition is nearly gone. We are now using the cartridges from the boxes of our wounded comrades." TG

"The one word "bayonets" rings from Chamberlain's lips like a bugle note, and down that worn and weary line the word and the action go. The lines were in motion before the word of command was completed, and Col. Chamberlain does not know whether he ever finished that order. *In an instant, less time than has been required to tell it, Lt. Melcher has sprung ahead of the line,* the colors are advancing, and with one wild rush the devoted regiment hurls itself down the ledge into the midst of the gray lines, not thirty paces distant. Officers and men are striving for the lead." HLP

"Lieutenant H.S. Melcher saw the situation and did not hesitate. With a cheer and a flash of his sword that sent an inspiration along the line, full ten paces to the front he sprang. The color sergeant and the brave color guard follow, and with one wild yell of anguish wrung from its tortured heart the regiment charged." TG

"When the charge was made it was in a direction directly to the rear from the way the rest of the regiments of the brigade were facing and fighting; and the enemy, or the most of them, were driven in their flight, at first, directly to the rear of the line of battle of our army, and accounts in part for so few of them escaping." HSM*

"They went to the rear without resistance, and those in front broke, *not so many towards the Round Top as to the rear, and many ran and corralled themselves in the worm fence lane.* Some of these, attempting to escape, were shot down, as they climbed the fence, and others surrendered." E.S.**

This quote is from the article: Little Round Top, *by Holman Melcher, first published March 13, 1885 in the* Lincoln County News. *The article, without this important paragraph, was later reprinted in* Battles & Leaders of the Civil War.

**Taken from the memoirs of Ellis Spear, currently in possession of grandson Abbott Spear of Warren, Maine. The "worm fence lane," was located on the eastern slope of Little Round Top, near the Jacob Weikert farmhouse.*

These two previous quotations demonstrate that the majority of Confederates captured by the 20th Maine, were fleeing towards the Taneytown Road and not in the direction of Big Round Top. The Confederates that fled into that farm lane found themselves trapped, and were compelled to surrender.

140 *With a Flash of His Sword*

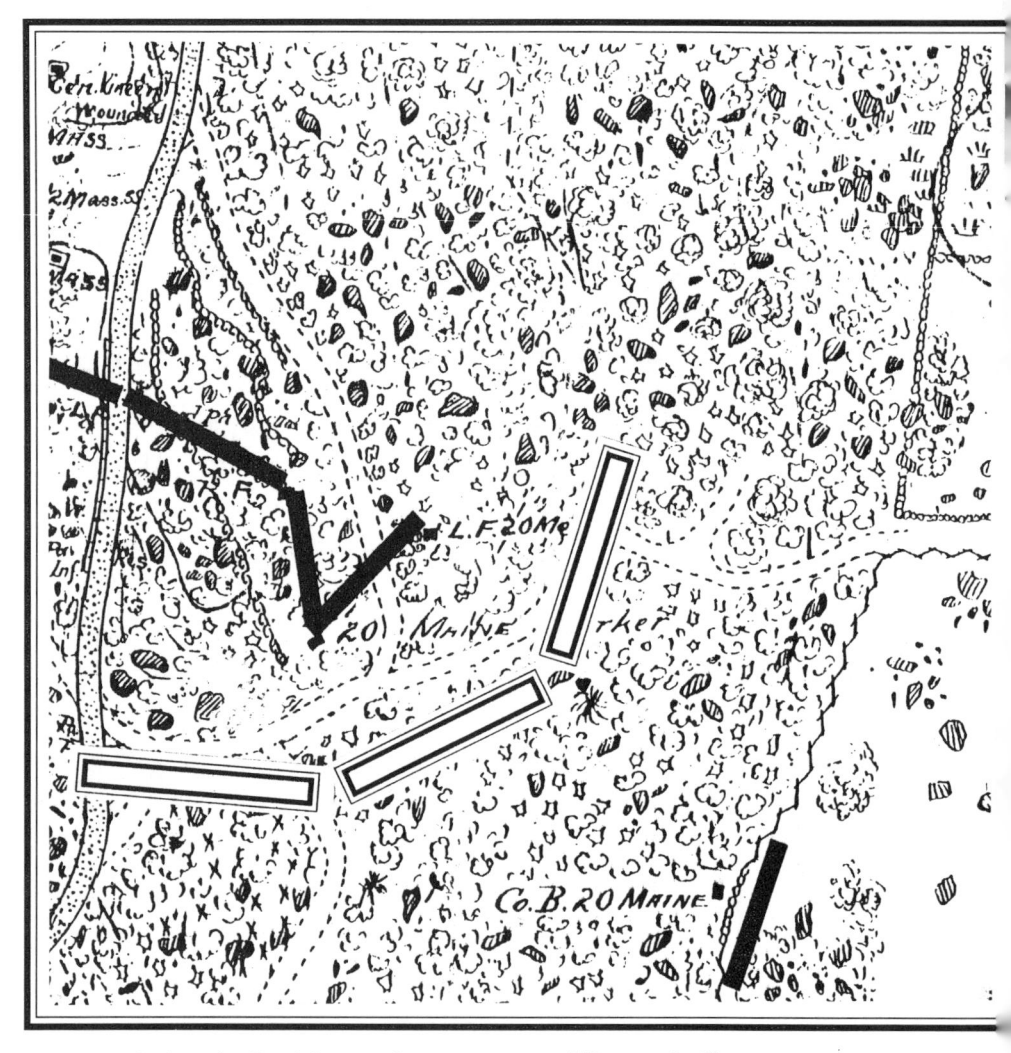

(Above) Positions of troops upon Vincent's Spur.

Union ■■■■■   Confederate ▭▭▭▭▭

(Right) 1895 Battlefield Survey Map, showing Little Round Top/Vincent's Spur area.

A. Twentieth Maine Monument   C. Chamberlain Avenue
B. Company B Marker   D. Weikert Farm Lane

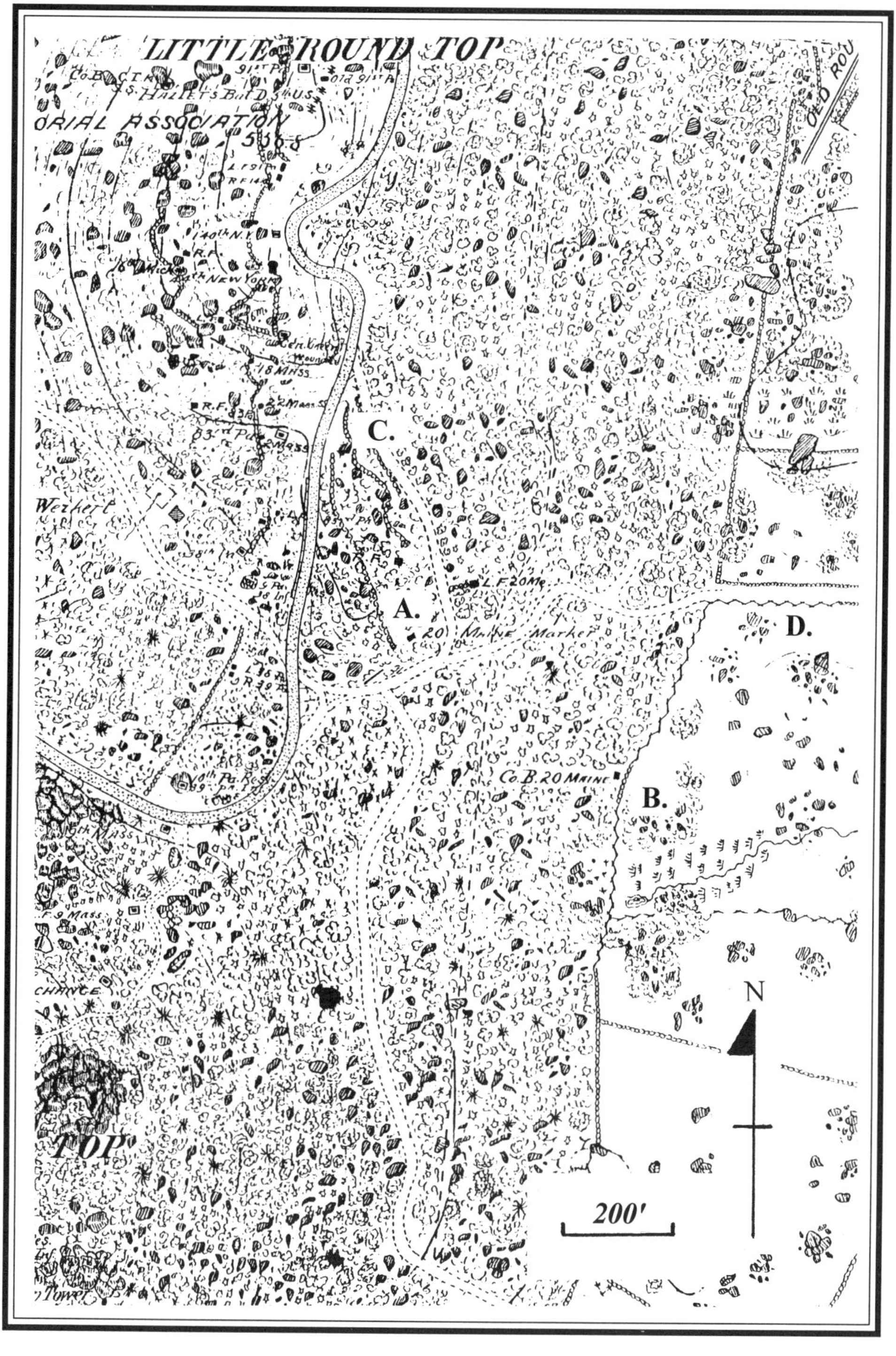

LITTLE ROUND TOP
ORIAL ASSOCIATION
140th N.Y.
44th New York
83rd Pa.
C.
A.
20 Maine Marker
L.F. 20 Me
D.
Co. B. 20 Maine
B.
N
200′
TOP

Sixteen-year-old Miss Tillie Pierce lived in Gettysburg with her family. They fled from their home on July 1st and sought refuge in the Jacob Weikert farmhouse on the eastern slope of Little Round Top for the duration of the battle. On the afternoon of July 2nd she witnessed the same scenes in the Weikert farm lane as those described by Ellis Spear. Twenty-six years after the battle, Tillie wrote about her experience in the book: At Gettysburg or What a Girl Saw and Heard of the Battle. *Unfortunately, many historians did not lend credence to her story. Most believed that the Confederates never reached the clearing east of the Round Tops.*

Between four and five o'clock in the afternoon, I heard some of the soldiers about the house saying:

"The Rebels are on this side of Round Top, coming across the fields toward the house, and there will be danger if they get on the Taneytown road."

Just then some one said the Pennsylvania Reserves were on the way, and having a brother in the First Regiment of the Reserves I was anxious to see whether he would be along.

As I went out to the south side of the house I looked in the direction of Round Top, and there saw the Rebels moving rapidly in our direction.

Suddenly I heard the sound of fife and drum coming from the other side of the barn. Then some of our soldiers shouted:

"There come the Pennsylvania Reserves!" And sure enough there they were, coming on a double-quick between the barn and Round Top, firing as they ran.

The Confederates faced toward them, fired, halted, and then began to retreat. I saw them falling as they were climbing over a stone wall and as they were shot in the open space. The fighting lasted but a short time, when the Confederates were driven back in the direction of Little Round Top. I think they passed between the Round Tops.

The conclusion of facts:

1. The charge of the Twentieth Maine was an impulsive and spontaneous effort in order to protect their wounded comrades in their front. "Bayonets," was the only command given.
2. A "right wheel forward," was never ordered by Chamberlain. His first report stated that, "an extended right-wheel" was made only after the initial charge and the breaking of the first enemy line.
3. Approximately 170 men of the Twentieth Maine made the final charge. It was described by all as one wild rush.
4. Col. Chamberlain did not lead the charge. Lt. Holman Melcher was the first officer down the slope.
5. Col. Oates was planning to retreat before the charge was made. The two "regiments," that Col. Oates saw in his rear were Capt. Morrill's Co. B, and the 2nd U.S. Sharpshooters. Their "well-directed fire," was the reason for Col. Oates' order to retreat. Oates mistakenly thought the sharpshooters were dismounted cavalry.
6. Over 80 Confederates retreated to the northeast and were corralled in the Weikert Farm Lane.
7. Approximately 300 Confederates were taken prisoner in the charge, including 100 wounded. About 60 were dead on the field.
8. According to Chamberlain, the placing of the monument of the 20th Maine Regiment does not mark the position where the colors stood during the fight.
9. The construction and the subsequent removal of Chamberlain Avenue forever altered the terrain where the 20th Maine and 15th Alabama fought.
10. On July 2, 1863, the Federal left was saved by the tenacity of the 20th Maine Volunteer Infantry.

CHAPTER FOUR
WE HAVE DONE MUCH,
BUT SHOULD HAVE DONE MORE

After Gettysburg the contending armies returned to Virginia. A complicated, chess-like campaign would follow for the next six months. To frustrated Northerners, it seemed that Gen. Meade had allowed Lee's Army of Northern Virginia to escape, and had failed to maintain the strategic initiative. Disillusionment set in; the men in the ranks realized that after three summers of bloody fighting, little had been gained. Though Lee's army had been defeated, it was still dangerous. Each side was unwilling to waste lives in assaults without a clear tactical advantage. Melcher placed his fate in the hands of God and his commanding generals. He knew that only a decisive effort could vanquish this redoubtable Confederate army.

Bivouac 20th Me. Vols.
in the field, Loudon Valley, Va.
July 18, 1863

Dear Brother N.

 Once more we find ourselves in the "Old Dominion," but Gen. Lee says he is going to drive us out within 4 days, but he will finally have to go ahead, like he did before, to get around us.

 I suppose you are all confounded that we did not "pitch into" him at Williamsport. Well I don't wonder. I am afraid that some of the officers of the regular army wish the war to continue, [Maj.-Gen. George] Sykes for example. Yet I hope they used the best of their judgement when they objected to the advance on the rebels Monday. If Gen. [Oliver O.] Howard could only have his wish!!

The rebels had a strong position naturally, and well fortified, at least that part that I saw. Good rifle pits in front, earthworks for their artillery and behind these a hole for every man working the battery to jump into when they saw one shell coming. Gen. Meade seemed to be impressed with idea that Lee was going to attack him and so went to work and throw up rifle pits and earthworks for his guns, but Tuesday morning discovered their cannon gone and our pickets advanced taking the whole line of their pickets. Out of 15 prisoners that our regt. sent in at one time, only one had shoes.

A lady, at whose house rebel officers had stopped, told us that they said, "they came into Maryland with 80,000 men, well clothed and shod, but now they could not get back with over 40,000 and those all without shoes. We advanced forward to the river and finding that the advance had taken care of all the rebels left behind, bivouaced for the night, and the next morning started for Berlin. This was far the hardest march that we ever had. Marched via Antietam Battle-field, Cedarville, South Mountain and encamped just this side of the range, the men being too tired to go further. Thus we passed two memorable battle-fields in one days march. The graves and shattered trees showing the fierceness of the struggle that raged there.

Next morning started at 5 o'clock and after a very pleasant march of 8 miles through a beautiful county, such as Maryland can boast of, and the pretty little village of Burkesville, arrived at Berlin at 9 o'clock A.M. Went into camp and other Corps continued to arrive till every field was white with tents.

Capt. Keene came back, having been sick at Middletown one week. Remained here till next afternoon and then crossed the Potomac once more on a pontoon, only one of which was across the river. Marched about 5 miles down the valley, bivowacked and this morning again started marching about 6 miles and are now camped in a beautiful oak grove with a field thick with blackberries. We shall go in the morning, but how I should enjoy being home to attend Church instead. May this soon end, but I am ready to labor earnestly till a "right" end is obtained--"God speed the right." How great has he blessed us of late! May the people realize it, and return heart-felt thanks to the Father of all our blessings. I rejoice to see the President's and Gov. Bradford's call to Thanksgiving. I will have to march instead of attending with them in houses of worship, yet my heart goes up with theirs in Thanksgiving for I have seen the destruction that their beautiful state has been spared from.

We rejoice in the news from the S. West and Charleston. "Good! Good!! Good!!!" Hope they will have a good time in general in N.Y. City, perhaps some of them might have a chance to "die at home" and they will also learn, copperheads and all, that "U.S." is able to whip rebels and draft at the same time. It won't hurt New York to fortify it a little.

You would be pleased to see the feeling manifested towards the riots by the soldiers. Not a one has a word of justification for them, but all seem to want to see them exterminated. New York regiments are very bitter against them.

I thank you heartily for your kind letters, and your kindness in keeping me supplied with postage stamps. Write very often, whether I answer or not. I write just when I can while on the march.

Truly,
Holman

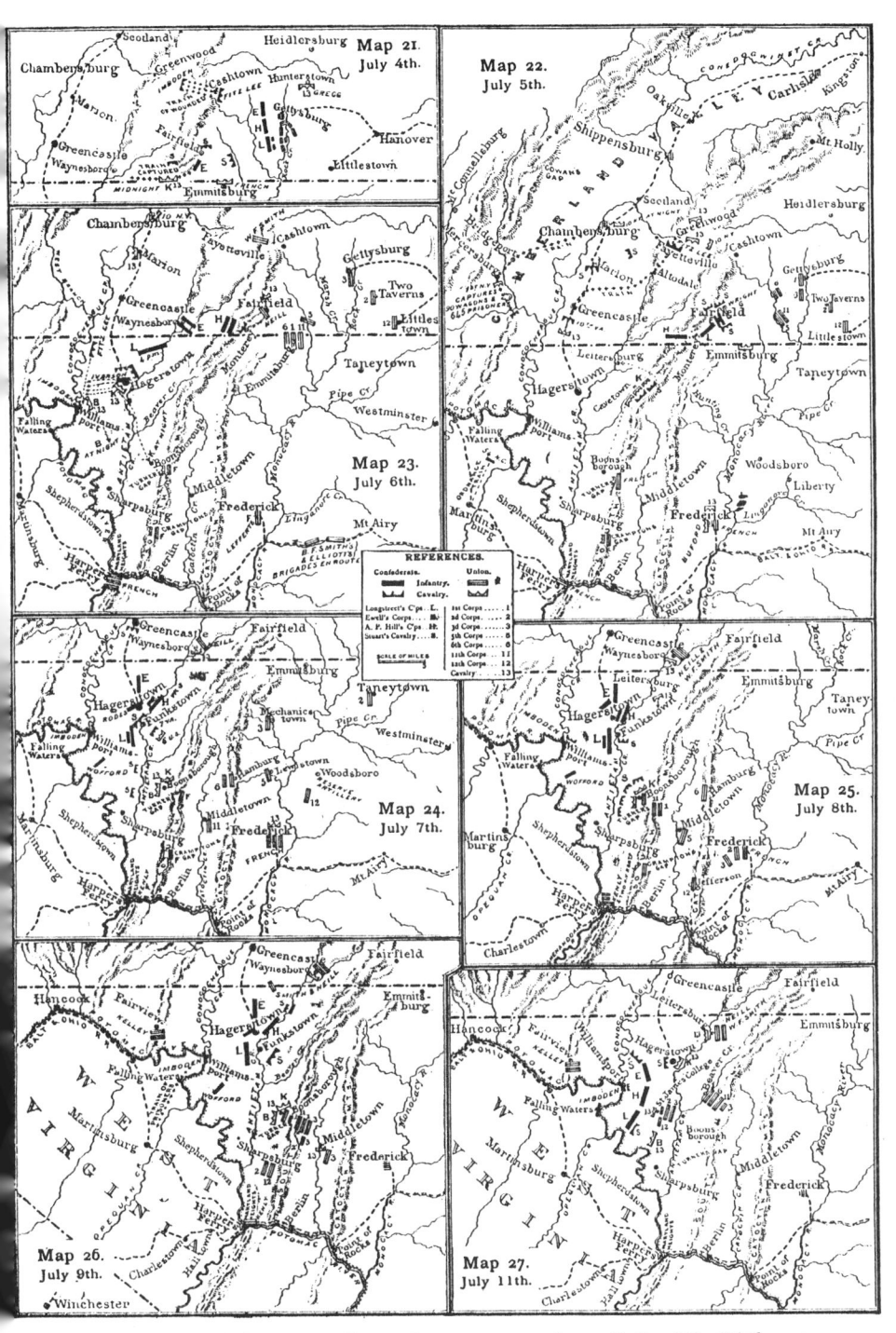

Map of the post-Gettysburg campaign, July 4th–11th.

(No. 26)
Camp 20th Me. Vols.
Near Warrenton, Va. July 28, 1863

My Dear Brother:

    I am happy to find a few moments in which I can write to you. For two months past it has been march & march, skirmish & fight. We have taken an immense circut up around into the Free States, and are now nearly back to where we started from. It has been a hard, very hard campaign, and the protruding bones of the Artillery and Cavalry horses, the tired look of the Infantry, and their thinned ranks, all show how hard has been the campaign and how wearing to all departments of the army. I am afraid that the army is almost worn out, and I know that we all need rest. I know that our ranks are much decimated by the severe marches and battles; but I also know that the enemy are more tired and worn than we. They are much demorilzed and I know that if we stop here to rest, the enemy will also halt behind the Rappahannock, face about, throw up entrenchments, and when we get ready to resume active operations, they will be already to meet us behind strong works. We have done much, but should have done more.

    Williamsport & Chester Gap both are examples of........ ....I won't say blunders, and I hope it was not intentional. Perhaps I am too "avericious" but I do want to "gobble up" a crowd of them before they get away. I don't feel contented to go into camp this side of the Rappahannock, but probably shall although I think we shall move forward to Bealton, or Rappahonnock Station. We are now encamped in a spendid field with acres of Blackberries around us, and I can assure you that we do justice to them, at any rate, we don't intend for many of them to ripen and fall...We have them at every meal, and as I write there is a dish of them on the desk that receive my compliments very often. I dine with Col. Chamberlain since I have been in the Adjutant's position. I enjoy the position very much and consider it an honor to be on the staff of such an officer as Col. Chamberlain, and I hope he will remain with us for it would be a dark day to this Regiment, should he leave us. He is a noble officer, a brave man, an energetic leader and, as you all know, a Gentleman.

I forgot where we were when I last wrote you, as we have been so much wasted around of late that I have hardly time to think of more than the crowded present. We have been into nothing of late that would interest you much, so I will not attempt to describe our march through Loudon Valley, our halts, etc.

We arrived at Rectortown near Manassas Gap, evening of the 22nd and the next morning started into the Gap, preceeded by the 3rd Corps. It is a horrid place to march an army through. The road is narrow, rocky and crossed by many little brooks, so the men's feet were constanly wet. We arrived in front of the enemy's position; a strong one near the further end of the Gap. At 3 o'clock P.M. we found the skirmishers of the 3rd Corps already engaged, and the Corps advancing in column of battle. It was a grand sight, for I was impressed with the soleminity of being shot and buried in such a place. As soon as we came up with the 3rd Corps, we deployed into column of battle and to do this, had to go onto the sides of the mountains which gave us a perfect view of all the operations.

There were both lines of skirmishers, which looked but a few rods apart, with the rapid flashes of their rifles, followed by their sharp reports. Steadily our skirmishers pressed them back from bush to fence to another shelter, till they fell back upon their lines. Closely following the skirmishers were the glittering rifles of the massive thousands, their silken banners waving over the steadily advancing columns, contrasting with the dark blue of their uniforms. As soon as the enemy made a stand, a brigade immediately deployed into line of battle and advanced upon them, till within a short rifle range, halted, fired a volley and then with a shout rushed upon them driving them back in perfect disorder. No artillery had yet been engaged, but we knew well that a battery was there in the distance, and we had not long to wait to know its exact locality. For as soon as the enemy broke, a flash burst forth from a top of a distant hill followed by a cloud of white smoke, and another, and another, till five guns had belched forth their contents upon our columns. It did not cause them to waver. They halted and waited for our batteries to move forward into a new position as those in position were to far off to be effective, and night came on before further advances. In the evening we went to the front and relieved the 3rd Army Corps and after sleeping on our arms through the night, prepared for an advance early, but after going far into one of the worse places--bushes, rocks, etc., where we supposed the enemy were, found that the enemy had fled and we prepared to return. We buried the dead rebels, which were many. Meanwhile one division of the 3rd Corps advanced into the Shenandoah Valley, to Front Royal, and found that the enemy all fled.

In the morning we started back out of the Gap, about 7 miles. The railroad runs near the highway, and it shows the result of war in Virginia. Every sleeper is taken up and burned in piles with the rails lying in heaps, all warped out of shape by the burning of the bon-fires.

Write very often please.
Your brother Holman.

We Have Done Much 151

Bivouac 20th Maine Vols.
at Rappahannock Station
Dec. 3rd 1863

My Dear Brother:

Eight days ago we started on the movement that is about ended to-night, as most of the army is in their old camp now. Our Corps is assigned to the very unpleasant duty of guarding the railroad from this place to Centreville, and enter upon other duties to-morrow. I wish I had the pleasure of writing of a grander result, but one satisfaction is that but a very few of our noble men have fallen. Only one of our regiment, wounded in the left arm.

Thursday, Nov. 26th. We started early from camp and marched to Culpepper Ford, between Ely's & Germanna Fords on the Rapidan. Crossed about 3 o'clock P.M. and marched about 4 miles through the "Wilderness," rightly called, and bivouacked. That afternoon our regiment did the flanking for the Division and picketed that night, which made it very hard for them. I about beat out my horse that day. The next morning we struck the "Plank Road," from Culpepper to Fredericksburg, and marched to near Chancellorsville, passing the house where the Rebel General Jackson had his arm amputated, and afterwards died.* Before reaching Chancellorsville, we turned to the right through a bye-road leading to Orange Court House. Did not go far when the Cavalry in front began to cannonade, indicating that the enemy had not all gone to Hanover & Lynchburg. We, (5th Corps) supported by the 1st Corps, went to Hope Church, where we found the cavalry Division of Gregg, warmly engaged with the enemy. Two divisions of our Corps already deployed in line of battle and driving the enemy before them. Our Division massed behind a piece of woods ready to render any assistance, but we were not needed, the enemy leaving our front in the night. The enemy loss was much

---

The Old Wilderness Tavern is where Jackson was brought after he was wounded. Afterwards, he was transferred to a house near Guiney's Station where he died on May 10, 1863.

larger than ours, besides the many prisoners that we captured.

Friday, Nov. 27th. In the morning we moved to the right, to Locust Grove on the Turnpike leading to Orange Court House, it raining hard. Sharp skirmishing was going on all the while in front. We arrived at the Grove to find all the roads filled with troops moving forward into position. It stopped raining about noon, but was muddy and unpleasant. The enemy continued to fall back closely pressed by our advance, until they got a strong position behind "Mine Run." They made a stand and threw up fortifications. We bivouacked for the night when we were, and early the next morning, moved to the front, and occupied an extreme advance in the centre. Our regiment sent out six companies to occupy the Rifle Pits, and the rest lay in reserve behind a hill. Corp. Neil, Co. C, was wounded severely in the arm while advancing to the Pits, which were all the casualties in our regiment. There was much firing during the day between the skirmishers and our regt. Our men brought down many of the "Grey Coats," but not one of the regt. got hit. There was no cannonading although our artillery was all in position.

Monday Morning. Nov. 30th, came clear and cold. Everything was ready for the assualt, batteries all planted, the storming column had piled up all their knapsacks, and were formed in the woods in three lines. The noble and brave 5th & 6th Corps lay side by side on the right. The 1st Corps in the center, and the 3rd & 2nd Corps on the left. The order had been issued for the batteries to open at 8 o'clock, and the troops to charge at 9. At 1 minute after 8 o'clock, a cannon on the right sent a shell shricking through the air, and quick as thought every gun was manned and the fire ran from the right to left along the whole line. The artillerymen sent their deadly missles with wonderful accuracy and rapidity. The Infantry grasped their rifles with a firm hold, ready to spring to their feet, and rush forward when the bugle sounded the "Charge."

My position that morning was in the centre, about half way

between our batteries and the enemies front line, with 35 pieces of artillery, including four, 32 pounders, sending their shot and shell directly over my head. It is impossible for one to have any conception of such a scene till he has seen and heard it, and I will not attempt a description of it. The howling of the shells attracts ones attention the most, yet the crash of the 32 pounders' discharge was enough to make one reel.

The enemy concealed himself behind his works, and replied only on the right and left. Although we could count 40 pieces of artillery in the works in his centre, but they could not be worked without having many of the gunners hit. This furious cannonading lasted about 30 minutes when it ceased to an occasional discharge along the line during the day, when the enemy would dare show their heads above the fortifications. The order for the charge was countermanded, and the fearful carnage that would have followed was spared. After the firing had ceased, a long train of Ambulances was seen coming to the enemies' front, telling plainly, that the shrieking shells had carried with them, death to the traitor.

Three times during the afternoon, our skirmishers drove the enemy out of their front pits in the center. No general advance was made. When the rebels would start out of their pits, our batteries would drop shells amongst them, scattering them in every direction. We killed many, and took some prisoners without scarcely any loss.

Tuesday all was quiet. Not even the skirmishers fired at each other, although within easy rifle shot. They seemed to have satisfied their desire of shooting at each other. In the afternoon the troops commenced moving to the rear. At dark nothing but the skirmish line was left, which consisted of details of the 6th Corps, our brigade being the detail from the 5th Corps.

In the evening the order was whispered to the officers that we should march to the rear at 3 o'clock A.M., and cross the river at Germanna Ford. Till then we supposed that we were going to Fredericksburg heights, which could of been done without trouble, but Gen. [Henry] Hallack would not let us. Had the enemy knew our position, it would have been very hard for us to have got off all right. But we did and not a gun was fired, or a man left behind, for I rode along our line to see all had left.

We marched 12 miles and crossed the river and bivouacked at Stevensburg that night. The next morning the troops went to their old camps, excepting this Corps, to which was assigned the unpleasant duty of guarding the railroad.

> Friday evening, Dec. 4, 1863
> Camp at Rappahannock Station, Va.
> Adj'ts Office, 20th Maine Vols.

Dear N.

I will add a few words to my already long letter. This morning it was reported that the enemy were crossing the Rapidan in force, and we waited to know what they were up to, but at noon, we received orders to go into Camp, and moved into a camp ground, and had been very busy all the afternoon in fixing up our Winter Quarters. Probably the enemy will keep quiet behind the Rapidan. We are garrisoning the forts that were so gallantly stormed and taken by the 5th Wisconson, and the 6th & 20th Maine, on the 7th of November. The graves of the fallen Brave are near our camp, but no fear that they will be disturbed. If we remain here I am going to have a fence built around their graves, and a monument erected to their memory.

I suppose all in the North are surprised at Gen'l. Meade's movement, and call him incompetent. I fear the result. But he is far more popular with the army now, than before the movement. He saw the strength of the enemy and the sacrifice necessary to drive them from their position. He saw that the fruits would be far less than the cost, and was BRAVE enough to withdraw, and save thousands of his army. Had the charge been ordered, we should have taken the works, but the slaughter would have been great, and before we could have reached Richmond, Longstreet would have joined Lee, and then we would have been outnumbered, and probably driven back.

For 8 days we have not received a word from the world, so that you can imagine our joy at receiving the news of Grant's great VICTORY this morning.* And then to get a large bundle of letters from home. Two from home and two from you, and also the [1865] Diary. How thoughtful and kind you were in sending it. Thank You. It is late and I must stop. Excuse the errors in this hastily written jumble, for I have not time to correct it. My love to all Dear Friends. My prayers and kind wishes to you. Remember me in your prayers.

As ever your affectionate Brother,
Holman

Adjutant's Office 20th Me. Vols
Camp at Kelly's Ford, Va., Nov. 13, 1863

To the Editor of the Portland Press:

I take this opportunity of sending you a list of the casualties in the 20th Maine in the action at Rappahannock Station, on the 7th inst.

It may not be generally known that the regiment took an active part in the affair, as official reports do not mention it; and it is true that the regiment was not under infantry fire, but the 1st Division of the 5th Corps was covered that day by skirmishers detailed by the 3rd Brigade, and the 20th furnished three officers and eighty men. They joined on with the skirmishers of the 6th Corps, on the right and when the 6th Maine charged the enemies' works the skirmishers of the 20th charged also, and shared with them the dangers and

---

Grant's victory at Lookout Mountain and Missionary Ridge, near Chattanooga, Tenn., Nov. 24-25, 1863.

glory of that brilliant achievement.

The officers engaged were Capt. Morrill, Co. B; 1st Lieut. Keene, Co. I; and 2d Lieut. Morse, Co. G. They displayed the greatest coolness and bravery. The men fought only as men can who are contending for the right. The loss was,

KILLED

Private Frederick Kinsel, Co. E, of Waldoboro.

WOUNDED

Corporal Sanford A. Carpenter, Co. I, Portland, toe, slightly.
Pvt. George H. Richardson, Co. B, Oldtown, shoulder, slightly.
Pvt. John W. Ramsdell, Co. D, Exeter, ankle, slightly.
Pvt. Wm. D. McKinn, Co. E, Bristol, arm, slightly.
Pvt. Wm. G. White, Co. G, Woolwich, shoulder, slightly.
Pvt. Joseph Winslow, Co. H, Plantation No.9, arm, slightly.
Pvt. Seth McGuire, Co. H, Linneens, thigh, severely.

Very respectfully yours,
H.S. Melcher,
Lieut. and Act Adj't.

Gallery of Portraits

Officers and wives of the Twentieth Maine Regiment standing underneath an arbor marking the entrance to the camp at Rappahannock Station on March 21, 1864.

1. Unidentified
2. Capt. Samuel F. Keene
3. Mrs. Keene
4. Unidentified
5. Capt. William Morrell
6. Capt. Walter Morrill
7. Lt. William Bickford
8. Lt. Holman Melcher
9. Unidentified
10. Lt. William Donnell
11. Mrs. Spear
12. Major Ellis Spear
13. Capt. Atherton Clark
14. Capt. Prentiss Fogler
15. Unidentified
16. Mrs. Plummer
17. Capt. Rufus Plummer

Adelbert Ames, Col. 20th Maine Vols., Maj. Gen. U.S. Army

William Bickford, 2nd Lt., Co. H, 1st Lt., Co. E, 20th Maine Vols.

Joshua Lawrence Chamberlain, Lt. Col., Col. 20th Maine Vols., Brig. Gen., Maj. Gen. U.S.V.

Thomas Davee Chamberlain, Lt., Capt., Brevet Lt.-Col., 20th Maine Vols.

Atherton W. Clark, Capt. Co. E. Major, 20th Maine Vols.

Albert E. Fernald, 1st Lt. Co. F, Brevet Captain, 20th Maine Vols.

Prentiss M. Fogler, Capt. Co. I, 20th Maine Vols.

William Griffin, Capt. Co. B, 20th Maine Vols.

William H. Harrington, Capt. Co. F, 20th Maine Vols.

Samuel F. Keene, Capt. Co. F.   KIA Petersburg, Va., June 22, 1864.

Joseph F. Land, Capt. Co. H, 20th Maine Vols.

Holman S. Melcher, 1st Lt. Co. F, Capt. Co. H, Brevet Major, 20th Maine Vols.

Alden Miller Jr., 1st. Lt. Co. G, 20th Maine Vols.

Nahum P. Monroe, Surgeon 20th Maine Vols.

William W. Morrell, Capt. Co. A. KIA Luarel Hill, Va. May 8, 1864.

Walter G. Morrill, Capt. Co. B.   Lt.-Col. 20th Maine Vols.

Hiram Morse, 1st. Lt. Co. I, 20th Maine Vols.

Rufus B. Plummer, Capt. Co. C, 20th Maine Vols.

Edmund R. Sanborn, 1st Lt., Co. A, 20th Maine Vols.

Abner O. Shaw, Surgeon 20th Maine Vols.

Henry F. Sidlinger, 1st Lt. Co. E, Capt. Co. K, 20th Maine Vols.

Ellis Spear, Capt. Co. G, Major, Lt. Col., Col., Brevet Brigadier-General U.S.V.

James H. Stanwood, 1st Lt. Co. C, 20th Maine Vols.

157

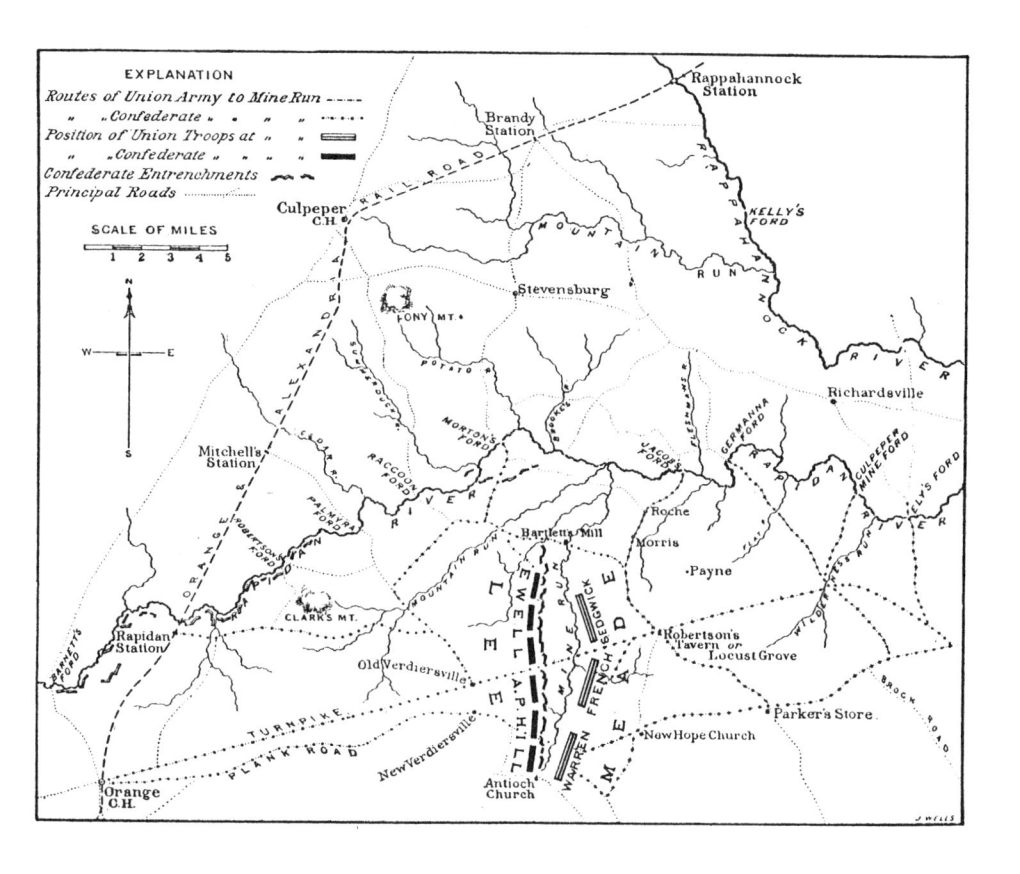

Positions of troops at Mine Run, Va.

CHAPTER FIVE

1864:

THE TROUBLED DREAM

OF THE TERRIBLE NIGHTMARE OF WAR

During the third winter of the war, a victorious outcome seemed more certain to Lt. Holman Melcher and the men of the 20th Maine Volunteers. Re-enlistments in the Union army were surprisingly high, and their numbers increased with the draft instituted in the North. Lt. Melcher knew the upcoming campaign would be bloody, but, the superior strength and will of the North would have to prevail. In the spring, the army and its new commander, Lt. Gen. Ulysses S. Grant, would meet Robert E. Lee's Army of Northern Virginia in a blind struggle to the death in the dark forest known simply as The Wilderness.

In preparing for this campaign, Holman Melcher was relieved as acting Adjutant of the regiment and placed in command of Company F. The 22 year-old lieutenant felt the burden of this new responsibility. Worried about the men in his charge and his performance as a company commander, Melcher relied on his sense of duty which instilled in him the courage to continue through the carnage.

(No. 49.)
Adjutant's Office, 20th Maine Vols.
Camp at Rappahonnock Station
Tuesday morning Jan. 5, 1864

My Dear Brother:
 I intended to have written you last evening so that the letter could go out in this morning's mail, but it took me until 11 o'clock to finish the business of the Office, and then thought it too late to write. So I will improve the moments this morning in that pleasant exercise.
 Your (I ought not say best, for they are all good), No. 44 came to hand yesterday morning. You cannot guess how much satisfaction it gave me and pleasure. I had waited so long for it, that I begin to think you considered it hardly worth your time and paper to write me.
 It is different with you than it is with me. You can have "sleigh-rides," make visits, call on the Ladies when you want, recreation and the like, but it is all the same in Camp. No sleighs, no skates, no "Tea Parties," NO LADIES!, and letters from friends are the only source of our pleasure. So if we do not get them when we expect, I feel very much disappointed. But such a letter as received yesterday, is something worth getting, I read it and reread it.
 Who would ever have thought that you would have hired a team to give the ladies a sleigh ride, (how deceitful) but then, man is not proof against everything. It seems that the beauty, the purity of mind, the sweet disposition and the charming manners of the Pastor's Fair Daughter, was more than you could contend with, and you had to "strike your colors," and surrender to the Fair Jenny. Soldiers think it a matter of much importance into whose hands they fall prisoner. Perhaps you did, and so did not fight so gallantly. But

let me think, I am not so sure, but you are the attacking party! All the time!! I should think one should be forcibly reminded of how a snow ball would feel planted into ones eye.

I have been fearing it, yet I hoped you would not think of enlisting. I have already, in previous letters said enough about your business, but having been in the army long enough to learn by experience, and feeling a deep interest in your prosperity and happiness and success, I am going to say, don't come into the army as a Private. You are fitted to be an Officer, and so don't be too modest in asking for a position, not that you would get a high position. But if you come as a private, you have got some very hard labor before you, such as I fear you could not endure.

You need not come as a Private. If you intend to enlist in the Army of the Union, go directly to Col. Chamberlain, who is now at home, and don't be afraid to ask of him that you want a position in some of the new regiments, the Cavalry if possible. He will tell you as I do, and I believe will try to get you a position.

But if you enlist and do not try to get a commission, and come as an enlisted man, by all means come to this regiment. I have a little influence here yet, and of course it would be my greatest pleasure to exert it for your benefit.

All this is said supposing you enlist, but do not enlist. You are needed there. I want you to see you graduate first now so near the close of your course, only one term. All are not needed in the army. Men are needed, but so are they at home. This war is to be a matter of time, than fighting in future, and during that time we want to preserve all our Christian Institutions perfect at the North. There influences will be needed when the soldiers return. If you want to go into the army very well, but if you think it is duty, I think otherwise.

I have just been down to the R.R. Station to see Major Spear off for home. He is gone on a 14 days leave, this leaving the Regt. without a Field Officer. Command devolves upon Capt. [Atherton]

Clark.

We received orders last evening to be ready to march at very short notice, but we have not gone yet. It will be very hard to leave our good comfortable tents and sleep on the cold wet ground, nights without shelter.

I congratulate you on the receipt of your nice slippers; a Christmas present--the gift of Cousin Mary. Wish some Dear Cousin had thought of me too. "Santa" C. did not find any stockings, perhaps he didn't visit the army. Perhaps he did not dare to get into my chimney for fear of getting covered in a heap of stones, pieces of bricks, dirt, soot, ashes, and the old barrel that tops it. Rather a rough looking place for a man to get into, I will acknowledge, especially with a bag of presents on his back.

Several of the officers had boxes of pastry on the way for a Christmas dinner, but did not get here till two days after, of course there was some disappointment, but then we get used to most all kinds of disappointments and learn to "keep quiet." I was invited to a very rich dinner by Capt. [Joseph F.] Land, on the 27th, intended for Christmas. Could guess that the rich cakes and pies were made by a sister.

I forgot to acknowledge the receipt of my watch-key in the last letter from you. It corresponds well with my chain, which proves itself to be gold by wear.

Reenlistments are very rapid here in the army, surprising all. Certainly I did not think so many would reenlist who had service since the breaking out of the war. Almost every one in our Regt. who came has reenlisted for three years more, and I have prepared their papers for a Furlough of 34 days, which I send up to Corps Hd. Qtrs. to-morrow for approval.

No one can reenlist and receive the bounties unless they have served two years, and have a year or less to serve. Consequently our Regt. cannot receive the benefit of the orders. Those of our regiment who have reenlisted were formerly members of the 2nd

Maine Vols., 14 in number.

One Regiment in our Brigade went home in a body, taking with them their Colors and arms.

It is a daily occurrence to see regiments going by on the cars leaving for furlough home, having all reenlisted.

This is what is going to give us efficiency when the campaign opens in the Spring. Old troops, willing volunteers, fresh from the respite of a rest at home and aided by the 300,000 new troops. I trust we shall deal some very heavy blows upon Rebellion.

Now in closing, let me say, Don't Come into the army in the ranks. I will labor more earnestly, and strike some more blows in each battle for you (and family) if you will remain and finish your College course.

      Write soon. Write often.
      Yours affectionately,
       Holman

(No. 55)
Rappahannock Station, Va.
April 9, 1864

My Dear Brother,

Your excellent No. 51, was just received and read with the greatest pleasure. I should have written you before, but since I received yours, I have had no opportunity to write. By the consolidation of the Corps, the 3rd Brigade was consolidated with the 2nd and the Staff broken up, so that [Lt. William E.] Donnell was sent back to this Regiment, and of course I was relieved from Actg. Adjt. I am now in Co. F, as before, with little to do, and having a good time in general. Capt. Keene is detailed on Court Martial so that I have the care and drilling of the Company, which I enjoy very much. We have now have Target Practice three times a week, (30 rounds ammunition per man) which adds much to the interest of camp life.

Donnell is learning his duties by severe experience. His first trials at "Guard-Mounting" were blunders, that he was made aware of it by the shouts of the whole Regt., who were out to see the "fun" as they call it, but I could not help pitying him. If he was a man of fine sensibility, he would not again have tried it.

We expect Col. Chamberlain back to the Regiment next Tuesday. He is at Gettysburg now to look over the battlefield. I suppose you have the reorganization of the army in the papers so that it will be of no use to note it here. The changes among Generals have been more severe than any other grade. Colonels who have commanded Brigades will now have to command Regiments. We all have much confidence in Gen'l. Warren, our present Corps Commander. He is the Hero of Bristow Station, you know.*

I suppose you are expecting a movement soon, but don't think of it, as long as this weather lasts. Yesterday and the day before were pleasant, but another storm we are getting to-day in real earnest, in the shape of a cold "Northeaster." We should probably move just as soon as the mud dries. Received orders yesterday to send to the rear all supplies, baggage and stores at once. I am going to send a valise of books etc., home, such as I cannot carry. Shall direct it to Father, Brunswick, that it may remain in the Express Office till some of you call for it. It will probably arrive about the last of next week.

All Civilians, Citizens, Sutlers, and Ladies have been ordered to leave at once, so that their will be no "hangers on" to impede our progress, when we start. I hope our efforts will be rewarded according to our preperations. Be sure to send your photograph in your next letter.

April 10th--The tremendous storm of rain yesterday and last night carried away some of the bridges between here and Washing-

*The Battle of Bristoe Station, Va., was fought on Oct. 14, 1863, where Gen. G.K. Warren defeated Gen. A.P. Hill's Corps.

ton and no trains have run so I could not send this letter. The water is higher in the river than I have ever before seen it. The mountains are yet covered with snow and one may expect bad weather for some time to come.

H.S.M.

Camp of the 20th Maine Vols.
Rappahannock Station, Va.
April 22, 1864

My Dear Brother:

I last wrote you that we should move before this day, but we yet remain in our old camp on these heights by the Rappahannock Station bridge. It is a pleasant camp and I hope we shall remain here till a general movement of the army takes place, for it would be very uncomfortable to have to camp on the ground without floors in our tents, when it is as wet and cold as it is now. Yet, many of the troops have had to do so, by the consolidation of the Corps. We being on duty along the Rail-Road, are still needed where we are to protect the Road from Guerillas, who are desirous of cutting our communications, but they have failed thus far in reaching the Road, but they did get twenty-five of the Guard at Bristow this week. They have never yet made an attack on the fort on this line, guarded by our Brigade.

I suppose you are expecting every day that this army will move. So are we, yet we cannot guess how soon it will be. Everything seems to be in readiness as far as this army is concerned, but I suppose we are to cooperate with other armies and perhaps they are not yet ready.

In obedience to orders, all the Ladies, Sutlers, Photographers etc., have left the army. All baggage not actually needed has been sent to Alexandria for storage. The sick who would not have been able to march with their Regiments were sent to the General Hospitals yesterday. The weather for the past few days has been very pleasant and springlike. It seems doubly pleasant after having such very stormy weather as we have had for a month past.

It is with feelings better felt than expressed that I look forward to the coming campaign. The army is large and its numbers are being constantly increased by the daily arrival of new troops. The enemy cannot and do not fail to see that we are to make this the principle field of action, and they are massing all their available force to oppose us. And these two mighty armies are to be hurled against each other in deadly conflict, by the two most skillful Generals that the Country possesses, each having the full confidence of the troops under them. We that have taken part in, and witnessed the scenes of such battles as Fredericksburg and Gettysburg know what is before us. That the Rebels will fight, and fight desperately too, no doubt for their all depends upon this campaign. For should they be defeated, with their present situation, all is lost to them. And how glorious! How grand! will be the results to us and the cause of Liberty throughout the world!

When I think of the magnitude of our cause and the glorious results to come from the successful termination of the war, I am glad that I am where I can give all my strength to the work, although as with thousands, I may never live to see the end. But the cause is worth of all the sacrifices we shall make. How much bloodshed and suffering will be spared the people, if this campaign does result in success to our arms! Never since I have been in the army has it been in such good spirits, and looked so well as it does now.

Our Regiment is in a fine condition, which reflects much credit upon Major Spear who has commanded it since Nov. 18, 1863.

Those of the 5th, 6th & 20th Me. Vols., who were killed at the storming of these heights, Nov. 9, '63, are buried near where they fell, which is close to our Camp. During the winter our Regiment

has built a nice fence around the graves and erected a monument in the center of the enclosure, ten feet high, made of plank and painted white. The following inscriptions are neatly painted on the different sides of the Monument:
On one side,
"DIRIGO"
and the side opposite
"Sixth, Fifth and Twentieth Maine Regts."
On the third side
"In memory of the brave men of Maine, who fell leading the way to these Heights. Nov. 7th 1863"
and on the side opposite
"Erected by the 20th Maine Vols. March, 1864."

The graves are marked with wooden headboards, on which are engraved the name, Regt., and place of residence, of these brave men of Maine, who fell in one of the most brilliant actions of the war. Died fighting, for Liberty, Justice, and Humanity. Gave freely their lives for their Country.

(No.59)
Bivouac 20th Maine Vols.
Near Culpepper, Va.
May 3, 1864

Dear Brother.
It was with pleasure, better felt than expressed, that I received your kind and interesting No. 55, to-night.
We had marched from Ingel's Station this after-noon and I had just had my tent pitched when my Sergeant handed me my mail. Among which was the long waited for and almost despaired for, letter from you. Every mail for over a week, have I expected would

bring me a letter from you, but have been destined to disappointment till to-night.

My accommodations are very poor to-night and I will have to be very brief. My seat is a rubber blanket spread on the ground, and my writing desk is my knees. It is late too, and we are expecting to be far away from here by morning. And before another night, to have taken part in the great struggle on which so much is pending. It is with pain, that I look forward to the conflict, for I know its scenes, and I know my responsibility for I have been relieved from the duties of Adjutant and assigned to the command of a Company numbering 38 men, whose wants and interests I am to look after in battle. While it is my duty to urge them on to great deeds, yet I must use discretion and protect them from the enemies fire in any possible way. I need wisdom. Pray Brother that the Lord will give me wisdom, and that Christ will strengthen me.

The other Corps of the Army, other than ours, have orders this afternoon to have everything packed in readiness to move at dark to-night. But I do not know if they have gone yet. As our Corps was on the move already we received no other orders, than to hold ourselves in readiness to move at any hour during the night, and perhaps by the time I get asleep, the bugles will sound the "Strike Tents."

Our whole Division of over 10,000 strong is camped in a beautiful green field. The troops are in fine condition. The thousands of white tents dotting this green surface, and the many wagons, and ambulances, which go with the marching column, makes a really grand sight. And the bands have been playing all the evening, making music sweet and soul-stirring, which floats forth in the pleasant evening air, all making up a scene grand and lovely. But I am moved when I think that before another evening, this beautiful scene will be stained in the blood of the thousands who are to-night, happy actors in it.

My love to all the family.
Holman

An Experience In The Battle Of The Wilderness
By Brevet-Major Holman S. Melcher

Read before the Military Order of the Loyal Legion on September 4, 1889.

In the Commonwealth of Old Virginia there is a tract of forest land about fifteen miles square, extending south from the Rapidan River toward Spottsylvania court-house and equidistant from Fredericksburg on the east and Orange court-house on the west; or to be more specific, from Chancellorsville on the east to Mine Run on the west.

The forest of this historical region is occasionally broken by small farms and abandoned clearings, and watered by numerous streams and brooks there designated as creeks and runs, which flowing northerly empty into the Rapidan and Rappahannock Rivers. This country is generally level, or slightly undulating, with several eminences that might be called hills near the center of this tract.

The region rests on a belt of mineral rocks, and for more than a hundred years extensive mining operations were carried on, in its early history by Alexander Spotswood, then governor of Virginia, whereby he received the title of Tubal Cain, not only of Virginia, but of North America.

To feed the mines, the timber of the country for many miles around was cut down, and in its place there had arisen a growth that did not have the ordinary features of a forest. With the larger growth there arose a dense undergrowth of low-limbed and scraggy pines, stiff and bristling chinkapinks, scrub-oak, and hazel.

It is difficult to make way through this growth except by the paths and wood-roads that intersect it in many directions, but known only to those familiar with the region. Ways for travel were opened from east to west by the Orange Court-house turnpike, and the Orange Court-house plank road, which run nearly parallel from Fredericksburg to Orange some five or six miles apart, and south of the plank road there was a railroad unfinished at the time of this narrative.

The traveled way from north to south was by the Germanna plank road from Germanna Ford of the Rapidan to the Wilderness Tavern, thence by the Brock Road to Todd's Tavern and Spottsylvania court-house.

It can be truthfully said that there is nothing in or about this region that was either interesting or attractive. One writer says of it, "It is the region of gloom and the shadow of death."

This condition was terribly emphasized when in the course of events there met in battle in that horrible thicket nearly two hundred thousand men. Through it lurid fires played, and though no array of battle could be seen, there came of its depths the crackle and roll of musketry like the noisy boiling of some hell-cauldron that told the dread story of death until twenty-five thousand brave men were swallowed in its fiery vortex.

When the Army of the Potomac was organized, preparatory to the campaign of 1864, by an order from the War Department, dated March 23, the five infantry corps were consolidated into three, the Second retaining its number and receiving into its organization the Third, excepting one division assigned to the Sixth Corps, and the Fifth retaining its number and receiving the First Corps (or what remained of it after its sacrifice at Gettysburg), which constituted the Second and Fourth Divisions of the new Fifth Corps, now numbering about twenty-five thousand men, - too large an organization of be handled to the greatest advantage in the densely wooded country in which occurred the campaign of 1864.

The brilliant and able commander of the magnificent corps was Major-General [Gouverneur Kimble] Warren, and his division commanders were Major-Generals Charles Griffin, John C. Robinson, Samuel W. Crawford and James S. Wadsworth, - all brave and tried officers.

The Third Brigade of Griffin's First Division was made up of seven veteran regiments, 1st and 16th Michigan, 83d and 118th Pennsylvania, 44th New York, 18th Massachusetts and my own regiment, the 20th Maine, all under the command of the gallant soldier, Brigadier-General Joseph J. Bartlett.

In the absence of Colonel Chamberlain on court martial duty, my regiment was commanded by Lieutenant-Colonel Ellis Spear. About two weeks before the opening of that eventful campaign, I was assigned to the command of Company F, the company in which I held the commission of first lieutenant but had been detailed from, acting as adjutant of the regiment since the battle of Gettysburg. Captain Samuel Keene of the company, being second in rank, had been assigned to the duty of acting-major; and on account of his rank it gave my company the left in right line of battle.

During the winter a large number of recruits had been sent to the regiment, mostly substitutes and bounty jumpers, and I found on assuming command of the company, that there was quite a quantity of the rawest kind of recruits to be drilled up to the standard of soldiers. But it took only a short time to satisfy me that, with few exceptions, this new material was not the proper kind out of which to make good soldiers, and only the most persistent drilling and careful instruction would bring them to the grade of doubtful efficiency. The work was pushed forward as fast as possible by the aid of my non-commissioned officers and example of the veterans of the company, true men and tried, who survived that fearful slaughter on Little Round Top the July preceding, when ten were shot dead and thirteen fearfully wounded in this company of forty-three that carried the colors of the regiment through that terrible conflict.

The position of my regiment, guarding the railroad bridge over the Rappahannock, was favorable for all kinds of drill, as the isolation from the rest of the brigade gave room for skirmish drill and long range target practice, which was made much of during the two weeks I had for this purpose, so that considering the character and utter lack of knowledge of all military matters on the part of these recruits, not one of them knowing how even properly to load a rifle, much more correctly to aim in firing, we got them up to a fair standard when the grand movement came, and we marched at midnight, May 3-4, crossing the Rapidan on a pontoon bridge at Germanna Ford, plunged into the Wilderness, and there settled down on our fated veteran First Division of the Fifth Corps the terrible nightmare of the troubled dream of war.

To explain what I mean by this statement it is only necessary for me to say that in the three days' battle in the fearful thickets of the Wilderness our First Division lost six thousand men out of the twelve thousand that entered so fearlessly into the contest on the morning of May 5.

Pushing forward with all possible haste, we reached the Old Wilderness Tavern about two o'clock p.m. on the fourth of May, and moved westward along the Orange Pike, bivouacking about one mile out toward Orange court-house on both sides of the road, to await the coming up of the Sixth Corps, which went into line on our right, and the Second Corps, which moved off toward the left near Chancellorsville.

The night was quiet and restful after our long forced march, but the bugles sounded an early reveille for the forward movement. Coffee had been made and drank, and when about ready to draw out into the pike to resume the march, some cavalry scouts that had been out far in our front during the night came galloping down the road, with word that the rebel army was advancing along the pike from Orange court-house and were already this side of Robertson's Tavern, and not over two miles away.

Affairs changed very suddenly; arms were stacked, shovels and picks brought up, and every man worked with a right good will to throw up earthworks along the line we had bivouacked on during the night, which was on a slightly wooded crest of a ridge running across the road. The pioneers cut down the trees in front of the works to give range for our fire, and sharpened out the limbs to make a temporary abatis.

A battery of Napoleon guns came up and took position between our regiment and the one on the left, and by ten o'clock, covered by a goodly line of works and supported by batteries, we expected and hoped for attack, but that little arrangement was too much to our liking to be realized. You know we almost always had to take hold of the other end of the poker, and so it was in this case, for after waiting for an attack of the enemy till about twelve o'clock, orders came to "advance and attack in force," and climbing over the line of works we had erected with so much interest and pleasure, we pushed out through the thick woods in our front, - the right of my regiment resting on the pike, - till we came near an open field, where lines were carefully formed, my regiment being in the second line of battle. The bugles sounded the "Charge" and advancing to the edge of the field, we saw the first line of battle about halfway across it, receiving a terribly fatal fire from an enemy in the woods on the farther side.

This field was less than a quarter of a mile across, had been planted with corn the year before, and was now dry and dusty. We could see the spurts of dust started up all over the field by the bullets of the enemy, as they spattered on it like the big drops of a coming shower you have so often seen along a dusty road, but that was not the thing that troubled us. It was the dropping of our comrades from the charging line as they rushed across the fatal field with breasts bared to the terrible storm of leaden hail, and we knew that it would soon be our turn to run this fire.

As we merged from the woods into this field, General Bartlett, our brigade commander, came galloping down the line from the right, waving his sword and shouting, "Come on, boys, let us go in and help them!" And go we did. Pulling our hats low down over our eyes, we rushed across the field, and overtaking those of our comrades who had survived the fearful crossing of the front line, just as they were breaking over the enemy's lines, we joined with them in this deadly encounter, and there in that thicket of bushes and briers, with the groans of the dying, the shrieks of the wounded, the terrible roar of musketry and the shouts of command and cheers of encouragement, we swept them away before us like a whirlwind and scattered a part of [Maj-Gen. Edward] Johnson's and [Maj.-Gen. Robert E.] Rhodes' Divisions of [Lieut.-Gen. Richard S.] Ewell's Corps, namely, [Brig.-Gen. John M.] Jones' Brigade of Johnson's, and [Brig.-Gen. George] Dole's and [Brig.-Gen. Cullen A.] Battles' of Rhodes' Division, and pursued them like hunted hares through the thick woods, shooting those we could overtake who would not throw down their arms and go to the rear.

This pursuit with my company and those immediately about me continued for about half a mile, until there were no rebels in our front to be seen or heard; and coming out into a little clearing, I thought it well to reform my line, but found there was no line to form, or to connect it with. I could not find my regimental colors or the regiment . There were with me fifteen men of my company with two others of the regiment. I was the only commissioned officer there, but my own brave and trusted first sergeant, Ammi Smith, was at my side as always in time of danger or battle, and with him I conferred as to what it was best to do under the circumstances.

There was nothing in front to fight that we could see or hear, but to go back seemed the way for cowards to move, as we did not know whether our colors were at the rear or farther to the front. I was twenty-two years old at this time, and Sergeant Smith twenty-three, so that our united ages hardly gave years enough to decide a question that seemed so important to us at that moment.

While earnestly considering this question, one of my men came to me and said, "Lieutenant, come this way and let me show you something." Following him, he led me to the Orange Pike, and pointing back down that straight level road he said, "See that!" I looked in the direction he pointed and saw that which froze the blood in my veins and made my heart almost cease beating for a time. Some half a mile down the road from where we had just charged up through in our advance, I could see a strong column of rebel infantry moving directly across the road into our rear, completely cutting us off from the direction we had come.

I quickly surmised what I learned soon after was true, that the First Brigade that charged with us on the right of the pike had been repulsed in the advance, and that my regiment had been ordered to halt when this was discovered, and being outflanked on the right, had fallen back. But my company being on the extreme left of the regiment, I had not heard these orders, nor seen the colors halt, on account of the thick woods, and so had rushed forward beyond the rest of the regiment. But now the question was, what should we do?

I called all my men together, stated to them how I understood the situation, and said, "Now, my men, as for myself, I had rather die in the attempt to cut our way out, than be captured to rot in rebel prisons. Will you stand by me in this attempt?" It was a moment that tried men's souls, and boys' too, but the resolution was quickly formed, and every one said, "Yes, Lieutenant, we will and gladly, too." I looked in their faces and I knew there was not one that would fail me. They were all men who had been tried in the fires of Antietam, Fredericksburg, Aldie, Gettysburg, Rappahannock Station and Mine Run, and had never been found wanting.

None of my "recruits" were there. They had all been lost in the first shock of the charge, of course. I said, "Every man load his rifle, fix bayonets and follow me." And with Sergeant Smith at my side we started to cut our way out to "liberty or death".

In order to pass around the right of the rebel line if possible. I took a course as far from the pike as I dared to and keep a direction so as to come out somewhere near the works we had thrown up in the morning, in case we succeeded in getting out, as that was the only spot on earth that seemed a desirable objective to me under the circumstances.

The hope of getting around the rebel right proved vain, however. On approaching their line, we found it extended farther to the right than we could see. Our only chance was to cut our way through.

Forming our "line of battle" (seventeen men beside myself) in single rank, of course, with Sergeant Smith on the left while I took the right, we approached quietly and unobserved, as the "Johnnies" were all intent on watching for the "Yanks" in front, not for a moment having a suspicion that they were to be attacked from the rear, until we were within ten or fifteen paces, when on the first intimation that we were discovered, every one of our little band picked his man and fired, and with a great shout as much as if we were a thousand, we rushed at them and on to them, sword and bayonets being our weapons. "Surrender or die!" was our battle-cry.

They were so astonished and terrified by this sudden and entirely unexpected attack and from this direction, that some of them promptly obeyed, threw down their arms and surrendered. The desperately brave fought us, hand to hand; the larger part broke and fled in every direction through the woods, and could not be followed by us or our fire, as our rifles were empty and there was no time to reload.

This was the first, and I am glad to say, the last time that I saw the bayonet used in its most terrible and effective manner. One of my men, only a boy, just at my side, called out to a rebel to throw down his gun, but instead of obeying he quickly brought it to his shoulder and snapped it in the face of this man, but fortunately it did not explode, for some reason.

Quick as a flash, he sprang forward and plunged his bayonet into his breast, and throwing him backward pinned him to the ground, with the very positive remark, "I'll teach you, old Reb, how to snap your gun in my face!" And this was only one scene of many such I saw enacted around me, in that terrible struggle. How I wished my sword had been ground to the sharpness of a razor, but the point was keen and I used to the full strength of my arm.

I saw a tall, lank rebel, only a few paces from me, about to fire at one of my men and I the only one that could help him. I sprang forward and struck him with all my strength, intending to split his head open, but so anxious was I that my blow should fall on him before he could fire that I struck before I got near enough for the sword to fall upon his head, but the point cut the scalp on the back of his head and split his coat all the way down his back. The blow hurt and startled him so much that he dropped his musket without firing and surrendered, and we marched him out with the other prisoners.

In less time than it has taken me to tell this we had scattered the line of battle and the way was open for us to escape. Two of our little band lay dead on the ground where we had fought, and several more or less severely wounded, but these latter we kept with us and saved them from capture. By spreading our little company out rather thin we were able to surround the thirty-two prisoners we had captured in the melee and started them along on the double quick, or as near to it as we could and keep the wounded along with us.

When our prisoners discovered how few were their captors and how near their many friends, they slackened their pace, refusing the orders to double quick, and seemed inclined to turn on us. Seeing this I drew my revolver, and I have always regretted I did not have it in my hand instead of my sword during the struggle we had just been through; but it served me a good purpose now as its seven barrels were loaded, all of which might be needed. Halting the squad and cocking my revolver I said, "The first man who does not keep up in his place will be instantly shot." As this little speech was made in as fierce and emphatic a manner as a boy could do it, they appeared to think that the threat might be carried out, and when I shouted, "Forward, double quick!" they trotted along right lively.

As we were rushing along I noticed one of our "recruits" squeezed up behind a log. I said to him, "Come on, come along with us, George, or you'll be captured." His only response to my order was, "Don't let them know I am here." We could not stop to drag him out and so had to leave him to his fate.* He was captured and never returned to our regiment. I afterwards learned that he starved to death in the Andersonville Prison Pen, as all of us undoubtedly would, had we not dared to act on the one chance that we had to escape.

One of our prisoners was a captain, who was badly wounded in his side, and though we made the other prisoners take turns in helping him along, it was very painful to him to be moved at the rate at which we were marching, so that when we got well away from the enemy's line, and came to one of our own regiments that had not previously been engaged, but had been sent forward to cover the falling back of our broken line, I asked the colonel commanding to take this wounded captain off our hands until we could get our prisoners to a place of safety, and left another prisoner to take care of him while we pushed on with the others. After turning over our prisoners to the provost marshal, we went back to take out the two we had left behind, but the regiment had changed its position and we did not find it, and so did not get the balance of the prisoners we captured in the first instance.

I was too much excited and exhausted to ask the colonel who he was or what his regiment, and never had an opportunity to ascertain afterwards. I have never ceased to regret that I left those prisoners with him, as he was a very pompous officer, and I suppose he claimed them as his legitimate captures. Had we retained them in our ranks we could have safely got them out by taking more time,

*George Steward of Co. H, 20th Maine Vols. died on August 8, 1864, and is buried in grave 4596, Andersonville National Cemetery. --Atwater List.

but I was fearful that we might not come out as we planned, possibly might fall in with some of the enemy's skirmishers in the woods, and with the embarrassment of a badly wounded officer on our hands might lose all of our other prisoners.

In taking our prisoner out we struck our main line some distance to the left from the place where we had thrown up works in the morning, and finding ourselves safely within our lines marched directly to our division headquarters where we delivered the thirty prisoners that we had in charge. After our captured were disposed of, we made our way to the point in our line from which we had moved out to make the charge, where we found the survivors of our regiment already comfortably established in the works.

As we came to the regiment we were greeted with exclamations and inquiries, as it was supposed we had all been killed or captured in the fight. Captain William W. Morrell, commanding Company A, a young officer only a few years my senior, said to me, "Well, lieutenant, how did things look down at Rappahannock Station?" When you recall the fact that Rappahannock Station was our winter quarters, you will at once see the sarcasm and implication carried in the remark. It implied that we had been panic stricken in the battle and fled to the rear, not stopping in our flight until we were back to our winter camp, and after recovering from our fright, and desiring to return to our regiment, had fixed our bayonets and were marching in order to give the impression that we were a provost guard and not a band of cowards and stragglers. His remark stung me like a viper, and had he thrust me through with his sword the wound would not have been more painful, nor would it have taken as long to heal had it not been for what occurred three days later, when in the hand-to-hand contest with the enemy at Laurel Hill, Spottsylvania, on the night of May 8, he was shot dead at my side, and in attempting to drag off his body after the battle I became unconscious from the bleeding of my own wounds and we were both carried back together, he to be buried in the woods where we had been fighting, I to the hospital and recovery after a long and painful experience. Thus death established its truce over its victim. As has been intimated in this narrative, it was a very delicate thing for an officer to lead those under his command to the rear during a battle, and I had felt very anxious for fear I had made a mistake in so doing, for had I not been correct in my premises and the regiment had not gone back before we did, I should have been exposed to the charge of cowardice and conduct unbecoming of an officer; but as our little company brought out more prisoners than all the rest of the regiment I had begun to feel very comfortable, and to think I had not made a mistake after all; but when met by this implied charge of misdemeanor, I was too astonished to make answer to the cruel words, but recognized the importance of having proof that we were not guilty of the charge he made; so hastening back to division headquarters, and tearing a piece of paper from a letter in my pocket, I wrote a receipt for the prisoners we had turned over and for which I did not think of asking a receipt at the time. The provost marshal signed it and it has been carefully preserved till this day and I will read from the original:

H'd. Qrs. 1st Div., 5th Corps.
May 5, 1864.
*Received of Lieut. H. S. Melcher
Thirty (30) Prisoners (rebel).*
Jas. D. Orne,
Capt. Pro. Marshal,
1st Div., 5th Corps.

I returned to my command tired and with wounded feelings, yet I had in my pocket, where it has ever since remained, an unanswerable defense to the charge made.

Referring to my diary which I kept during the war I find recorded under date of May 5, 1864: "We packed up to march this morning, but hearing that the enemy were advancing on us we threw up earthworks, waited till noon, but as they did not attack we charged them. It was a severe charge and a bloody battle, but I got off safe bringing out thirty prisoners."

You will see that all I have told in my story is covered by the brief account in my diary, and perhaps it would have been more agreeable to you had I used the diary to tell the story of this "Experience in the Battle of the Wilderness."

5th Army Corps Hospital
in the field.
near Spottsylvania Co. House
May 10th 1864

Dear Brother:

I will just write you a line this morning as I understand that a mail will be sent to Washington to-day. As you see by this, I am in the Hospital, but do not be alarmed, for my wounds are not dangerous, only a minie ball through my right thigh. No bones broken. It has been very painful till midnight last night, since when it has been very easy and now I am real comfortable.

I am having every attention paid me possible by the Medical Dept., and Sanitary and Christian Commissions. I suppose we shall be sent to Washington as soon as possible. But the ambulances are so much engaged bringing the wounded from the field, for the battle still goes on, the 6th day of its continuation. As I am now writing the thunder of artillery reverberates through the morning air. Our line of battle is about two miles in front of us. Lieut. Howard L. Prince is lying by my side. He is wounded just in the same place as I am, and also his right thumb is shot so badly, he will have to have it amputated. One ball did it all for him. He wants you to tell Maxwell that he is comfortable and "am coming home to Commencement."

I have not time to tell you of our doings since we crossed the river, but will in some future time. The battle has been one of terrible fierceness and slaughter. The three first days of the battle was in the Wilderness, and no artillery could be used. But such volleys of musketry never before was heard! Our Regt. fought there three successive days. Lieuts. [Frederick W.] Lane and [John M.] Sherwood, Capt. [William W.] Morrell were killed, and Lt. [Hiram] Morse wounded. And about 100 men killed, wounded, and prisoners. My company lost two killed, and four wounded.

On the night of the 7th, we drove the enemy back and pursuing, overtook them again at this place 12 miles distant. At 9 o'clock A.M. on the 8th, we were under fire all day and at about sunset, made a charge through the woods, terrific indeed! I was wounded in the early part of the engagement, but remained with my company till the firing ceased. But in attempting to get off Capt. Morrell (W.W.), who was shot, I fainted and was carried off by my Sergeant. The battle goes bravely on. We have captured many prisoners.

Make the best of it to Mother.
Pray for us Brother.
Holman

On May 20th, Lt. Melcher was transferred to the Armory Square General Hospital in Washington, D.C. On June 7th, he was granted a leave of absence to return home to Topsham for recovery, and being reunited with his family brought joy to the wounded soldier.

The healing of his wound would be slow and painful for Lt. Melcher. For the next five months doctors treated the gangrenous leg, saving it from amputation and possibly saving young Holman's life as well. On October 21, 1864, Holman S. Melcher returned to active duty in the Twentieth Maine and was promoted to Captain of Company F, commission dating from July 12, 1864.

Armory Square General Hospital, Washington, D.C.

Gen. G.K. Warren and his Staff in 1864.

(No. 10)
Hd. Qrs. 5th Army Corps.
Nov. 17, 1864

Dear N.

I will try and not write such long letters in future or at least, I'll not say much about Miss Hattie, for when I write about "H" it is, or seems to be a sign for you to cease all operations in writing to me. I don't allow myself to imagine bad things when I can prevent it, but it is hard for me to do so in this case.

I wrote you as soon as I got settled in my present position which you have probably received, but I do not know, as I have received no reply. I enjoy my position very much, find it easier to get along than I was afraid it would be. I am very politely used by all the Staff and think I will not be wholly unpopular if I do not drink "Cocktails" with them. There is no playing cards here so I am safe from that temptation. See but little of Gen. Warren, as he has a private mess and keeps himself very close. There are about 15 staff officers in our mess, have a well regulated table of good food. Breakfast at 8 1/2 A.M. Dinner at 4 P.M. My servant is a colored boy about 18, named George.

I admire your patriotism and courage, but please do not enlist, or it may be your misfortune to know how bullets feel, as well as "sound" and then you will be compelled to walk--if you could walk at all--with a cane, like I still have to do. One cripple in a family is bad enough, so do take care of yourself.

Write soon,
Holman

(No. 14.)
Hd. Qrs. 5th Army Corps
"Jerusalem Plank Road"
December 20, 1864

Dear N.

I was happy to receive your good No. 10, but disappointed to know that you cannot make me a visit this Winter. I had allowed myself to believe that you would come, and had even been laying out in my mind, plans of operations while you would be here, and when your letter was received last evening I hastily broke the seal hardly stopping to read any of it till I came to the reply, and then with an air of disappointment carefully examined your picture, and read the letter again from the beginning. I thank you heartily for the picture, though had rather you had come yourself.

I am afraid you will know nothing about the "Army of the Potomac" now that other departments are attracting so much attention just now, and so I must remind you that we "still live."

After the object of the late expedition had been successfully accomplished, the 5th Corps returned to find their nice, comfortable quarters occupied by the 6th Corps just back from the Shenandoah Valley, and so had to go into camp on new ground. It is interesting to ride along the lines and hear the rapid blows from thousands of axes, and the crash of falling trees, as the gallant 5th Corps go about building Winter Quarters.

The 9th, 6th & 2nd Corps of this Army occupy the works in front of Petersburg, from right to left in the order they are named. Our Corps is parallel to them facing in an opposite direction, occupying a line about six miles from Petersburg. We hear all the firing in front, which is cansiderable of late, but are exposed to none ourselves.

Some 20,000 men from the "Army of the James" have gone South to cooperate with the great Naval expedition which left Fortress Monroe a few days ago.

A salute of 100 shotted guns was fired last Sunday at sunrise in honor of [Maj. Gen. George H.] Thomas' Victory.*

It is notoriously evident that, confidence was not at all misplaced by those who believed that "Hood & Co. would get a licking." Only "licking" fails entirely to express the thing that Thomas has done, is doing, and is going to do. We feel exultant, and prone to boast. We certainly have reason to rejoice. We will rejoice and will at the same time return thanks, and give the glory to the "God of Battles," who has given us the victory, given wisdom to the Generals, and strength to the Soldiers, to defeat the hated foe.

You are having quite a winter, both snow and cold. Perhaps riding in a sleigh with such fair, beautiful, and angelic beings as Misses Clara, Addie, Laura, and numberless others, may have had much to do in raising you to the dignity of a Portly Gentleman, in connection with the thoughts of that Dear One, who wears such beautiful curls, and is so faithfully conducting herself worthy of a true and absent Lover.

The week past has been delightful, so good for our men to put up their quarters. I am occupying a tent with Capt. Malbon, Chief Ambulance Officer of the Corps. He is a Maine man, and a nice fellow too, and I enjoy his company much. It is more pleasant to me thus far than it was to be alone. I enjoy my Official position as well as at first.

If we take Richmond, it will be a Merry Christmas to us. I sincerely wish you a Merry Christmas. You will probably enjoy it and the Holidays, but amid all pleasures, don't so far forget your Soldier Brother, as to neglect to write the weekly letter.

Holman.

*At the Battle of Nashville, Dec. 15-16, 1864, Gen. George H. Thomas thoroughly defeated Gen. John Bell Hood. The Civil War, Day by Day.

CHAPTER SIX
1865:
CAMPFIRES OF VICTORY!

In the final months of the long and bloody war, Holman Melcher knew that only absolute victory for the Union could atone for the sacrifices that had been made. Still not fully recovered from his painful leg wound, Captain Melcher's lameness prevented him from marching with his company in the upcoming spring campaign. To pass the idle hours, he began to record his thoughts in a diary that Nathaniel had given him.

While recuperating from his wound, Melcher served on the staff of the Fifth Corps as Postmaster, a position which permitted him to ride horseback. Although duties were light and comfortable in camp, during the campaign he would act as Assistant Aide-de-Camp to General Warren, the Fifth Corps Commander. In this position, Holman Melcher rendered service possibly even more crucial than his action on Little Round Top. During the battle of Hatcher's Run, it was Melcher's quick initiative and gallant actions that steadied a routed Federal unit heading for the rear. Melcher, the only mounted officer present, rallied the fugitives and formed a defensive position that held the Confederates in check, and helped change the battle's outcome.

Sunday, January 1, 1865
Let this day and all others of this year be spent as it should and may the experiences of the past enable me the better to spend the days of future probation--and while I use wisdom and reason to direct my course, let me remember that action is more creditable than words.

Monday, January 2, 1865
General Warren invited the officers of his staff and corps to call on him unceremoniously--as a New Year's Call. Many officers of the Corps came and we of the staff had much to do to entertain them, and officiate at the tables. With the General and the Staff I attended the sword presentation to Gen. [Henry] Baxter this evening.

Tuesday, January 3, 1865
Am glad enough to keep quiet today--for after the exertion of yesterday my wound demands in plain unmistakable terms, rest, and so I do rest. How glad I am that my position is such that I can take care of myself until my wound gets well.

Wednesday, January 4, 1865
Was the recipient of a good recommendation from General Chamberlain today. Am happy to know that he is willing to express himself in such commendable terms of me. I must remember that this is all of the little benefit to me unless I strive to fit myself for higher positions by close application and attention to duty. Faithfulness will be rewarded.

Thursday, January 5, 1865
Went to City Point on business this morning on the 8:30 train. Did my business and then called on Mrs. Mayhew. Had a real pleasant visit indeed--and a good social chit-chat. Learned interest-

ing matter about Miss C.M.F. Started on the three o'clock train for camp--but did not arrive there till 7 o'clock.

Friday, January 6, 1865
Replied to General Chamberlain today--and spent the day in writing and filing papers. It has rained most all day, wind southeast but is quite warm and pleasant. Spent the evening in writing business letters and one to Brother Nathaniel. Mail did not arrive til 10 o'clock this evening. My wound is quite painful this afternoon.

Saturday, January 7, 1865
A very cold windy day--which I spent in reading and studying Bookkeeping. I am having a fine opportunity for mental improvement and let me be wise and improve it as I should. Spent the evening at the [20th Maine] Regiment-- and not an unpleasant one.

Sunday, January 8, 1865
Why this coldness of heart and spiritual desires? If I have been regenerated through the blood of Christ it should be reason enough for me to spend my life in the service and honor of my Master. May I ever be ready to own and bless Him who has saved me. The day has been a very quiet one to me. Pleasant.

Monday, January 9, 1865
It has been the most lovely day imaginable. Such days are what makes the Southern Clime so much more pleasant than the North--and would make life so delightful if one was settled in this State. Have shown far too much "Tameness" today. Ought to strive to be more interesting.

Tuesday, January 10, 1865
It stormed all last night and all day-- rain falling in torrents--and

tonight the brooks are full and running over their banks. Mail arrived at 9 o'clock. I have spent the day in a very quiet manner--not improving the time as I ought. Yet I have learned something. I do wish I could make myself more agreeable in company and not be so reserved.

Wednesday, January 11, 1865
I have been superintending the building of an Office today. Am vexed with myself because I did not assume more authority and have it all as I wanted it; by not doing it, I get a building extremely different from what I intended it should be. Thus I live in constant warfare with myself.

Thursday, January 12, 1865
Had a very pleasant call from Lt. Col. [Ellis] Spear yesterday and a good social chat with him, the best I ever did have. We received the intelligence of the death of Capt. [Burrage] Rice, 189th NY, shot while in charge of a Foraging, by Guerillas. It has been a truly lovely day--just cool enough for winter. Had a call from Capt. [Thomas] Chamberlain, and a letter from Brother N.

Friday, January 13, 1865
It has been a day truly delightful. I have personally superintended the work on my Office today. Am better satisfied with my conduct than I am sometimes. My Leave of Absence was granted me, but I cannot seem to go tomorrow. I have thought considerably about the remark of Col. [Frederick Thomas] Locke about my going Sunday. I must be more careful and live on principle.

Saturday, January 14, 1865
Spent a very pleasant day riding out with Captain [Joseph H.] Malbon, first to Army Hqs., then to my Regiment, where we had a very pleasant call, then to the Hqs. of the Artillery Brigade. Made

preparations to go to Washington as Col. Spear and Gen'l Chamberlain leave tomorrow.

Sunday, January 15, 1865

As Lt. Col. Spear, Gen'l Chamberlain, and other officers of my intimate acquaintance were going, I decided to accompany them as far as Washington--excusing myself that it would be desecrating the Day no more than if I remained in camp. We had a very pleasant and agreeable party--and a lovely day.

Monday, January 16, 1865

We arrived at Washington about 8 o'clock this morning after a very pleasant journey. Went to the National Hotel with Col. Spear, took breakfast, and then was paid for four months by Maj. Sabine. Invested $300 in Seven thirties.* Visited the Patent and Post Offices and went philosophically to Grover's Theater to see Miss Avonia Jones play Judith. Learned something.

Tuesday, January, 17, 1865

A day in the Metropolis. Called on Mrs. [Charles D.] Gilmore and in the evening had the pleasure of the company of Miss Nellie to the Opera. The Opera was good-- "Il Trovatore", and the audience brilliant in the extreme. It would hardly seem that such a man existed to look on such an audience.

Thursday, January 19, 1865

Went to Mason's Island, Virginia, today to see what I could do about a servant for Father. Found affairs more favorable than I anticipated. Was not severe enough in settling my bills at Dyer's Hotel. Taking the Horse Cars, I got to the Steamer in good season. Found much ice in the Potomac, but the "Webster" butt her way nobly through.

*3-Year Treasury Notes. Interest paid was 7 3/10%, i.e. "seven-thirties." -- Treasury Historical Assoc.

Friday, January 20, 1865
When I got up this morning, we were at Fortress Monroe. Had a pleasant passage up the James. The time passed rapidly in conversation with a Masonic Brother and reading. Reached City Point at 2:30 o'clock and Corps Hqs. at 4:30 P.M.--to find everything quiet. Have been too extravagant and manifested inferior judgement during my stay in Washington.

Saturday, January 21, 1865
I found my box of luxuries from home awaiting me at Corps Hqs. Was most happy to receive it for I was in want of its contents. It has been a very severe storm today--ice in the morning and rain in the afternoon.

Sunday, January 22, 1865
A dark, cloudy day. Went over to the 20th Regiment to carry the letters to Col. [Charles D.] Gilmore from his wife as it rained so yesterday that I could not go. Had a pleasant call and a good social talk with Dr. [Abner O.] Shaw and Capt. [Joseph F.] Land. Spent the afternoon in reading. I wish there were religious meetings that I could attend. No mail tonight.

Monday, January 23, 1865
It has been a dark, drizzly day. Capt. Marvine left for home today, having resigned. It makes one uneasy to have their friends going home--but I know my own situation and business in this matter and must be governed by my good sense and not by my feelings.

Tuesday, January 24, 1865
Have been engaged in business of my office and in Official Communications. The day has been quite cold. Last night the cannonading was very heavy, continuing all night--and today we

hear that the Rebels attempted to capture and burn City Point, but their gunboats got aground and so the attempt completely failed. It seems almost a special Providence that saved the place, for all our fleet was away and there seemed to be no protection from the Rebel gunboats. The feat by which the Rebels were to "astonish the world"--and that too like the whole Confederacy is going to soon--In noise, fire, and smoke.

Thursday, January 26, 1865
It has been a severe cold day, and one thought more of keeping near a large fire than most anything else. Such cold days are very unpleasant in camp for our canvas tents furnish but little protection from the cold without a large fire. Rode over to see Capt. Carne this afternoon. No mail arrived tonight, probably on account of the ice. It is hard to be shut off from all news.

Friday, January 27, 1865
It was the coldest night of the season last night and has been very cold today. The Potomac is frozen over so that the mail steamers are compelled to go via Annapolis. I learned to play chess today and have questioned myself if I ought to have done it-am conscious that it would have been better to spend the time in reading, but one gets tired of reading all the day long.

Saturday, January 28, 1865
It has been another severely cold day, coldest of this winter I should think. Have kept very close in my tent and burned immense quantities of wood. Am not particularly pleased with the labors or the fruits of them today. Wrote Cousin Mary this evening. Another week gone into the past never to return.

Sunday, January 29, 1865
It has been a cold, windy day but a pleasant one. Have spent

the day in reading the papers that Father sent me and other matters. Rode over to the 16th Maine with Capt. [Joseph H.] Malbon after dinner and made the acquaintance of Col. [Charles W.] Tilden. The evening spent in pleasant conversation. How pleasant it would be to have an opportunity to attend church these Sabbaths.

Officers of the 16th Maine Vols. Capt. Joseph Malbon is seated at right.

Monday, January 30, 1865

I went up to Fort "Hell"--and had a nice opportunity to see Rebel movements.* The lines are close together there. A little incident of interest occurred there today--that the pickets met together, cut up a tree, and divided the wood. How friendly--and yet enemies. Many rumors about Peace. It was said that [Confederate Vice-President Alexander] Stevens and [Senator Robert M.T.] Hunter came into our lines to proceed to Washington.

Tuesday, January 31, 1865

I made the application for an appointment as [Assistant Adjutant General] in the U.S. Army--with assurances from prominent offic-

During the siege of Petersburg, Fort Sedgwick was nicknamed "Fort Hell."

ers that it would be granted. It will be a fine position for me if I am appointed and quite an important one too. The day has been truly beautiful and the evening made pleasant by the music of the band.

Wednesday, February 1, 1865
We received orders last night to be ready to march but have not gone yet. The day has been one of unsurpassed loveliness. Have not spent the day particularly advantageously to myself. Made a bargain for "Dick" to be my servant. I was very much disappointed at not receiving a letter from Brother N. in the mail this evening.

Thursday, February 2, 1865
With the greatest anxiety I looked for a letter from Bro. N. but was disappointed. The day has been very pleasant, but the orders for marching were not enforced and we remain quietly in camp. I have realized the importance of being versed in knowledge--and, knowing the importance, let me improve every moment to reading and study of instructive works.

Friday, February 3, 1865
It has stormed the whole day--hail and rain intermingled. The rumors of a move seem to have been quieted. We get the satisfactory intelligence that the 13th Constitutional Amendment passed Congress on the last day of January--119 to 56--so we are at last a Free Nation with the approval of the States. Thank God!

Saturday, February 4, 1865
There was considerable picket firing last night. The enemy seem to be moving to their right. I went to the 19th Maine Vols. today, had a pleasant ride and a pleasant call there. [William L.] Gerrish who came out as 1st Sergt. is now a 2nd Lt. and acting adjt. We get orders this evening to march at 6 o'clock in the morning.

Sunday, February 5, 1865

The corps marches at 6 o'clock this morning--meeting the enemy after 11 o'clock on a branch of Hatcher's Run. After a sharp little fight we charged across the stream, capturing the works and 25 prisoners of the 26th N.C. Regt. I was sent back to Gen'l Meade with dispatches and got back just as the Corps was going into camp. Rode till 3 o'clock next morning.

Monday, February 6, 1865

I came in to get the mail last night and after 3 hours sleep, mounted my horse and led the mail wagon to the front. The Corps was building works. At 3 o'clock we assaulted the enemies' lines but were repulsed. Our men acted rather cowardly and displayed more of the panic principle than I ever saw before. I lost my hat in the battle and had my horse shot under me. Was exposed to a terrific fire and can ascribe my safety only to the pressing care of a preserving God. Was complemented all I could desire by Genl. Warren after the battle. Genl. [Samuel W.] Crawford fought all day, gaining many important positions.

February 6, 1865

Dear Brother,

I have just returned from the battle-field at Hatcher's Run, and while waiting for my Servant to fix my bed, will write you just a line or so to let you know that I have survived the first day's campaign although I am emphatically tired. Since 7 o'clock yesterday morning I have hardly got off my horse until this moment.

Our Corps moved out on the Halifax Road, meeting the enemy about 11 o'clock, and after a sharp little fight, drove them taking some prisoners-- have skirmished some since. The 2nd Corps moved on our right and have had the brunt of the fighting. The enemy attacked them furiously, two successive times and were severely repulsed each time. I cannot give losses or particulars as I have been constantly on the go with dispatches from Gen'l Warren to Gen'l Meade, and back. The Corps being so far apart made it much more severe for the Staff Officers. It has seemed but little like Sunday, I assure you.

I shall go to the front at 8 o'clock this morning with the mail and dispatches for the Corps, but in the intermediate time, hope to get some sleep, and as my servant has got my bed ready, I will cease writing and subside and sleep. We expect a severe battle to-morrow. God grant us success.

In haste,
Your Brother, H.

Tuesday, February 7, 1865

It has rained all day--cold and dreary--and our troops have suffered severely as very few of them took their tents. I rode over the battlefield today. What sights sickening and horrible met my eye. Pools of blood and other scenes incident to a hard fought field.

Wednesday, February 8, 1865

Everything is quiet today, and our skirmishers do not meet the enemy in their advance.

Thursday, February 9, 1865

It is a cold and disagreeable,--and our men are suffering severely (while they) are at work on the fortifications preparatory to holding the line we have established. I rode into camp this afternoon. It seemed like getting home after having had such a severe campaign. I did enjoy a good bed a bit, if not more.

Friday, February 10, 1865

I remain in camp today attending mail duties and writing letters. Sent my agent to the front with the mail instead of going myself. Everything is quiet along the lines. Our troops are engaged in building fortifications. Gen. Baxter's Brigade came into camp after their tents; return this morning.

Saturday, February 11, 1865

I went to the front today--to find all quiet. The Corps is going into camp today, and Genl. Warren is out putting them into position while we wait in the mud near Hatcher's Run in our old Bivouac. The day is quite pleasant and is a good one to be at work on the fortifications. The new line is to be established.

Sunday, February 12, 1865

What a miserable way to spend the Sabbath! One of the demoralizing things of war. It is impossible for subordinate officers to escape it, but we will be happy that, if while compelled to endure it, we close ourselves against its polluting influence. The Hqs. of the Corps went into camp today. I was in the saddle all day.

Monday, February 13, 1865

We have just got set down in our new camp but are anything but comfortably situated. Tents without floors and other such unpleasant surroundings. We are unfortunate to be going into camp at such a cold time as it is now, but the weather is pleasant if it is cold. I sent to the old camp and had my office hauled up here.

Tuesday, February 14, 1865

A cold but otherwise pleasant day. It has seemed a miserable day to me, partly on account of my being out of humor--by not knowing where to put my office when I had all the lumber ready and only waiting for others to decide where it must be. If I was planning the camp, I would do it at once and not put it up one tent at a time.

Wednesday, February 15, 1865
Have been quite closely engaged all day attending to matters of business pertaining to my office. I must apply myself more closely to reading now that I have so much time and not live in ignorance. I never will regret that I improved all my leasure moments in study, but will if I neglect it and fool away my time and opportunities.

Thursday, February 16, 1865
Everyone has been at work all day in fitting up our new quarters. The day has been one of unsurpassed loveliness. Did not need any fires. I have spent a part of the day in playing chess, believing it to be a good discipline, giving me opportunity to apply my mind.

Friday, February 17, 1865
All are very clearly engaged in fitting up our new quarters. Military movements are a non plus just now in this Dept. but we are looking with much interest to Gen. [William T.] Sherman just now. South Carolina is at least drinking in full from the bitter cup of secession.

Saturday, February 18, 1865
I have been busy all the afternoon in fitting up my tent, having had a tent assigned to me for my personal use. It was in a bad condition when I began on it, but by night I had got a real comfortable tent. Am glad that I am situated as I am, which is very pleasant.

Sunday, February 19, 1865
This is a beautiful day, and I wish opportunities offered to spend

it in a more proper way than we shall. Army life is really demoralizing. I feel interested in reading from the Book "Grapes of Eshcal"--an interesting and refining work. Spend the evening in writing to the Rev. Mr. Gurney.*

Monday, February 20, 1865
Another lovely morning enough to almost inspire one. I arise after a rich night's sleep--the nights are just cool enough to sleep well. Had a grand view of the two armies and the opposing works from the top of the Signal Tower--a really grand sight.

*The Rev. Leander Gurney was a minister in Brunswick. His daughter Hattie would marry Nathaniel Melcher on August 16, 1866.

Signal Tower near Petersburg, Va.

Tuesday, February 21, 1865
   The weather is really delightful. We are rejoiced beyond measure by receiving the glorious news that Charleston has fallen! That nest of secession. The hotbed of treason. Thank God that our efforts to restore the Union have thus been blessed to such a glorious extent. That seems good news enough for one day, but in addition we learn that Columbia has surrendered too.

Wednesday, February 22, 1865
   We got orders late last night to look out for an attack from three Brigades of Genl. [Henry] Heth's Division, which moved down to our right. A salute was fired at 12M. in honor of Washington's Birthday. How we ought to be inspired with feelings of Patriotism on such a day as this and renew or vows to strike earnestly for right and our government handed down to us.

Thursday, February 23, 1865
   It has been raining gently all day. The attack which we expected from Genl. Lee was not made this morning--which is well for the Rebel Army. Genl. Warren and ladies arrived in camp tonight and our evening has been made pleasant by music by the Band. I spend the evening in writing to Father.

Friday, February 24, 1865
   We are rejoiced this morning at receiving the glorious news that Wilmington, NC was captured on the 22nd. We can hardly realize how great blessings God is bestowing upon our Nation. We deserve wrath and displeasure, but the "Lord is merciful and gracious." Deserters are numerous and said this morning that Lee was preparing to evacuate Richmond and Petersburg.

Saturday, February 25, 1865

It has rained all day--gently--and the review ordered was thus prevented. I have felt foolishly "Blue" today. Must have more will to overcome little repulses. I feel such too keenly, yet others do not know it. The ladies went home this P.M. At 5 o'clock the batteries opened up to feel if the enemy evacuated. Furious shelling for an hour. Result not learned tonight.

Sunday, February 26, 1865

It has been a warm and lovely day, but it has seemed little like Sunday--and to make the day more hideous the Paymaster came and as he would leave early in the morning, we had to receive our pay or go without. Sometimes I think I ought to go without instead of receiving pay on the Sabbath. God grant that while exposed to these demoralizing scenes I may keep my heart closed against them.

Monday, February 27, 1865

There is general quiet reigning today. I suppose I ought to be more social with the other Officers. We each have our individuality.

Tuesday, February 28, 1865

The last day of the month, the shortest in the year to be sure and it has seemed very short to me. How very little I have done during the past month. I ought to be more earnest in reading and general improvement. The day has been rainy and dull. Considerable picket firing last night.

Wednesday, March 1, 1865

I have spent so much of the day in reading that my head aches severely this evening. Have been thinking if there is any probability of my being appointed A.A.G. Think there is very little as I have little political influence to help me. Should much prefer to be appointed on my application in a military way than any other.

Thursday, March 2, 1865

It rained all last night and it has rained about as hard as it ever does all day, and there is very little prospect of clearing away. Have accomplished but little today. Two letters written is about the whole extent of my labors, I regret to be compelled to say. Let me arouse and be in earnest in life.

Head Qrs. 5th Army Corps.
March 2, 1865

Dear Brother:

I'm not exactly "Blue" to-day, but you know how unpleasant a stormy day always was to me even at home. And here in camp, with an old wounded leg to add unpleasantness, to dark rainy weather, by a dull heavy pain. "Thank my stars," that I am not called onto the road by business to-day, for the mud is appalling. It has been raining since last evening. I cannot find better amusement than in writing you, so you will pardon me if I inflict on you a sheet of writing very much more uninteresting than a sheet of white paper. I was much interested in your good No. 4, for you wrote so freely. I did really feast the evening of its arrival. Was much interested in your account of Miss Addie, still up to your old habits of finding any number of Darling beauties, in your pathway. I wonder if she knows that your heart is all possessed by a Fair Lady who wears curls, "Down East"! I hope you will continue to write me such incidents for they are far more interesting than stories. Who would you write to if you would not to me? Until you are married, who can have greater claims in your confidence than your only Brother, if he is unworthy even?

Am most happy to learn of your success in speaking in behalf of the cause of Christ. By all means accept the invitation to speak to the people.

Jimmy Maxwell has got to the Regiment at last, and they have given him the position of Regt. Clerk, an easy unexposed place, but small chance of promotion. But if he does well, he may get an appointment of Sergt. Major some day in the future. I met him when I went to the regiment a few days ago. He tells me that you shot six (6) Guerillas!!! Should think your slumbers would be disturbed by the ghosts of so many dead men. That is more Rebels than I have shot or expect to shoot in the whole of my three years. There is no need of your enlisting to do something for the Country, for there is not a soldier in the Army of the Potomac who has shot more than that probably.

I was considerably surprised that you should for one moment think that I exposed myself as I did in the last battle, just to gain popularity and "serve my worthy General well." I had hoped you believe me to have higher motives to govern me than that. I, with most of the other Staff Officers, were by the temporary Hd. Qrs. established just in rear of the line of battle. All was going well, the General had gone away by himself, when the line began to break and fall back. The General was not there to give orders. Something must be done quickly, a few rods behind us was our Ammunition and Ambulance Trains. And behind them was Hatcher's Run, with only one narrow bridge across it. I thought what if we are driven back onto that stream, and attempt to recross on that bridge. All would be lost. The line must be rallied here. I drew my sword and spurred my horse to the point, calling on the retreating soldiers to fall about and hold the pursuing enemy, and thank God we did hold them there. Back and forth across that field, for an hour or more the battle raged with terrible fury. We would be driven back across it when rallying by the most strenuous efforts of what officers there were left. We would in turn drive the enemy back till the field was so thickly strewn with dead that my horse could hardly step without striking his foot against a noble fallen. I was the only mounted Officer left on the field. We had got a good line established and I was riding along in front, instructing the men not to fire and waste their shots until they could see the enemy. My hat had been knocked of, and my horse covered with foam. When Gen'l. Warren came riding onto the field, from a distant point of the line. Of course I had nothing to do then, but obey his orders. and I was the only Staff Officer left. My horse was shot when I was riding by Gen'l. Warren. Pardon this illusion to myself. I have to let you know how affairs were that you would not think that I was intently selfish in my conduct. I would not expose myself again for half of this Nation, if that is what I was doing it for.

                Write often please.
                Sincerely,
                H.S. Melcher

Friday, March 3, 1865

Another dark and rainy day. The enemy continue to desert as rapidly as ever--so much that it has become necessary to make their vedettes walk in the rear of the picket line instead of in the front as our men do. I should think the demoralization would spread through their whole army. When officers begin to desert, it looks as if the army must be low in morale.

Sunday, March 5, 1865

I rode over to the Ambulance Camp with Capt. Malbon, so as to escape the monotony of the day in camp. Visited the 6th Corps hospital, decidedly the most tastily arranged of anything I have ever seen in the Army. Let me strive to keep myself above the vices of this life. God save me for Christ's sake. It pains me to see this total disregard for the Sabbath by so many, but they are left to their own destruction, which they are rapidly making complete.

Monday, March 6, 1865
It has been a lovely day. I have kept myself quietly in my tent, writing and reading but little. Col. Locke returned this evening from a leave. "Tempus Fugit."

Tuesday, March 7, 1865
It has been a lovely day. The 1st and 3rd Divisions were reviewed by Genl. Meade. He was accompanied by Genl. [Horatio G.] Wright and Staff and a company of Fair Ladies from City Point and Washington. It was a gay afternoon for us--a strange sight for us to have Ladies to accompany us on military movements. Genl. Crawford's Division did splendidly. The evening is one of unsurpassable loveliness, and the delicious air is made melodious by the smart music of numerous bands. I wonder if I like this kind of life.

Wednesday, March 8, 1865
The morning was pleasant but afternoon dark and evening stormy. I have felt out of bias and unhappy all day for no reason at all. I wish I had full control over myself. Have been engaged in writing an account of the battle of Dabney Mill [Hatcher's Run].

Friday, March 10, 1865
The morning was rainy; the afternoon it hailed and snowed; and near night the clouds broke and the sun shone down in its brightness. Spring is struggling with winter for the mastery, but like the union cause is sure to come off triumphant. The day has been much more pleasant than yesterday.

Saturday, March 11, 1865
It has been a pleasant day, but my feelings have been anything

but pleasant. The thought has been raging triumphant that I had rather not be than not be one of the first in the world, but that is not my business I suppose. I ought to do what I think is right, be diligent in business, and then look to God for the blessing and leave all with Him. It is not for me to say that I will not arise.

Sunday, March 12, 1865
I had to sit up late last evening for the arrival of the mail so that it was late before I got up this morning, but with a rich bath last night and a sweet quiet sleep I rise refreshed and in a proper state to spend the day in worship, but how the surroundings are calculated to draw one away from the substantial duties of life! God rules in wisdom and we are not excusable if we neglect his service and the things that relate to our everlasting destiny. I pray that wisdom may be given me to act as becomes an intelligent and responsible being.

Tuesday, March 14, 1865
It has been a lovely day. The corps assembled for a review at 1 o'clock, but considerable time was occupied in clearing the ground. The appearance of the Corps was very fine. Mrs. Griffin rode with General Warren and staff in review--quite a novelty in military matters. Am more satisfied with myself today.

Wednesday, March 15, 1865
I went to City Point on the 9:35 train--called on and took dinner with Dr. [Granville M.] Baker,[20th Me] a pleasant call. Mrs. Mayhew was at the front so that I did not see her. Came up on the 3 o'clock train. The day passed more pleasantly than common. Sent Father by Express a $50 "seven thirty" Treasury Note.

Thursday, March 16, 1865
The day has been cloudy and windy with showers of rain. The Corps was reviewed today by Genl. Meade accompanied by

Secretary of War [Edwin M.] Stanton, the French officers and a large party of ladies and gentlemen. The appearance of the Corps was very fine, but the wind and dust made the review very unpleasant.

Friday, March 17, 1865
"Saint Patrick's Day"--a real Irish celebration--horse races, mule races, and man races. The races were a general breakdown with the severe injury of some four men. There was quite a large party of ladies on the stand. The day has been beautiful. Popularity may be well enough in its place, but, when it is attained at the loss of principles, it is good no more.

Saturday, March 18, 1865
I reviewed the horses and wagons of my department this P.M. and found them in good condition. Rode over to the picket line near the battlefield of Hatcher's Run--and down to the Goshen House. They day has been really lovely and summer like.

Sunday, March 19, 1865
This has been another beautiful day. How I longed to attend Church! but know of no place. I have had a long earnest talk with Capt. [Emmor B.] Cope. He disbelieves all the Bible that is not in accordance with his ideas of propriety, and that man has come up from the lowest part of the vegetable creation. Both ideas I think to be entirely wrong. God give me a right understanding in such matters of vital spiritual importance is my sincere earnest prayer.

Monday, March 20, 1865
Have spent the day in reading and writing. The day has been very warm, almost unpleasantly so. In asserting my dignity, I said too much perhaps. Let me set a careful guard on my tongue. "Let the words of my mouth and the meditation of my heart be acceptable

in thy sight, O God, my strength and my Redeemer."

Tuesday, March 21, 1865
As I write this, the rain is pattering on the roof of my tent right merrily--but though thin, the canvas roof affords me good shelter--and sitting at my desk before a bright fire am more comfortably situated than many brother soldiers. It is those on picket and guard that really suffer on such a night as this.

Wednesday, March 22, 1865
It has been a windy day and quite cool, have kept myself very quiet indoors and spent almost the whole day in conversation--an accomplishment that I am very much lacking. Let me improve.

Thursday, March 23, 1865
I spent the morning in writing and receiving visitors. A grand review of the 2d Corps was to take place, but about 2 o'clock when we were all ready to go, a terrific wind arose, filling the air with dust and smoke so that we did not go, but there was a partial review near night. The evening that I intended to spend in writing was spent in conversation.

Friday, March 24, 1865
This day and evening has been one almost void of benefit to me only that which I received from conversation--having spent the day in visiting. Dr. [William H.] True of the 20th spent the evening with me, with whom I had a very pleasant chat. Wrote Mother today.

Saturday, March 25, 1865
At daylight, 25,000 Rebels charged our lines in front of Petersburg, capturing Fort Stedman and 3 batteries but were driven back with the loss of 2000 prisoners besides the killed and wounded. Our picket line was advanced along the whole line under cover of

a terrific cannonade--which has continued all day. Pres. Lincoln was in the army today. We have captured some 3000 prisoners and killed and wounded many.

Sunday, March 26, 1865
    I rode in company with Capts. Malbon, [George B.] Halsted, and out to and along the picket line of the 2nd Corps, all in sight of the enemies' lines--we hold all their old picket line--and are close to their main works. The battlefield of last evening was interesting to ride over. Have never seen the bushes cut down by bullets as there.

Capt. George B. Halstead

Tuesday, March 28, 1865

It has been a warm, pleasant day, and we have all been busy packing up for the extensive movement which is to take place tomorrow morning. [Maj. Gen. Philip H.] Sheridan has arrived with his cavalry, and everything seems to be ready for a grand advance. God grant that it may be successful. Sent a box home by express.

Wednesday, March 29, 1865

We marched at 5 o'clock as ordered--crossing the Rorsach at 8 o'clock, finding no enemy. Went to near Dinwiddie, thence up the Quaker Road, where we met the enemy just across Gravelly Run, who charged on our advance, consisting of Genl. Chamberlain's [First] Brigade, but he repulsed them after a sharp fight of one hour, being wounded twice himself.

Thursday, March 30, 1865

We spent a miserable night it being rainy and we had no tents. This morning we firmly establish ourselves on the Boydton Plank Road. About noon the enemy attempt to break our lines on Genl. [Charles] Griffin's front, but were promptly repulsed--this, with considerable shelling on the part of the enemy, was all the fighting of the day.

Friday, March 31, 1865

The 2d Corps extended to the left, relieving the 1st Division [5th Corps], which massed in the rear of the 2d and 3rd Divisions. About 10 o'clock, General Warren and Staff went to the immediate front just in time to find the 2d and 3rd Divisions being driven back from the Oak Road, which they had taken in the morning. They could not be rallied until they had crossed the Run, when the 1st Division arrested the advance of the enemy after a short sharp fight. I was very much exposed today and seemed to be a miracle that I escaped. Capt. Halsted A.A.G. was wounded. We drove back the enemy and occupied the White Oak Road.

Saturday, April 1, 1865
 The Corps moved and formed a junction with Genl. Sheridan's Cavalry--and advanced on the enemy at "Five Forks" completely routing them, capturing 7,000 prisoners, 5 guns, 20 battleflags. It is pleasant to fight such battles, for we obtain material results.

Sunday, April 2, 1865
 The morning is beautiful, and only a little skirmish fire to be heard. We march early but proceed along the Oak Road but a short distance and halt, the 2d Corps not needing our assistance. News reaches us of the capture of the works around Petersburg. We return to the Grand Road, cross Hatcher's Run with little opposition, capture the [Southside Railroad] and a train of cars, and push on to Williamson's Farm--a beautiful place--and go into camp.

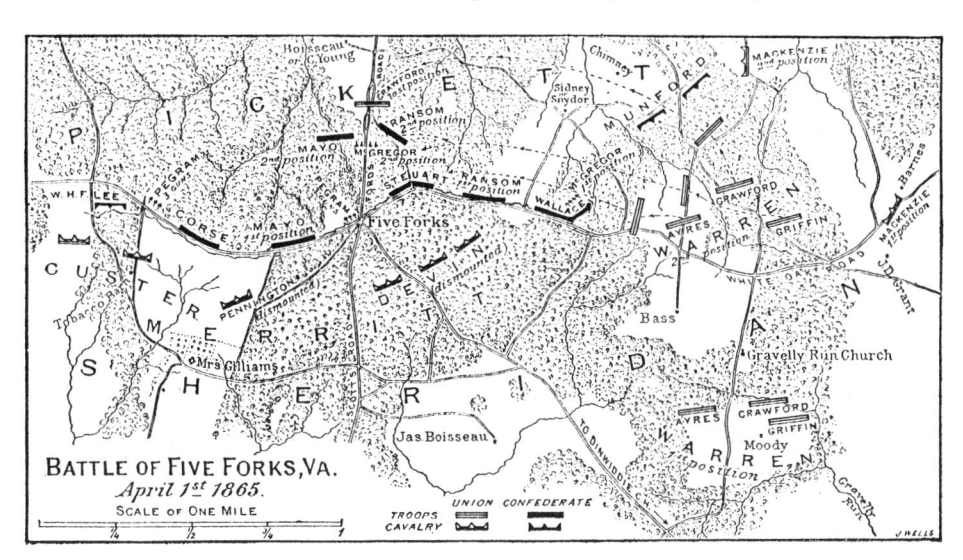

Map of Five Forks, Va.

H'd Qr's 5th Corps.
Near Petersburg, Va.
April 2, 1865

Dear Brother:

By the "Camp fires of Victory!!" I write. Since March 29th, we have fought every day, and with one slight repulse, our operations have been a complete success. But yesterday was the crowning climax. When, in conjunction with Sheridan's Cavalry, this Corps attacked Longstreet's Corps, and all the Rebel Cavalry behind works at Five Forks. And after a sharp battle we routed the whole army. And pressed them until our men were so exhausted that they could not move faster than a walk. Darkness covered the enemy from total destruction. We captured over 7000 prisoners, five pieces of Artillery, 20 battle-flags, and a large train of wagons and ambulances.

I should completely fail to describe the enthusiasm of our men, should I attempt it. Their cheers drowned the roar of battle, that rolled through the woods.

To-day we have captured the "South Side R.R.," and a train loaded with Rebel wounded, with engine and all. And have pressed far across the road and right in the rear of Petersburg. [Maj.-Gen. Wesley] Merritt's Cavalry have cut off Johnson's & Pickett's Infantry, (Rebel) and Lee's Cavalry, while we hope to capture the whole concern to-morrow morning. Our Division of our Corps. is skirmishing bravely as I write now--11 o'clock P.M.

We have been capturing prisoners all day. The Rebel army is completely demoralized, while our men cheer as they press on, filling the air with their shouts. It is a time of Jubilee for this army, but whilst all this rejoicing, we have to mourn the death of many of our noble officers and men. I have been much exposed, but God has spared me from wounds thus far, and trusting in Him, I shall strive to do my duty through the Campaign.

Before this reaches you, you will have heard of the brilliant success of the 9th and 6th Corps to-day, so I will not detail it here. I have had only a few hours of sleep since we started from camp, and have been in the saddle all day and a large part of the night. Sleepy enough, but have taken the time to-night to hastily write. Will write you again the first opportunity, but I do not know when that will be.

            Truly,
            H.S. Melcher

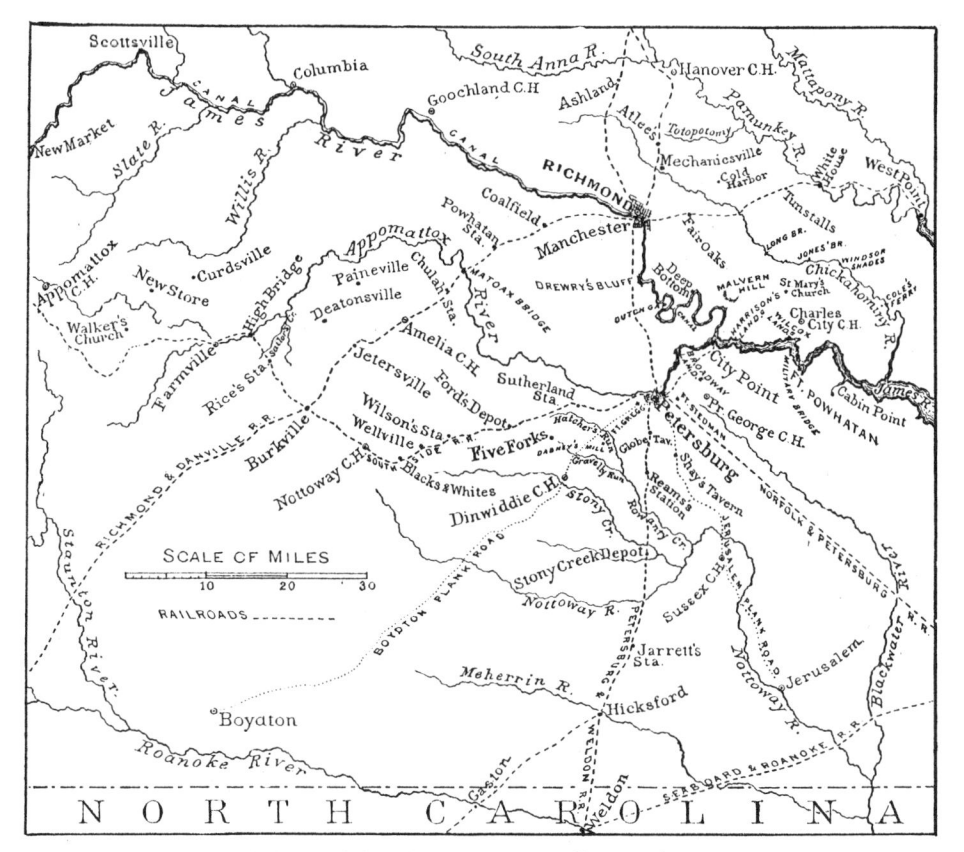

Map of the Appomattox Campaign.

Major-General Charles Griffin and Staff. Gen. Griffin replaced Gen. Warren as commander of the Fifth Corps after the Battle of Five Forks.

Monday, April 3, 1865
This morning we remain in camp until quite late in the morning and advance on the creek in two columns, capturing many prisoners, some guns and wagons, push on to Sweet House Creek, and camp; but, having marched away from all our wagons, we had to sleep without tents or blankets.

Wednesday, April 4, 1865
We march at 6 o'clock through a pretty country. I had the duty of looking out the road to travel--riding ahead had the opportunity of making acquaintance of inhabitants--the most interesting being Miss Booth. Took dinner at Dennisville and obtained a good insight into southern society. Interesting Land Lady. Reach Jetersville on the Danville R.R. at 5:30 o'clock and captured one passenger car.

Wednesday, April 5, 1865
We were about to go into camp when word arrived that the enemy were demonstrating in our front, consisting of Sheridan's Cavalry--and formed in line of battle, but no attack was made on us, and throwing up entrenchments we waited the arrival of the 2d and 6th Corps, which got here about 3 o'clock today. Genl. Meade arrived and took command. The Cavalry got rather badly handled, Genl. [J. Irvin] Gregg's Brigade being almost cut to pieces.

Thursday, April 6, 1865
This morning the whole army advances--our Corps taking the Amelia Courthouse Road--thence around to Painesville--which we reached at noon--we captured large numbers of prisoners and material along the road. We passed some 300 wagons that had been destroyed in the road, or abandoned. We encamped near "High Bridge" with the Headquarters at Mrs. Sheppard's, a pleasant time. Union people.

High Bridge

Friday, April 7, 1865

We reach "High Bridge" this morning in time to witness its capture by the 2d Corps and see it partially burned by the enemy. Our efforts to put out the fire were successful after 4 spans had been burned. We turn to the left and crossing Bush Creek about noon. After a disagreeable delay we press forward to Prince Edward Court House. I had the duty of putting Genl. [Joseph J.] Bartlett's Division in camp.

Saturday, April 8, 1865

March at 6 o'clock. I was assigned the unpleasant duty of searching the House of Mr. Price for Guerrillas; found none; spent a short time very pleasantly with Miss Price, who presented me with the enclosed Geranium sprig--without my requesting it! Halt at Prospect Church for dinner--and then push on until 11 o'clock-- marching 25 miles. A terribly hard march.

Sunday, April 9, 1865

The Day of Jubilee! We march at 4 o'clock and arrive at Appomattox Court House just in time to meet the enemy as they were breaking through our Cavalry, and hastily forming in line, advanced on them, compelling them to surrender. We had them nearly surrounded in a great natural ampitheater, and it was either surrender or total destruction. Genl. Grant, who was with the 2d and 6th Corps, was at once sent for and arrived in time to arrange the terms with Lee. It is impossible to express the joy that reigned throughout our army, and even the enemy cheered heartily when they learned that their General had surrendered them to their blue clad conquerors.

Head Quarters 5th Corps.
Appomattox Court House
April 9, 1865

My Dear Brother:

Let me write you a line this evening to unite with you in Thanks! and praise to Almighty God, for the great thing He has done for us, in saving our Country. I fail to express my joy of the events of the day. Joy supreme reigns in every heart here in the army to-night. And stern officers who have never failed on the bloody field of battle, wept like children, for joy, and grasp each others hands in silence and tears, unable to speak from emotions of joy.

All our labors of four years of bloodshed and strife are today over, with complete success. And in the present, we fought the trials and hardships of the last two weeks, sleepless nights, weary marches and terrible conflicts.

After almost superhuman efforts, we at last succeeded in surrounding Lee's army today and were about to crush him between our forces, when he sent a flag of truce, and the afternoon has been spent arranging terms and in the morning the formal surrender will be made. The whole Rebel Army now in plain sight of us, consisting of some 22,000 men with artillery wagons etc.,etc., surrendered to us unconditionally, but they will be paroled and sent to their homes. Lee and Gen'l. Grant arranged the terms.

This we all believe is the close of the War. Can it be? God be praised! We all rejoice together. It is dark and I must stop here while I can still see.

Affectionately,
Holman

Monday, April 10, 1865

Today I saw [Confederate Generals] Robert E. Lee, [James] Longstreet, [George E.] Pickett, [Charles W.] Field, [William H. F.]Lee, [William N.] Pendelton, [John .B] Gordon, and their staffs. They were all well dressed.

Tuesday, April 11, 1865

By distributing rations to so many prisoners we come quite short ourselves. I rode in company with [New York] Herald correspondent [Mr. L. A. Hendrick] and officers of the staff through the Rebel camps. An interesting scene, but the artillery was most interesting of all. A mixture of horses and mules constituted the transportation for guns and wagons. Lee was sitting in one tent that constituted his Hqs. looking dejected enough.

The following article appeared in the New York Herald, April 17, 1865.

A VISIT TO THE ENEMY CAMP

Headquarters, Fifth Army Corps,
Near Appomattox Court House, April 11, 1865
THE PAROLING OF LEE'S TROOPS

The work of paroling General Lee's army commenced to-day. It proves to be a matter requiring more time than was generally supposed. About four thousand have been paroled to-day, belonging chiefly to the artillery, cavalry and scattered commands. It will probably take two more days to get through.

VISITING THE REBEL CAMP

I spent several hours to-day in the rebel encampment in company with General Crawford. We visited the headquarters of several general officers, at all of which General Crawford met some of his old associates in the regular army. During an interview with General Lee, General Crawford told the former that if he should go North he would view the President's treatment and consideration and he would find out that he had hosts of warm friends there. "I suppose all the people of the North looked upon me as a rebel traitor," remarked General Lee, and his eyes filled with tears, showing the great depth of emotion and feeling. A throng of rebel officers most of the time crowded General Lee's tent. It is evidently a busy time with him and them. His tent by the way is an eight by nine wall tent; his staff sleep under fly tents; his headquarters are in the edge of a piece of woods in the rear of the infantry. All of the surroundings were of the plainest kind; but, as is well known, his army life has always been marked by great simplicity, and giving to no luxuries other than those used by the majority of his officers. At other headquarters I found the same scarcity of accommodations. More than one officer, in asking General Crawford to renew his visit, coupled it with the remark--"Bring your rations with you, if you expect anything to eat, for we are hard up for eatables, you know."

I remarked yesterday that they had been supplied with rations from our army, and the supply is still kept up.

The rebel camp is very much mixed up, and with very little seeming regularity. Many, I suppose from the scarcity of tents, sleep shelterless, as far as I could see. Most seemed to be in excellent spirits; so much that I infer, and I think very justly, that to a majority the surrender is more welcomed than regretted. We found among the officers that the Fifth Corps is held in the highest estimation of them, and that they always feared defeat when brought to battle with the wearers of the Maltese cross.

Wednesday, April 12, 1865

Today is the most interesting of all. The Rebel Infantry marched out and stacked their arms in front of the 1st Division [5th Corps], which was drawn up to receive the surrender. They realize today, I hope, that they are really surrendering to us. Genl. [John B.] Gordon objected very strongly to this but was brought to it. Let Capt. Halsted have $50 today.

Thursday, April 13, 1865

The Corps has been engaged all day in taking care of the ordnance and ordnance stores formerly of the Rebel army and disposing of the wagons and other property. The artillery was sent to Burkesville some on the cars and some attached to wagons. I have been to the station to make arrangements about the mails for the Corps.

Friday, April 14, 1865

This morning we were all made glad by the arrival of supplies and five days mails for the Corps. I sent Baily away yesterday, so that it brought considerable labor upon myself, and I have been hard at work all day distributing the mails. A party went to Lynchburg today. I would like to have accompanied them if my other duties had not prevented.

Saturday, April 15, 1865
Orders were issued last night to march at 12 noon today. We awoke to hear rain pattering on the canvas roofs, but it was necessary to go in order to get our rations, and at 12 we march on the ridge road, passing Pamplin's Station at 5 o'clock, and went into camp this side. The march was a muddy one.

Sunday, April 16, 1865
We march to Farmville today over a very bad road, but the day was pleasant and we got along very well--the men marching on the Rail Road. The Hqs. arrive at Farmville at 2 o'clock P.M. It is a very pretty village with a paved street and Female School, a Bank, and the "Randolph House." The sad news of the assassination of President Lincoln was received, with emotions of sorrow and indignation.*

Monday, April 17, 1865
We march at 7 o'clock A.M. Roads very bad. March via Rice's Station to Burkesville, thence to Sandy River--making a march of 27 miles when we might have reached our camp with only a march of 18 miles all from carelessness and stupidity of some of the army staff.

---

*President Lincoln was shot at Ford's Theater on Friday, April 14th and died the next morning.

Tuesday, April 18, 1865

Our camp is on William G. Woodin's plantation with the Hqs. at his house--a pleasant location but orders come today to move back to near Burkesville--right onto ground that we marched over yesterday. We have had a good opportunity to get rested today and I have improved it by a good refreshing sleep. Mail comes this evening, but no letter for me.

Wednesday, April 19, 1865

A day of National Mourning for our President. The army as well as the whole North observe the day by Religious ceremonies--the firing of minute guns at noon and refraining from all labor. The day has been one of unsurpassed loveliness and has seemed solemn to me. The bands have played appropriate pieces during the day.

Thursday, April 20, 1865

We march at 7 o'clock this morning--threatening rain, but cleared away towards noon. Go to Army Hqs., thence to Nottoway Court House--after a pleasant march. Nottoway is a very pleasant place consisting of a Church, a Court House, Jail, several stores, and a number of very fine residences. We establish Hqs. at the Court House.

Friday, April 21, 1865

I stopped at the house of Mr. Fregna last night--a refined family of good Common Sense. How much more we respect people of refinement than we do the common uncultivated. Today we have been busy getting up tents and have now got a beautiful location.

Campfires of Victory!

H'd Qr's. 5th Army Corps.
Nottoway Court House, Va.
April 21, 1865

My Dear Brother:
I think I wrote you last when at Appomattox C. H., and on the eve of that eventful day, for this army and the Country. But important events follow in such close and rapid succession that I can hardly keep accountings. Gen'l. Warren was relieved at the battle of "Five Forks" on the 1st of April by Gen'l. Sheridan.* The Corps is now commanded by Gen'l. Griffin, an able officer and a gentleman. I was detailed Aid on his staff, for my conduct at the battle of "Five Forks." Of course, I appreciate the compliment.

The 5th Corps was given the honor of receiving the surrender of Lee's Army -- a great honor. But much labor with it, as it proved by experience. It was a proud day to us when drawn up in line, the rebel army was marched between the long rows of glistening bayonets of the Blue Clad Conquerors, and laid down their dirty, hated, flags and their arms. You can guess that we felt somewhat proud, and a good amount of happiness. I met Lee, Longstreet, Gordon, Pickett, Johnson, W.H.F. Lee, Fitz Lee, Pendleton, Fields, and their Staffs quite often and became acquainted with many of them. After a week of hard work, we summed up accounts to find we had paroled 26,115 men, sent to Burkesville 151 pieces of artillery, 700 wagons, with small arms by the thousands, horses and mules in large numbers, but many are poor worn down ones, and a good amount of war material. There was a good feeling the Officers and men of the two armies and we had many pleasant meetings. Gen'l Grant set us the example by his conduct at the surrender. I must confess that a feeling of indignation would rise within me

---

* *Relieved for dilatory leadership, Gen. Warren waited 14 years before he could defend himself at a military court of inquiry in which Melcher would testify in his commander's behalf.*

when I would think of all the bloodshed and mourning these same men had caused. But it is honorable to be magnanimous to a conquered foe. And as civilized men and gentlemen, we strive to keep such feelings of hatred in subjection. After sending to their homes, the Rebel army, and disposing of the property, we began our march towards Petersburg, stopping one night at the beautiful village of Farmville. Here it was that our joy was turned into mourning, by receiving the sad intelligence of the assassination of President Lincoln. Many of our Corps were strongly in favor of burning the town, to express their indignation at this horrible deed. Though that was not done, there is an intense feeling of hatred aroused against the Southern people, by those who believe that this outrageous deed was of their instigation.

We halted in our march last Wednesday, in honor of the burial. Minute guns were fired and appropriate services held in each Brigade.

This Confederate Flag/Bookmark was "captured" by Melcher at Saylor's Creek. The note attached reads, "Taken from a Bible, belonging to Nathl. V. Watkins, captured in the Rebel Wagon Train at Sailor Creek April 6 1865."

Saturday, April 22, 1865
It has been a beautiful day. We are getting settled down to the quiet of Camp life. I have spent the day in getting up back in business and writing. Had a good long talk with Mr. Fregna this evening and find him to be an interesting and intelligent man--one who understands matters of Politics as they now are.

Sunday, April 23, 1865
It has been a bright and cool day and has seemed more like the Sabbath day than any I have experienced since I was wounded. [May 8, 1864] I attended church this afternoon and listened to an able discourse from Rev. Mr. Mead, the Methodist Clergyman of the Town. Am disappointed in not receiving any letters this evening.

Monday, April 24, 1865
Engaged today in the duties of my office during the morning. In company with Capt. Malbon I ride out into the country several miles this evening. The country south of here is heavily wooded and little land under cultivation. More open west and east, but the land seems to be poor. I would not like such for a farm, and if I purchased South it must not be here.

Tuesday, April 25, 1865
It is beautiful weather here now, and there seems to be nothing to prevent one from enjoying life as well as possible in the army. Our duties are light and pleasant. It does seem real good to be encamped here in the South and not necessary to be fenced in with Pickets.

Wednesday, April 26, 1865
What is to be my life business? Why am I not decided on some occupation? These are questions that I am constantly thinking about

but cannot come to any decision on them. I am vexed at myself for my indecision. I seem to be waiting for a kind of Providence to decide my course and yet constantly thinking about it.

Thursday, April 27, 1865
I do so wish I was entirely decided on some business--that which I would be ready to give my whole might and mind to--but I am a responsible being and must act like one and do that which I sincerely think is best. God give me wisdom is my sincere prayer.

Friday, April 28, 1865
It has been another beautiful day. I have been closely engaged in the office during the day. Received a communication from Col. Spear. Though glad to render the Col. any assistance in my power I felt that it was not my duty to sign the document--and was firmly decided on it. I may have selfish motives governing me but not more than others in the case.

Saturday, April 29, 1865
I had callers from my Regt. and entertained them the best that I could under the circumstances. I have been unguarded in my conversation today and have not heeded that wise counsel "If you can say no good of a man, say nothing." Let me be more careful in future and speak after thinking.

Sunday, April 30, 1865
It has been a beautiful day. I attended church this morning and listened to a sermon from Rev. Mr. Pryor. His opening remark spoiled my interest in the sermon though it was quite able, but one could not fail to see that he was a rabid old Rebel--who had taken the oath from the force of circumstances. The Church was so full that I could not get a seat--and so I spent the afternoon in writing.

Monday, May 1, 1865
This morning we leave our lovely camp and march to Wilson's Station (via) Blacks and Whites. Genl. Sheridan overtook us there. He was just returning from his march to assist Sherman, but he was not needed. Genl. [Joseph E.] Johnston surrendered before he got there. Only two divisions of our Corps move today.

Tuesday, May 2, 1865
We march at 6 o'clock this morning, passing Sutherland's Station at noon--camping for the night at the Booth Plantation, five miles out of Petersburg. I rode with the General over the Rebel works about this City in the evening--and intensely interesting it was to me too.

Wednesday, May 3, 1865
This morning we march at 7 o'clock but were long delayed in our passage through the city by the streets being filled by the 25th [Army Corps] which was on its way to City Point. Our Corps cheered Genl. Warren, who was standing on the sidewalk. March up the Richmond Turnpike, encamping within the 2d line of fortifications of Richmond with Hqs. at Drury's.

Thursday, May 4, 1865
Visit Fort Darling and was astonished to see what a strong position it was. The ruins of the Virginia projected above and the water and fragments lay on shore blown there. 13 guns in position: 1 Brooks Rifle, 10 Columbiads, and 2 ten inch smooth bores. March at 6 o'clock encamping at Manchester.

Friday, May 5, 1865
I visited Richmond last evening, going through Libby Prison and the Capitol. Visited the principle places of interest in the City today and had a grand view of the city from the roof of the Capitol.

The statues of Washington, Henry, Mason, Jefferson, and Clay in the Capitol yard are very good. The burnt district of Richmond looks dismal enough. 4 miles out of Richmond on Brock Pike is the prettiest place (country scenes) that I have seen in Southern Virginia.

Saturday, May 6, 1865

This morning we march through Richmond, followed by the 2d Corps. The display was really grand. The 24th Corps was drawn up in the streets and received us with flying colors, music, and cheers. There were some ladies who waved flags and handkerchiefs. We found two quite strong lines of works on this side of Richmond, not as strong as on south. Camp on the Hanover battlefield and saw many graves.

(No. 14)
Head Qr's 5th Army Corps.
Arlington Heights, Va.
May 17, 1865

My Dear Brother:

We arrived here in sight of Washington Friday last (12th), accomplishing our long march two days sooner than we expected. We made about 20 miles per day. I am with a cold which I got during a severe cold shower when directing the Divisions to their camps, and have kept my bed nearly all the time, but I am better this morning and will use what "spunk" is left me in writing you.

On our march through Richmond, the advance was the Provost Guard, Army of Potomac, composed of the 10th, 12th, & 14th Regulars and two Regiments of Cavalry. Then came our Corps, marching in column by company. The 24th Corps was drawn up along the streets through which we passed and received us with

Campfires of Victory!

arms at a "present," and hearty cheers. Of course we flaunted our banners and the men-stepped-like-conquerors. We passed down Carey Street on which are "Castle Thunder" & "Libby Prison," were labeled with large letters, so that all the soldiers would recognize these noted places. Thence to Main St., passing a part of the burnt district, past the Custom House, Capital to the Court

Castle Thunder (Above) and Libby Prison (Below) held Union prisoners during the war.

House, on the steps of which were Gen'ls. Meade & [Henry W.] Halleck, their Staffs and the noted visitors. Grace, Franklin & Broad Streets were passed through after passing the Court House, thence to the pike leading to Hanover C.H., camping that night on the battle-field of Hanover of 1862.

The 8th of May we passed near the place where I was wounded, one year ago, I did not care to visit the battle-field. We camped on the evening of the 9th at Falmouth opposite Fredericksburg. I visited the City, the heights over which we had fought so hard, bringing freshly to mind those scenes of blood and carnage, on the cold December days of 1862. I could hardly realize that all these battles were over, no more to curse our Land,--God grant. I went through the house in which I lay wounded last spring. The room looked familiar, and I selected without hesitation the spot where my stretcher set, on which I lay. The dark blood stains had been washed from the floor and nothing remains to indicate that it had been a place of so much suffering and death. The "man of the house" gave me a piece of the cornice as a trophy, which I shall carefully preserve.

The march the next day, over our camp ground of 1862-63, was of deep interest to me. In fact the whole march was intensely interesting to me, and I rejoice that I was able to accompany the army. Sherman's Army is expected here to-morrow. Then the grand Armies of the United States will be encamped with the towering dome of our Capital in view. It is a proud and happy day to us. I think the grand review, so much talked of will not come off. Corps may be reviewed separately.

The Cavalry is being mustered-out, as fast as possible, and the Infantry will also be discharged soon, but I do not know yet, how soon our Corps will be mustered-out. And I can make no calculations for the future, though I so think a good deal, but to little effect. Am quite firmly decided not to enter the Regular Army.

Your interesting No. 10, was gladly received, and set me all a glee over the thought that you will visit me here. Come by all means, and we will go to Richmond & Petersburg together, and over the battlefields about there, and visit all the places of interest here. Should the 20th be sent to Maine, I suppose I would have to go with it, so as to be mustered-out...

          Truly,
          Holman

Tuesday, May 16, 1865

In company with Capt. Malbon, I went to Washington to settle my accounts with the government and was more successful than I expected to be. Received a certificate of "non-indebtedness" from the Ordnance Dept. and got my papers well under way in the Q.M. Dept. Capt. Halsted paid me the $55 that he owed me.

Wednesday, May 17, 1865

It has been a very hot day--so hot that I have not been energetic enough to do anything but a little writing. Have been trying to decide if I ought to enter the Regular Army. Letters from Father and Brother N. advise me to choose some civil profession. Oh for wisdom to decide on a proper course.

Thursday, May 18, 1865

I went to Washington this morning in company with Capt. Malbon and spent the day in arranging the settlement of my accounts with the Government. Had a very pleasant time though I never see the enjoyment of being around street corners and Hotels that some do; it always seems to be a waste of time and talent. I put my autograph with others belonging to the army--after much teasing--not intending to do so at first. I wonder if I have got no mind of my own at all?

Friday, May 19, 1865

Remain in camp all day being occupied in business matters and arranging my papers. It was a difficult question indeed for me to decide when asked by Maj. [Atherton W.] Clark if I would remain in the service with the remnant of the regiment. I did decide to remain a year longer. God forgive me if wrong is my prayer and lead me in the way I should go.

Monday, May 22, 1865
    It rained all night most and though not rainy this morning, the ground, trees, and all out of doors and part of indoors seems as wet and heavy as could be; but the sun shines out and makes Nature more cheerful. I attended the presentation of a badge to Gen'l. Griffin this evening by the officers of the 1st Division. A pleasant affair if the officers had not used the Whiskey Punch so freely.

Tuesday, May 23, 1865
    The morning dawns bright and clear. We breakfast at 3:30 and mount at 5 o'clock. The Corps moves across to the Capitol light in front and forms in company columns closed in mass. The Cavalry move at 9 o'clock precisely, followed by the 9th and 5th and 2d Corps. The display was indeed grand. I returned to the 5th [Army Corps] Stand after the Corps had passed and had the pleasure of seeing the Second Corps pass--and then accompany Miss Gilmore home and dine with her--a pleasant afternoon indeed.

Wednesday, May 24, 1865
    I go to the City and watch the grand review of Sherman's veterans--a sight of a lifetime. They marched as well as our army did though not dressed as well, but we look upon them with admiration and gratitude for the noble work they have done. It took 6 hours and 20 minutes for the Army to pass the Reviewing Stand--about the same time that the Cavalry and "A of P" occupied yesterday. I was in charge of our Corps stand a part of the day. Saw Genls. Sherman and all his subordinate commanders.

The Grand Review.

(No. 15)
Head Qr's. 5th Army Corps.
Arlington Heights, Va.
Sunday May 28, 1865

Dear Brother:
    I did not go over to the City to Church to-day, and will employ a part of the afternoon in writing you. I wish I could see you today, and talk thousands of things that cannot be written. But will write hoping to meet you soon.
    Will you not go home this summer after your school closes? I am in a very uncertain state of mind just now, but part of the doubt will be removed this week and then I will know better, what is to

be my future course, though I must see you and get some more advice.

My Regt. will probably leave for Portland this week, or all but the recruits, some officers are to be retained to command these men, and I do not know yet that I am to be retained for that duty. Now if I am retained here, do not fail to make me a visit when your term closes!

All the troops that entered the service in '62, will leave as soon as the muster-out papers can be completed, probably within two weeks. Everybody is busy in preparing to "go Home."

I had the honor and pleasure of taking part in the Grand Review of the Army of the Potomac, and Sheridan's Cavalry, last Tuesday and was a spectator to the Review of Sherman's Conquerors on Wednesday. It was truly magnificent. We marched in column closed in mass, and even then extended some 30 miles, taking over six hours to pass the Reviewing Officers, moving all the time. Everything moved along military, not the least crowding or confusion. The city was crowded with visitors, and they received us with hearty welcome too. Cheers from the men, and waving of handkerchiefs, and presenting bouquets by the Ladies. I got a beautiful wreath for my share. Sherman's Army did not look as clean and nice as our Army yet they marched finely and were as heartily welcomed as we.

The two days of the Review were cool and beautiful, and I am glad that the Review was ordered now, but at first I did not like the idea of being paraded through the streets of Washington, to be made a public show of. But we have left a better opinion of the army on the minds of the people, than existed before the Review, and that is well. The people seem to think the army is a demoralized, uncultured, and ignorant crowd, so that anything that will assist in disabusing their minds of that idea is good for us. The most beautiful, artificial sight I ever saw was the evening of the Review, when the whole army illuminated its camps. The night was cloudy and dark, with not a breath of wind to put out the candles. We are on the heights here so that we can look right down upon the whole army, and that night it looked like a sea of fire. After a time, brigades formed, and proceeded by bands of music, marched in columns to different Gen'l. Hd. Qrs., to honor their Generals, bearing aloft the torches. Gen'l Chamberlain made a very nice speech to his old Brigade that came to his Hd. Qrs. The 1st Division came to our Hd. Qrs., but as Gen'l. Griffin was absent, they had to go away without a speech from our Chief. I never expect to witness such a scene again. It seemed so appropriate, just now when the brilliant Star of Peace is illuminating our land, and dispelling the dark clouds of war.

Poor little Jimmy Maxwell was not strong enough to endure the hardships of war. He was taken sick on the march and died shortly after getting to the Hospital. How uncertain is life!!

Holman

Saturday, May 27, 1865
A cold wet dismal day which I spend in writing and reading--and the evening in sitting with the Staff around the large camp fire talking over the war. We are a collection from the different northern states with different educations and surroundings making different opinions so one learns broadness of ideas in conversation.

Sunday, May 28, 1865
The clouds struggle to break through the dark stormy sky but the day has been showery. I ride this evening with Capt. Malbon to the Arlington House--one of the most beautiful locations I ever saw. How insane must a man have been to take an active part in a wicked Rebellion who was so fortunate as to have this lovely place for a home!

Head Quarters 5th Army Corps.
Army of the Potomac
June 5, 1865

Dear Brother:

The 20th Maine Regt. left for Portland this morning. I am retained as the General's Aid, and cannot deny, but that it cost me quite an effort to remain here and see the regiment go "marching home," with happy hearts and their banner waving over them, on which are engraved the names of twenty (20) hard fought battles.

I went to the camp of the regiment last evening and bade them "good bye." It was a happy farewell for me, knowing that all were going home and not to the bloody battle field. Yet there is always a feeling of sadness connected with separation, even under the most happy circumstances. I did not accept the earnest invitation of Lt. Col. Morrill to accompany them to the depot in Washington, knowing I would be homesick to see them leave and I stay behind. Some 250 men, remains of the Regt., and so some officers would be retained with them. A Board was appointed to examine and decide who should remain. Of those who expressed a willingness to do so, and I was one of the number. I explained a willingness to remain for several reasons. I can perform my present duties, much better than most any business in the present condition of my wound. I was urged to remain by Col. Spear who remains, and by the Adjutant General of the Corps. Then I expect to go home, time enough to begin my studies this fall, if I should decide on such a course.

I do not expect the position of a Field Officer in the new organization, for Col. Spear remains and Captain Chamberlain, who is my senior in rank. And as the 16th Maine and 1st Maine Sharp Shooters are consolidated, an officer from one of these must have a position, as a matter of compliment and to "keep peace in the family." If not absolutely needed in the regiment, I expect to remain here until the army is broken up. Regiments are leaving every day, over 7000 are gone from our Corps. I think another order will soon be issued mustering-out others than those whose term of service expire before October 1. And the new 20th may go soon, but how soon I do not yet know.

Attended the Court where the assassins are being tried, last Saturday. And had a fine opportunity to study the character of that motley crowd of villains, except Mrs. Surratt, who kept her veil drawn so closely that I could not get a sight of her face. There is great interest here in the trial and the Court Room, (in the arsenal) is constantly crowded.*

Miss Nettie [Gilmore] remains the same to me as ever. I am much entertained and socially instructed by her frequent letters, but I have never been able yet to find out whether she was writing me to make camp life more endurable, (many ladies seem to be impressed with the idea that it is a duty to write soldiers) or because she loves to. I would hesitate about going to Wiscosset, just to visit her, were I in Maine. You know I have the least opinion of and confidence in myself possible, and a bad student of human nature. I suppose I ought not write her, but her letters entertain me, and so I respond, but I do believe she is a heartless Darling anyway.

I am all a glee that you are to come here. How happy I will be to welcome you. Write me when you will be here and I will meet you at the Depot in Washington.

Your Brother,
Holman

*After the Lincoln conspirator trial, Mary Surratt, David Herold, Lewis Paine, and George Atzerodt were hanged on July 7, 1865.

Monday, June 5, 1865
    It is pleasant and yet a thought that somewhat affects one to know that we are to separate from those with whom we have shared so many dangers and to go to different parts of this land perhaps not to meet again for life. My Regiment left this morning for Maine. I thought it best not to go with them to Washington and so remain in camp.

Tuesday, June 6, 1865
    Again "Good-bye." Capt. Malbon with whom I spent so many pleasant hours since I came to this staff left this morning for home. I respect him much and miss him greatly. Cloudy and cool. Went to the City this evening to make purchases.

Wednesday, June 7, 1865
    I have had the pleasure and satisfaction of going to Mt. Vernon, the home and tomb of the Great and beloved Washington. It is a lovely spot and a hallowed one. We cannot fail to be inspired with thoughts of his greatness as we have his memory called to mind by visiting his tomb. The grounds are in somewhat of a dilapidated condition but lovely still. A Harp, silver holster, Camp Equipage, a sofa, the bedstead on which he died, and the marble mantelpiece engraved in Italy are among the articles of interest. The key of the Bastille hangs in the Hall.

Monday, June 19, 1865
    I have kept quiet today--spending it in reading "Harper's" and "The Atlantic"; have been entertained if not instructed. Would have been instructed if I could remember and use what I have read. Everything has gone wrong in my Department; my driver got into the Central Guard House for Drunkenness, but it may be well for it will cause me to look about myself and discipline some of these fellows.

Wednesday, June 28, 1865
This is another beautiful day, and one of the happiest to me that I have spent for a long time. I found my horse would travel beautifully in a carriage and so went to the City and gave an invitation to Miss Nellie (which was accepted) to go with me to the Soldiers' Home and Fort Stevens. I enjoyed the ride and company much.

Thursday, June 29, 1865
This has been one of the bad days of my existence, and I have been on the go all this hot day, accomplishing almost all that I intended. This evening I went to the Depot to meet Brother N. and after waiting till 10 o'clock, was really disappointed that he did not come. The Farewell Order of Gen'l Meade and the Order breaking up the Army of the Potomac and organizing into a Provisional Corps to be commanded by Gen'l Wright were received.

Friday, June 30, 1865
Regiments are going home every day, and soon this grand army will be reduced to a small command. Went to the Depot this evening and waited till 1 o'clock for Brother N. in vain.

Saturday, July 1, 1865
I must confess my sincere disappointment on learning today that I was not recommended for a Brevet appointment and wrote Gen'l Warren about it--maybe foolishly. Capt. Halsted and Dr. [Charles K.] Winne go away today. I go to the City again to meet Bro. N. but am more disappointed than ever not to meet him. We had a terrific storm tonight.

Monday, July 3, 1865
This morning rode to Arlington, enjoying it very much. We ride in the evening to see Gen'l Bartlett's torchlight review; a very

Major General Joshua Lawrence Chamberlain

interesting and pretty sight it was too. The evening was one unsurpassed loveliness.

Tuesday, July 4, 1865
The morning is beautiful, giving joy to those who are to celebrate the great day of our National Independence. I do not take part in any celebration. So disappointed am I that Nathaniel did not come that I have little heart to celebrate. Witness the very splendid display of Fire works this evening in Washington south of the President's House.

Wednesday, July 5, 1865
Receive my orders as Inspector on Gen'l. Chamberlain's staff and have been busy on moving to his Hqs. It does seem almost sad to break up our associations of the Corps after being so long together and so pleasantly associated. Flies are getting intolerable.

Friday, July 7, 1865
We took breakfast with Gen'l Chamberlain this morning, and Capt. [Willam E.] Donnell and my self rode into town with him. I received my pay for the month of June and invested $50 in 7-30's at the Treasury. The day is terribly hot and streets dusty. We receive orders this evening to muster out the whole army at once.

Saturday, July 8, 1865
It has been a very hot day. I have suffered more from the heat than any other day. We had a refreshing shower this afternoon. I went to Corps. Hqs. on business, but as the Inspector General was absent, I could do nothing. I am trying to decide in my mind if I ought to study law for a profession. Took dinner at the General's table. Passed through another temptation--very severe.

Captain Holman Staples Melcher, July, 1865.

Sunday, July 16, 1865
The Regiment is mustered out today--and though I feel anyway but decent, I get up and attend to the packing of my things for the journey. I do wish that I felt better now that I am about to go home--but let me have more Faith and be willing to trust to God at all times, knowing that he doeth all things well.

Monday, July 17, 1865
We are up early this morning and packed ready to go at 9 o'clock but learn that we cannot have transportation until 1. Go to the City, where I make satisfactory arrangements about my Corps badge. Called on Miss Gilmore and bid her good bye. Made such arrangements with Col. Gilmore as to enable me to draw servant's pay due and pension. After waiting till everybody was tired out, we got off at 7 o'clock. Changed cars at Baltimore and arrived safely in Philadelphia about 8 o'clock. A good entertainment awaited us there--a hearty welcome.

Wednesday, July 19, 1865
We were received by the citizens all along the way with hearty cheers. Arrived in New York City and put the Regt. in Battery Barracks while we stop at the Washington Hotel, taking tea at the Stevens House. Rested well last night but don't feel very smart after all. Leave the city at noon on steamer. A pleasant trip out of North River. A windy afternoon.

Saturday, July 22, 1865
Arrived in Portland this morning at 6 o'clock after a pleasant passage. Went to Camp Berry and got permission from Col. Spear to go home and was pleased to find myself once more on my way home. Bro. N. met me at Brunswick and I enjoyed his company home, where I found all well and everything pleasant, *very much so to me!*

Reunion of the Twentieth Maine at Garland Pond, Maine, Sept. 17, 1898.

CHAPTER SEVEN
THE TWENTIETH MAINE
REGIMENTAL ASSOCIATION

At a reunion on August 10, 1876, the survivors of the 20th Maine Regiment gathered and a committee was chosen to form an association. Any veteran of the 20th who received an honorable discharge was entitled to be a member of the new organization. Major Holman S. Melcher was voted the first President of the Association. He would be reelected each year until his death in 1905.

This chapter presents the recorded events of the Association during the reunions that were held in 1876, 1881, 1894, and 1895.

Holman S. Melcher circa 1890.

At the Grand Reunion of the Soldiers and Sailors of Maine in Portland, August 9th and 10th, 1876, forty-six members of the Twentieth Regiment were present.

The members of the regiment, who arrived Wednesday, reported at Grand Army Hall, where the afternoon was passed in renewing acquaintances. At 4 p.m. the regiment formed under command of Brevet Lieut. Col. A. W. Clark, with Lieut. S. L. Miller as Acting Adjutant, and joined the column for escort duty, after which a collation was served by the city in City Hall. At 6 1-2 o'clock a column in three divisions was formed, each regiment wearing the badges and carrying the flags of their respective corps. There were about fifteen hundred veterans in line and it was said to be the most notable procession of men that ever marched in the State of Maine.

The men were conveyed by the barge and steamers to Little Chebeague, an island in Portland harbor, where tents had been pitched and immense bonfires were burning. An artillery salute and fireworks welcomed the veterans to the island.

After the supper of beans, brown bread, hard tack, cheese and coffee, the assembly was called to order and Gen. Chamberlain welcomed the guests. Speech making was kept up till after two a.m., and the balance of the night was spent in "howling."

Thursday morning after the arrival of the 10:30 boat, the different regimental organizations got together and held their annual meetings. As the Twentieth had never formed an association, the time was deemed favorable to perfect an organization. Accordingly, the men gathered in a grove where Gen. Chamberlain soon joined them. Bugler Tyler sounded the old 3rd Brigade call, "Dan! Dan! Dan! Butterfield!" and the

Twentieth responded with three cheers for the Bugler and the famous old call.

The organization was then perfected by the choice of the following officers:

    President—Holman S. Melcher, Portland.
    Vice President—James B. Wescott, Bath.
    Secretary and Treasurer—Samuel L. Miller, Waldoboro.

These officers constitute an executive committee with authority to act in all matters pertaining to the association. A communication from Sergeants Daniel Donovan and Ruel B. Jones, of Providence was read. Edmond M. Barton, Sanitary Inspector of the 5th Corps, who had associated with the Twentieth during the reunion, was chosen an honorary member.

The "boys" spent a short time recalling some of the incidents of the war, after which an invitation was accepted for an hour's sail in Gen. Chamberlain's yacht, which was found in charge of Color Sergeant Andrew J. Tozier. The party returned in season to take part in the Dress Parade and clam bake which followed. Seventeen hundred persons were fed at one time. At four o'clock the veterans embarked for the city and the grandest reunion since the muster out in 1865, came to an end.

SECOND REUNION AT PORTLAND

The second reunion of the surviving members of the Twentieth Maine Regiment was held at Portland, Aug. 23, 24 and 25, 1881, in connection with the grand reunion of Maine Soldiers and Sailors.

Through the efforts of Maj. H. S. Melcher, President of the regimental association, the veterans found upon their arrival four large tents arranged for their accommodation. The tents were decorated with a large campaign flag, while a small national flag and guidons bearing the division badge, the red Maltese cross, were stacked in front, and in large letters appeared "Headquarters 20th Maine Regiment." The headquarters tent was furnished with chairs, table, writing material and a book for registering names. The other tents were arranged for sleeping purposes. As the survivors of the Twentieth arrived at headquarters the greetings were most cordial. Comrades of many a weary march and hard fought battle, who had not met for sixteen years renewed their acquaintances and told again the stories of the war. As the veterans reported, their names were registered until one hundred and thirty-seven names appeared upon the roll. Several failed to register, so that the total number present at the second reunion of the Twentieth was at least one hundred and forty.

The Twentieth participated in the general exercises of the camp until Wednesday evening, when the special exercises arranged by the Executive Committee of the Association occurred. At half-past seven the regiment, led by Chandler's Band, marched to the grand tent. The Portland Press of the next morning said:

"The chief event of the evening was the reunion of the Twentieth Regiment, the gallant body of men which Chamberlain led to Little Round Top, and whose obstinate hold of that important position baffled the plans of Lee and made the battle of Gettysburg a Union victory. The meeting was held in the great Yale tent. Long before the hour for the exercises came the tent was filled by interested spectators, and the grey-bearded "boys" with the red Maltese cross upon their caps, found difficulty in making their way within hearing distance."

Not less than two thousand veterans and visitors were assembled around the stand when Maj. H. S. Melcher, President of the regimental association, called the meeting to order and requested Joseph Tyler, the old bugler of the Twentieth, to sound the brigade call. As the ringing notes of "Dan, Dan, Dan, Butterfield, Butterfield!" burst upon the evening air the veterans broke into cheers in which the audience enthusiastically joined. Maj. Melcher then very happily referred to the old battle flag of the regiment which had been promised for this occasion. As Corporal Coan came forward with the tattered flag borne by the Twentieth through the storm of iron and lead at Gettysburg, it was greeted by another cheer, and the band struck up "Rally round the Flag." This flag at Gettysburg was carried by Sergt. Andrew J. Tozier and Dr. E.S. Coan was the only surviving member of the color guard at Gettysburg present on this occasion, and to him the flag was formally entrusted for the remainder of the reunion.

The president then read a poem, written by a Portland lady and dedicated to the 17th and 20th regiments as they marched through the streets of Portland with their tattered flags on their return from the war in 1865. At the close of the reading of the poem, the historian of the Twentieth, Samuel L. Miller, was introduced and delivered the following:

Comrades of the Twentieth:
    It is now nineteen years since you were sworn into the service of the United States as members of the Twentieth Maine Infantry; more than sixteen years have elapsed since your military service expired. These fleeting years of toil and care

have sprinkled many of your heads with gray. The youthful recruit of '62 appears tonight in the vigor of manhood, and the middle-aged veteran of Fredericksburg, Gettysburg, Wilderness, Petersburg and Appomattox already feels the infirmities of age creeping on. Another generation is growing up around you, and your children and your children's children are eagerly listening to the story of your marches, your battles and your encampments. Comrades, this is the story it is my proud privilege to recall to your minds tonight.

With you enlistment was no holiday affair. For more than a year the war had raged. It had been a year fraught with disaster at least to the Union armies in Virginia. The advance upon Richmond from the Peninsula had been repulsed, and the troops of McClellan had been driven back with terrible loss. The second battle of Bull Run had been fought but three days before you left the State, and the victorious army of Robert E. Lee was already preparing to invade the free States. With a knowledge of these terrible events fresh in your minds, fully realizing the dangers and suffering before you and prepared to face death in any form, you moved to the front.

To give the full particulars of every march, encampment, skirmish and fight in the history of the Twentieth Regiment would fill volumes, and is not within the scope of an evening's address. I ask you, therefore, to overlook any seeming omissions or too brief representation of important events. The Twentieth Maine infantry was the last of the three years' regiments raised in pursuance of the requisition and authority of the President of the United States, dated July 2d, 1862. The regiment appears to have been formed from detachments of men enlisted for the Sixteenth, Seventeenth, Eighteenth and Nineteenth, and afterwards found to have been unnecessary to complete those organizations. A large proportion of the men were enlisted before the order for the formation of the Twentieth Regiment was promulgated. The authority for the organization was as follows:

Headquarters Adjutant General's Office
Augusta, August 7, 1862

GENERAL ORDER NO. 26

The secretary of War having requested that another regiment of Infantry be organized from the enlisted men of Maine's quota of an additional 300,000 volunteers, called for by the President, the Governor and Commander-in-Chief orders and directs that all companies already enlisted for new regiments under this call, and which shall be hereafter designated, the same not necessarily comprised in the organization of the Sixteenth, Seventeenth, Eighteenth and Nineteenth regiments of Infantry, report to Col. E. K. Harding, Asst. Q.M. General, and go into camp at the rendezvous established for this regiment (the Twentieth of Maine Volunteers) at Island Park near Portland, on or before the 12th Inst., where quarters and subsistence will be provided. The organization of this regiment will be completed forthwith.

BY ORDER OF THE COMMANDER-IN-CHIEF,
JOHN L. HODSON, ADJUTANT GENERAL

On the 11th of August, in pursuance of this order, squads of recruits began to arrive in camp, afterwards known as "Camp Mason", and in a few days the ranks of the Twentieth regiment were full. Adelbert Ames of Rockland, a graduate of West Point, who had already acquired a reputation for military skill and bravery, was commissioned Colonel; Joshua L. Chamberlain, of Brewer, Professor of Modern Languages in Bowdoin College, Lieut. Colonel; and Charles D. Gilmore, of Bangor, Captain of Company C., Seventh Maine, Major.

The Twentieth was supplied with an English arm, known as the Enfield Rifle Musket, with the regulation equipments, and the uniform consisted of the usual fatigue cap, blue frock coat, with the unusual dark blue trousers.

The men having received slight instruction in the "School of the Soldier", were mustered into the service of the United States by Capt. Bartlett, 12th U.S. Infantry, on the 29th, at which time the regiment numbered 965 officers and men. On the morning of the 2d of September the comfortable quarters at Camp Mason were abandoned, and the regiment quietly took its departure for Boston by rail, where it embarked on the steamer "Merrimac" and sailed the next morning for Alexandria, Virginia, arriving on the afternoon of the 6th. Sunday, the 7th, the Twentieth proceeded to Washington by steamer and occupied grounds near the arsenal. Having been assigned to Butterfield's famous "Light Brigade" of Morrell's Division, Porter's Corps, the regiment moved about sunset on the 8th, crossed Aqueduct bridge over the Potomac and marched to Fort Craig, Arlington Heights. This moonlight march of four or five miles was our first experience, and the soldier's privilege of grumbling was freely indulged. Looking back through the vista of years, it does not strike us as at all surprising that Col. Ames, disgusted with the conduct of his command on the occasion, should have exclaimed: "If you can't do any better than you have tonight, you better all desert and go home!"

The brigade to which the Twentieth had been assigned was composed of the Twelfth, Seventeenth and Forty-Fourth New York, Eighty-Third Pennsylvania and Sixteenth Michigan, and was then under the command of Col. Stockton of the Sixteenth.

September 12th the brigade crossed the Potomac to Georgetown and started on the forced march to Antietam. That night, after a march of sixteen miles, scarcely a corporal's guard of the Twentieth stacked arms when the brigade went into camp. The stragglers, however, came up in a few hours and the regiment marched with full ranks the next morning. On that day a march of twenty-four miles was made, and, during the day, a majority heard the distant roar of battle for the first time. The regiment marched through Frederick on the morning of the 15th and bivouacked that night at Middletown, arriving near Sharpsburg the next evening. The next morning the Twentieth moved forward with the brigade and took a position in reserve near the center, east of Antietam Creek. During the afternoon of the 17th our brigade and another were ordered to the right to support troops in that quarter. The emergency having passed the Twentieth returned to the former position, and the men lay on their arms that night. The next morning the brigade took up a position in the rear of Burnside, on the left. The infantry of Porter's corps took no active part in the battle of Antietam, but the position it held during that eventful day was a most important one.

On the 19th the command moved forward through Sharpsburg to Shepherdstown Ford, where the main body of the rebel army had crossed the Potomac. The next morning Morrell's division and a portion of Sykes' made an attempt to cross over and drive the enemy from their position. Sykes' division and the first and second brigades of our division, with a portion of the third, including the Twentieth, had crossed and pushed out a short distance, when the enemy developed such force that a retreat was ordered. During the recrossing of the ford under a sharp and severe fire from the rebels, who now lined the bank, the Twentieth was kept in excellent order and discipline, and the conduct of the regiment, for the first time under fire, was noticed and much praised. As soon as the regiment recrossed it was formed along the canal bank, and kept up a hot fire with the enemy across the river.

The Twentieth being a portion of the force left to guard the upper Potomac, remained near Shepherdstown three weeks.

On the 7th of October the brigade moved to the Iron Works, near the mouth of Antietam Creek, where it remained till the 30th. Colonel Ames now found an opportunity to give the regiment a taste of discipline and drill which it so much needed. Company and battalion drill, dress parade and inspection kept the men from idleness, and the line officers were obliged to apply themselves to the study of tactics until they become proficient in the manual of arms and in all the evolutions of the company and battalion. Col. Ames was an educated soldier and a rigid disciplinarian, and although at times his orders were severe in the extreme, yet the soldierly bearing of the regiment soon became conspicuous, and without question much of the fame which the Twentieth Maine afterwards achieved was due to the sense of subordination and attention to duty, instilled by the teaching of its first commander.

The hardships to which the men had been exposed, the forced march, the change of climate and above all the failure to supply the regiment with shelter tents, now began to show its results in the long list of sick borne upon the rolls. It is almost incredible but nevertheless true, that, when the advance was made into Virginia from Antietam, the Twentieth sent away three hundred invalids, and many of those who remained on duty were reduced to a condition from which they did not recover for months.

October 30th the regiment broke camp and marched in the direction of Harper's Ferry. The next day the Potomac and Shenandoah were crossed, and the column having wound around the base of Loudon Heights, continued the march down Loudon Valley. While the army was moving south through this beautiful valley, the enemy was moving up the Shenandoah on the other side of the Blue Ridge. November 2d an advance corps had a fight with them at Snicker's Gap, and that night we camped near a village with the euphonious name of

"Snickersville". On the 6th, marched through Middleburg, where eight months later the Twentieth and the Third Brigade had a spirited brush with the enemy. The next day the march was interrupted by a snow storm, and the troops camped in the woods near White Plains. November 9th we went into camp at Warrenton and remained till the 17th, during which time Gen. McClellan was superseded by Burnside, and a general reorganization of the army followed. Continuing the march, the Acquia Creek Railroad was reached on the 24th, at a point three miles from Fredericksburg, afterwards well-known to you as "Stoneman's Switch," where the regiment settled down to the monotony of camp and picket duty for three weeks.

At daylight on the morning of December 11, we marched in the direction of Fredericksburg, but did not cross the river till 2 o'clock on the afternoon of the 13th. Passing through the town under a terrible fire of shot, shell and railroad iron, the Twentieth formed and advanced across the field, while the enemy poured upon them a terrific fire of musketry and artillery. With Colonel Ames gallantly leading in advance of the colors, the line moved in admirable order over fences and obstructions, through the ranks of troops lying down, until the extreme front was reached. Relieving those already engaged, Colonel Ames placed his men as much under cover as possible and held his position for thirty-six hours, constantly under fire. During the night of the 14th the brigade was withdrawn from the front and bivouacked on the pavements of the city. The next night they were again moved to the front, and it soon became known that the movement was designed to cover the retreat of the army. The men were kept in position until the troops were all over, when they too approached the pontoons, and just at dawn of day reached the north bank in safety. The small loss which the Twentieth suffered at Fredericksburg may be attributed largely to the skillful manner in which the regiment was handled by Colonel Ames. With weary steps and thankful hearts, the Twentieth Maine found its way through mud and rain to their old campground and went into winter quarters. At Fredericksburg many of the men exchanged their Enfield for Springfield rifles, and in a short time the whole regiment was supplied with those muskets.

The duties of camp and picketing a few miles to the rear, were interrupted December 30th by a reconnaissance to Richard's Ford, and the celebrated "Mud March" January 24th, 1863. Towards spring by an egregious blunder the men were inoculated with small pox, and on that account the regiment was moved on the 22d of April to an isolated camp. On the 27th the Fifth Corps moved to Chancellorsville, and Colonel Ames volunteered as an aid on the staff of Gen. Meade. May 3d the Twentieth was ordered to Banks' Ford to guard the telegraph, returning to its former camp after the battle.

May 21st the regiment moved with the brigade three miles to the right, and went into a pleasant camp. Colonel Ames having been promoted to Brigadier General, the command of the Twentieth devolved upon Lieut. Col. Chamberlain, who was soon after commissioned Colonel. About this time Col. Strong Vincent of the Eighty-Third replaced Col. Stockton in the command of the brigade. Lieut. J.M. Brown, the efficient adjutant of the Twentieth, was promoted to Captain and A.A.G. The Second Maine Regiment having been mustered out, one hundred and twenty-five men, who had enlisted for three years, were transferred to the Twentieth, and joined the regiment at this camp on the 23rd. These men expected to be discharged with their regiment and at first refused duty, but finally accepted the situation and became a valuable acquisition to the command.

May 28th the brigade was ordered to guard the fords of the Rappahannock, the position of the Twentieth being at

United States Ford. June 5th another move was made to Ellis Ford. In a few days it became known that the army of Lee was moving north, and the army of the Potomac entered upon those movements which culminated in the battle of Gettysburg. At dark on the 13th the Twentieth broke camp and joined the brigade at Morrisville, marching the next day to Catlett's Station. The day following you will remember as one of the hottest days of your experience. The regiment marched to Manassas Junction. Sunstrokes were frequent and the men were weary, thirsty and footsore when they bivouacked that night.

June 17th the column marched to Gum Springs, and on the 19th to Aldie, where the cavalry had fought and driven back the rebels under Hampton and Stewart. The Third Brigade, having been selected to support the cavalry in a further advance, was put in motion at 3 o'clock on the morning of the 21st and marched to Middleburg, where the cavalry was already advancing. The force of the enemy was two brigades of cavalry supported artillery, which the Third Brigade was mainly instrumental in driving from one position to another, behind stone walls and creeks for some six miles. During this running fight of ten hours duration, the Twentieth lost one man killed, and one officer and seven men wounded. The next day the brigade returned to its former camp at Aldie. During this movement the Twentieth was commanded by Lieut. Col. Connor of the Forty-Fourth New York, Colonel Chamberlain being sick from a partial sunstroke.

The Twentieth remained at Aldie until June 26th, when it marched through Leesburg to the Potomac and crossed at Edward's Ferry. Continuing the march on the following day, it forded the Monocacy river and camped within two miles of Frederick for two days. At this time Gen. Meade was made commander of the army of the Potomac, and Gen. Sykes succeeded to the command of the Fifth Corps. On the 29th the march was resumed through Frederick to Unionville. On the last day of June a movement was made by a portion of the Fifth Corps to intercept the enemy or ascertain his position. The Third Brigade took the advance and marched with skirmishers in front during the afternoon, and camped that night about three miles from the Pennsylvania line. On the 1st of July, having crossed the state line amid great enthusiasm, the column pressed on and late that afternoon reached Hanover. Halting two hours, the march was continued by moonlight, the music of the bands mingling with the cheers of the soldiers. At midnight the exhausted troops went into camp, after a march of thirty-two miles.

At daylight on the morning of the 2d the troops were again in motion, and at an early hour arrived within supporting distance of the forces engaged at Gettysburg. At four o'clock in the afternoon the Third Brigade was hurried a mile or more to the left under a heavy artillery fire, and the Twentieth, moving "on the right by the file into line," took position in the woods on the crest of a small hill, now known as "Little Round Top." The position held by the Twentieth was the extreme left of the Union line, and of great importance. Company B. was sent forward as skirmishers, but had not deployed when brisk firing commenced on the right, and a large force of the enemy was soon seen marching rapidly to the left through the ravine in our front. So rapid were their movements that the skirmishers were cut off, and were obliged to secrete themselves behind a stone wall. To avoid being flanked, Colonel Chamberlain moved his left wing to the left and rear, making nearly a right angle at the colors. This disposition had scarcely been made when the enemy fell upon the left with great fury. The struggle was desperate, now one party and now the other holding the ground. The ammunition of the Twentieth was nearly expended when the enemy gave way. The men had scarcely time to collect cartridges from the boxes of the dead and wounded before the assault was renewed apparently by fresh troops. The Twentieth had now lost nearly half its number and began to waver. At this moment Col Chamberlain ordered the charge. Advancing on the run the Twentieth completely routed the enemy and at the opportune moment the skirmishers arose from behind the stone wall and gave them a volley. Thinking themselves surrounded large numbers threw down their arms and surrendered. After driving the enemy nearly half a mile the regiment returned to its old position. Having received a supply of ammunition the Twentieth supported by two regiments of Pennsylvania reserves, advanced up the steep and rocky sides of Big Round Top and secured a position which they held during the night with the aid of the Eighty-Third which came up later. The Twentieth went into the fight with 358 muskets and captured 308 prisoners. The regiment lost 32 killed, 97 wounded and 6 taken prisoners on the skirmish line in the night. Detachments sent out to bury the dead counted in front of the position occupied by the Twentieth on Little Round Top fifty rebel dead and it is estimated that the regiment killed and wounded at least 300 of the enemy. The colors of the regiment were carried by Sergt. Tozier and although exposed on the angle of the line the sergeant and two of the four guards escaped without even a scratch. The splendid fighting qualities developed by the Twentieth Maine on the 2d day of July, gave it a brilliant reputation throughout the army and gained for Joshua L. Chamberlain the well-deserved title of "Hero of Round Top."

On the morning of the 3d the brigade was relieved and moved to the rear of the left center and lay in reserve during the day. At two o'clock in the afternoon the enemy open upon our lines the most terrific artillery fire ever heard in battle. For two hours the earth trembled and the air was filled with shot and shell.

> "Then shook the hills, with thunder riven
> * * * * * * * *
> And louder than the bolts of heaven
> Far flashed the red artillery."

During the night of the 4th Lee's army retreated and towards the close of the next day we were again moving south. Nothing of importance occurred except hard marching through rain and mud till the 10th when Company E. had two men killed and six captured in a skirmish near Fair Play, Maryland. During the night of the 13th the enemy made its escape across the Potomac and the expected battle did not occur. The next day the Fifth corps moved to Williamsport and on the 15th crossed the Potomac at Berlin and encamped at Lovettsville eight miles south of the river. The march was continued down the valley to the 23d when our division relieved the Third corps at Manassas Gap. The next morning the whole division was drawn up in line of battle and word was passed along the lines that the heights in front were to be taken at all hazards. Wapping Heights proved to be the most difficult place over which troops ever advanced in line of battle. Up the almost perpendicular hill, through woods and tangled underbrush, the men toiled—and picked blackberries—expecting the enemy to open fire at every step. The summit was finally reached but the enemy had fled. The magnificent view of the Shenandoah valley obtained from the heights partially repaid the men for the ascent. The "recall" was sounded and the line faced about and marched two miles to the rear. On the 25th the march was resumed, and on the 7th of August the regiment arrived at Beverly Ford, which the brigade guarded till the 16th of September. The command of the brigade having devolved upon Col. Chamberlain by the promotion of Col. Rice, Lieut.

Col. Gilmore assumed command of the Twentieth.

September 16th the army advanced to Culpepper where it remained in camp till October 10th, when the Fifth Corps moved to Raccoon Ford on the Rapidan, but finding no enemy returned to camp at night. The next day the enemy having threatened our right flank, the army began to fall back to preserve its line of communication. That night we camped at Beverly Ford. In the morning we retraced our steps, crossed the river, advanced nearly to Brandy Station and bivouacked for the night. It was now ascertained that Lee was moving rapidly around our right and at one o'clock on the morning of the 13th the race for Centreville began. That night we camped at Catlett's Station having marched twenty-five miles. The bugle sounded "revelie" at an early hour the next morning and the march was resumed. Near Bristoe Station the division halted an hour for coffee and "hard tack" which had hardly been disposed of when a rebel battery opened upon us from the woods. The division pulled out hurriedly and the march from this point to Manassas was rapid and the files were well closed up. Arriving at Manassas, the corps was formed in line of battle with batteries in position and remained till late in the afternoon listening to the roar of battle some two miles south where the Second Corps under Warren was engaged—and all the while we were wondering why we had hurried away from them. About the time Warren had whipped Hill the Fifth corps was started on the double quick to his assistance. At nine o'clock the corps moved towards Bull Run which we crossed at half past two the next morning, having been on foot twenty-four hours and marched thirty-two miles.

From the 15th to the 20th the regiment oscillated between Centreville and Fairfax. The enemy in the meantime had destroyed the Orange and Alexandria

Railroad and begun to fall back to his old quarters across the Rapidan. As fast as the road could be repaired the army of the Potomac followed. On the morning of Nov. 7th the Twentieth, now under the command of Major Ellis Spear, was in camp at Three Mile Station. The Rappahannock river at Rappahannock Station was held by the rebel brigades of Hoke and Hayes which it was now determined to attack. Eighty men under Capt. Morrill were detailed from the Twentieth for the skirmish line which in the advance had gained a position behind the railroad embankment, when the Sixth corps moved to the attack on the right. Seeing the gallant advance of the line in that direction Capt. Morrill's party dashed forward with the Sixth Maine Regiment and entered the works simultaneously with them. The Twentieth lost in this brilliant affair one man killed and seven wounded.

The next day the regiment crossed the Rappahannock at Kelly's Ford and encamped two miles from the river where occurred the "hard tack" drill. Towards evening on the ninth we recrossed the river and passed a cold and uncomfortable night near the ford.

About this time Col. Hayes of the 18th Massachusetts took command of the brigade. On the 10th we crossed the river again and at sunrise on the 26th marched to the Rapidan which was crossed and the march continued with frequent halts till eight o'clock at night. On the 29th our advance was made to Mine Run where the brigade took a position under a brisk fire from the enemy's lines which were not more than three hundred yards distant. We remained before the works of the enemy until the night of Dec. 2d when we folded our tents like the Arabs and silently stole away, the Third Brigade forming the rear guard.

Dec. 4th the Twentieth went into camp at

Rappahannock Station for the purpose of guarding the railroad bridge during the winter. The rifle pits which had been captured a month before and which had become the last ditch for many rebel dead, were graded off and comfortable quarters erected thereon. The officers, lucky souls, sent to Maine for their wives and the rank and file contented themselves with an occasional furlough. Here was spent the gayest winter in the history of the Twentieth.

This old battle flag in which we naturally feel so much pride, had now become tattered and torn and a new set of colors were procured. The old flag was presented to General Ames and delivered to him in Rockland while on leave of absence that winter. You remember, comrades, how you stood by that flag at Antietam and Shepherdstown; how you planted it on Little Round Top and defended it through the fierce assaults of that memorable day; and you remember too how

> "In the brilliant glare of the summer air
> With a brisk breeze around it creeping,
> Newly bright through the glistening light,
> The flag went grandly sweeping;
> Gleaming and bold were its braids of gold,
> And flashed in the sun-ray's kissing;
> Red, white, and blue were of deepest hue,
> And none of the stars were missing."

Previous to the opening of the campaign of 1864 a reorganization of the army took place. The old First Brigade of our division was broken up and the Hundred-and-eighteenth Pennsylvania and the Eighteenth Massachusetts joined the Third Brigade. Gen. Warren was placed in command of the Fifth Corps, Gen. Griffin retained the First Division and Gen. Bartlett took the Third Brigade. On the first day of May the winter quarters of the Twentieth at Rappahannock were broken up and the Brigade marched across the river to a camp east of Brandy Station, where the Fifth Corps, now composed of thirty thousand men, was concentrating. On the morning of the 4th the regiment with about three hundred rifles, under command of Major Spear, crossed the Rapidan at Germania Ford, and entered upon those movements known as the battles of the "Wilderness," the memory of which appears to those who took part in those sanguinary conflicts, more like a dreadful nightmare than a reality. That night the brigade bivouacked on the Orange and Fredericksburg turnpike near the old Wilderness Tavern. On the morning of the 5th, the army was extended along the roads in the densest portion of the Wilderness and the enemy were soon found to be rapidly advancing for the purpose of crushing our line before it could be concentrated. Upon our division devolved the duty of engaging the attention of the enemy until the rest of the army could get into position. The Third Brigade which occupied the center, was formed in two lines, the Twentieth being in the second line. When the order was given to advance all three brigades started on the double-quick with a yell, driving the enemy in confusion back upon his reserves. Finding the Sixth Corps had failed to connect on the right, the First Brigade fell back while the Third continued to advance. The enemy quickly took advantage of this and opened a murderous fire on our right from across the road. At the same time the Second Brigade on the left was being driven back by a heavy force. The Third Brigade was now alone with both flanks exposed. In the confusion each commander acted on his own judgement and a large part of the brigade broke for the rear on the run. At length the order was given to retire. The Twentieth was the last to leave the field bringing off with them a large squad of prisoners and in the retreat was obliged to make a detour to the left to avoid a force of the enemy which held the open field across which the line had first charged. The breast works built in the morning were finally reached and the line re-established. The contest was short but the regiment lost about ninety men killed, wounded and missing, among them Capt. Morrill of Company B. severely wounded in the face. Nearly all the prisoners were wounded and taken by the skirmish line in our rear. At dawn of the 6th the regiment moved out to the open field where it fought the day before and on the right of the road, and established a skirmish line in the opening with the main part of the regiment in the edge of the woods, sheltered by the brow of a hill, where it lay all day under fire, losing two men killed and ten wounded. Towards night an attack upon the Sixth Corps swept it back until the firing appeared to be in the rear and there begun to be quite a panic among the regiments of our division but the Twentieth stood firm until the fighting was over when the brigade was ordered back into breastworks. At nine o'clock the next morning The Twentieth and Hundred-and-eighteenth were ordered to charge into the woods in front and develop the enemy's strength. The skirmishers were driven in at a run until the line came in sight of the enemy's old position when he opened with a battery which a larger force could have carried, but with two regiments it was impossible. It was evident, however, the main body of the enemy had withdrawn and our force retired a short distance where a skirmish line was deployed and the Twentieth placed in support. In this movement the regiment lost thirteen killed and wounded. All were brought off except Lieut. F. W. Lane, Company B. who was struck in the head by a piece of shell and taken prisoner. He died in a rebel hospital a few days later. Lieut. J. M. Sherwood was severely wounded and died that night. At dark the army began to move towards Spotsylvania and the Twentieth and Hundred-and-eighteenth remained on the line where they had spent the day as a part of the rear guard of the corps. At midnight they silently withdrew and followed the corps. Towards noon of the 8th as they approached Spotsylvania there was cannonading at the front and they then heard of the morning's battle in which the Third Brigade had suffered so terribly. The regiment had halted for breakfast when they were ordered to the front and placed temporarily in Crawford's division, supporting a skirmish line in front of the enemy's position at Laurel Hill. The regiment changed positions several times and during the afternoon was subjected to a severe shelling but had only one man wounded. At four o'clock the Twentieth was allowed to go a short distance to the rear to cook hard tack and make coffee—the first coffee the men had had for three days. At half past six they went to the front again and were placed in the third line for an attack on the enemy's position. The third line advanced up the hill and lay down until support should be needed. At dark the enemy charged. The lines in front of the Twentieth divided and fell back to right and left and the enemy came suddenly upon the third line, causing the regiment on the left to retreat in confusion and forcing the Twentieth back about two rods. Then ensued a desperate hand-to-hand fight in the darkness. Friend could hardly be distinguished from foe; men fought single combats; revolvers came into play and officers found their swords for once useful. The regiment took about eighty prisoners and lost six killed, fifteen wounded and two missing. Capt. W.W. Morrill was killed while cheering on his men and Lieutenants Melcher and Prince were wounded. Fighting ceased about nine o'clock but the regiment remained in the same position till morning when it rejoined the brigade. During the night troops in the rear threw out pickets and refused to believe that any Union force was so far to the front. The conduct of the officers and men of the Twentieth on this occasion was worthy of all praise.

During the 9th the regiment obtained rest for the first time since crossing the Rapidan. About five o'clock in the afternoon the brigade supported an attack in which the enemy were driven back. Towards the evening of the 10th the First and Third Brigades went to the front and prepared to charge in three lines upon the enemy's works, but to the great relief of all concerned the movement was abandoned. This was a lucky day for the Twentieth. During the 11th the brigade lay in reserve, exposed to the fire of artillery and musketry from the front. On the 12th the command went to the left and prepared for another charge but Gen. Griffin revoked the order.

The Twentieth moved to the left at ten o'clock on the evening of the 13th and arrived in front of the enemy at Spotsylvania Court House at five o'clock the next morning, having marched all night in mud, rain and darkness. The Twentieth remained in front of Spotsylvania from the 14th to the 20th, losing four men killed. On the 21st another left flank movement began and the next day the brigade was engaged in a skirmish with the enemy. On the 23rd our division reached the North Anna river at Jericho Ford and at once commenced crossing. The Twentieth forded the stream with the brigade and at six o'clock that afternoon assisted in the repulse of the sudden attack on Sweitzer's Brigade. In this action Major Spear, commanding the regiment, was slightly wounded. The night was spent in throwing up breast works behind which the regiment lay till five p.m. the next day when it moved to the right and front about a mile and bivouacked near the Virginia Central Railroad. On the 25th the column moved down the railroad and found the enemy strongly posted at Noell's Station. Breast works were thrown up for self protection and for two days a portion of the division was engaged in tearing up the railroad. During the heavy picket firing on the 26th the Twentieth had three men wounded. At dark the division withdrew from the front and marched with short intervals of rest till six o'clock the next afternoon. It was a hard march through a finely cultivated country which had never before been visited by the desolation of war. That night for the first time in more than three weeks the men slept without an apprehension of danger from any quarter. For twenty-two days the regiment had been almost constantly under fire, and the men who had survived the terrible ordeal wondered how they escaped unscathed.

  The Pamunkey river was crossed at Hanover Ferry and the march continued without interruption until the 30th, when still advancing heavy skirmishing occurred and the line of entrenchments covering the approaches to Richmond was reached. On the first day of June the enemy charged our line and was driven back. On the 3rd the Twentieth participated in the fight at Bethesda church, losing two men killed, one officer, Adjutant Donnell, and twenty-three men wounded. The brigade remained in this position till the night of the 5th when it was relieved by the Ninth Corps and the Fifth Corps lay in reserve till the 12th. The regiment moved on the night of the 12th and crossed the Chickahominy early the next morning. At nine o'clock on the morning of the 16th the Twentieth crossed the James river on a steam transport and halted a mile from the river, the Fifth Corps still being in reserve and the last to cross over. On the morning of the 18th the Fifth Corps moved to the front and was received with a heavy fire. The Third Brigade being in the center of the division was somewhat concealed by woods through which they advanced to an open field where they halted and commenced throwing up breast works. In the meantime the Second Brigade had gained a position close up to the enemy's lines and the First Brigade lead by our Colonel Chamberlain had made a charge in which its commander fell severely wounded. For gallant conduct on this occasion Colonel Chamberlain was made a Brigadier General on the field by Gen. Grant—the only instance of the kind in the history of the war.

From this time till the 15th of August, the Twentieth occupied works in front of Petersburg in close proximity to the enemy and generally under fire. These works were gradually strengthened and completed, bomb-proofs were constructed and vast covered passages were excavated in every direction. Every means were taken to provide protection from the mortar batteries and sharpshooters of the enemy but without success. On the 22d of June, Capt. Samuel T. Keene was killed by a sharpshooter, and the regiment lost three men killed and several wounded during their occupation of the works. July 30th the Twentieth from their position had a fine view of the grand explosion of the mine and the grand failure which followed.

Early on the morning of Aug. 15th the brigade was relieved by other troops and encamped in the rear. On the 18th marched to the Weldon Railroad which was struck about six miles from Petersburg and possession taken without opposition. That afternoon the enemy made an attack which was repulsed by the Second and Third Divisions. The next day another attack in full force was made and the Third Brigade went up to the right on the double-quick but were not needed. Sunday at the 21st, in the morning while the regiment was packing up for a move, the picket line was driven in followed by the rebels charging in several lines, supported by vigorous shelling from their batteries. The assault extended some distance to the right but their whole line was repulsed with heavy loss, our division capturing 38 officers, 300 men and four battle flags. The Twentieth held a splendid position, their fire enfilading the enemy completely. It was a smart fight and the victory though signal was a bloodless one for the Twentieth.

Sept. 30th the Division moved from the Weldon Railroad with the Third Brigade in advance, and found the enemy entrenched at Preeble's Farm. The works consisted of a small square fort flanked by strong lines of breast works. After some skirmishing the brigade charged across the open field in the face of terrible fire of musketry and canister and captured the works with one piece of artillery and seventy-one prisoners. The gun limber, six horses and two prisoners were secured by Lieut. A. E. Fernald of the Twentieth and an officer of the 32d Massachusetts while the rebels were trying to run it off. A division of the Ninth Corps then took the advance and being attacked just before dark were driven back in confusion. Our division was ordered to the front to check the enemy and after one of the fiercest fights of the campaign they were repulsed and Griffin's Division, and in particular the old Third Brigade, again covered themselves with glory. The Twentieth lost during the day one officer, Capt. Weston H. Keene, and six men killed and Capt. H. F. Sidelinger, Lieut. Alden Miller and fifty men wounded. The brigade commander being injured just before the assault, Major Spear, the only field officer in the brigade, took command, and the Twentieth passed into the hands of Capt. A. W. Clark of Company E.

On the 2d of October the Twentieth moved to the front and threw up earthworks where they remained until the 20th when the regiment took part in a reconnaissance to Hatcher's Run. The next day the troops returned to the works, the Twentieth acting as rear guard and losing one man killed and two wounded. Nov. 8th, Lieut. Col. Gilmore returned and took command and on the 5th of December the corps was relieved and moved to the rear on the Jerusalem Plank Road. The next day the corps moved out for a raid on the Weldon Railroad which continued to be used by the rebels as far as Stony Creek Station. About twenty miles of the road was destroyed and the corps returned to camp on the Plank Road Dec. 12th. This expedition you will all remember as the time when the Fifth Corps got gloriously drunk on "apple jack."

The regiment now supposed that winter quarters had been reached and both officers and men worked like beavers in the erection of comfortable huts many of which were quite elaborate. Major Spear and eight men went to Maine on recruiting service Jan. 15th 1865. Feb. 5th the regiment moved with the corps to Hatcher's Run and participated the next day in a second fight in the vicinity of that historic stream with slight loss. After the engagement the Twentieth went into camp at that place.

March 13th, Lieut. Col. Gilmore having resigned, Major Ellis Spear was commissioned Colonel, Capt. Walter G. Morrill, Lieut. Colonel and Capt. Atherton W. Clark, Major. About the same time a special order from the War Department made Charles D. Gilmore full Colonel and in consequence Maj. Spear could not be mustered. Lieut. Col. Morrill assumed command of the regiment and Major Spear was ordered on duty at Corps Headquarters.

The final campaign of the war was now about to

open. On the 29th of March the Twentieth moved across the run and supported Chamberlain's brigade in the action on the Quaker Road. The skirmish the next day resulted in the possession of the Boydton Road. On the 31st the regiment had a hand in the action at Gravelly Run having several wounded, among them Lieut. J.H. Stanwood, commanding Company E.

April 1st the Fifth Corps was ordered to report to Gen. Sheridan and acted as a sort of foot cavalry, if I may be permitted to use the expression, during the remainder of the campaign. On that day the Twentieth joined in the second attack on Five Forks and were among the first to gain the works, capturing one battle flag and a large number of prisoners.

Then followed the evacuation of Richmond and the pursuit in which the cavalry and the Fifth Corps by their rapid movements sealed the fate of Lee's army and when, on the 9th of April, the white flag of truce came over the field it was to the division bearing the red Maltese cross that it came. When the terms of surrender had been arranged Gen. J. L. Chamberlain, who received his first baptism of fire while an officer of the Twentieth Maine, was designated to command the parade before which the troops stacked their arms and colors and on the 12th the same grand old division was drawn up with our Third Brigade in the main line to witness the last movement of the confederate army of Northern Virginia.

The regiment arrived at Arlington Heights May 12th and participated in the great review on the 23d. Col. Gilmore resigned on the 29th and Major Spear was mustered as Colonel and Capt. A. W. Clark as Major. Col. Spear remained on detached duty. On the 4th of June 1865, the veterans of the Twentieth were mustered out of the service and started for Maine the day following under the command of Lieut. Col. Morrill, arriving in Portland on the 8th.

When the regiment left Washington the recruits of the Twentieth were consolidated with those of the Sixteenth and First Sharpshooters. This organization was known as the Twentieth Maine and remained in the service till July 16th.

Comrades—How vividly these scenes rush before our minds tonight, and though they seem more like the fantasm of troubled dreams, yet they can never, never be forgotten. Softened by the influence of time, the motley panorama passes rapidly before us—the weary march, the fierce assault, the hospital and the dreadful prison appear upon the canvas stretching from Antietam to Appomattox. Along the whole line may be seen the graves of our fellow-comrades, the memory of whose deeds remain fresh in our own hearts tonight and will be cherished by generations yet to come. Their achievements and your achievements made the history of the old regiment glorious, and as in the pride of your nationality you exclaim "I am an American citizen!" so in the light of your record as a regiment, you may exultantly add: "I, too, was a soldier of the Twentieth Maine!"

While Lieut. Miller was speaking Gen. Chamberlain appeared upon the platform and was greeted with cheers. At the close of the address J. L. Shaw's quartette rendered the song, "All Honor to the Soldier Give," in fine style, receiving much applause.

Gen. Chamberlain was then introduced and spoke briefly, touchingly and eloquently of the deeds of the Twentieth Maine. He complimented the graceful and modest manner in which the facts of the history of the Twentieth had been put together and said he was astonished to find how short a time he was directly with it. His experience with the Twentieth was the most honorable of his life. The red Maltese cross he was proud to wear above all the badges upon his breast. It was once crimsoned with blood but it was now blushing with undying love. No body of men who wore that badge was worthier than the Twentieth Maine, a regiment that he had the words of generals, from brigade commanders up to Meade himself, was held of as great account as any regiment that served in the war of the rebellion. They all eagerly gave recognition to its heroism and valor, its fortitude and patience. For discipline and morals, it bore a character conspicuous in the army. In Jeff Davis' history he told one true thing when he said, in speaking of the battle of Gettysburg, that it was those fellows up there on Round Top that spoiled his plans. The manly vigor shown by the Twentieth Maine had gone into history. In conclusion he said: "But I cannot speak. God bless the old flag and God bless you all, again and forever."

At the close of Gen. Chamberlain's remarks the band played a medley and then at the General's request the bugler sound "tattoo". Shaw's quartet sang "Larboard Watch, Ahoy," and all united in singing "My Country 'tis of Thee" and "Auld Lang Syne," when the audience was dismissed and the business meeting of the Twentieth Maine Regiment Association began.

The Association transacted the following business:

Reading the records of last meeting.

Reading letters from Gen. Ames, Col. Gilmore, Col. Morrill, Maj. J.F. Land, Major. J.B. Fitch, Capt. Howard L. Prince.

Lieut. E. R. Sanborn and Sergt. W. T. Livermore. (A letter from Col. Ellis Spear was received too late for the reunion.)

The following committee was nominated to select a board of officers for the Association: J. H. Stanwood, W. K. Bickford, Franklin True. The committee subsequently reported the following:

> President—Holman S. Melcher, Portland.
> Vice President—James B. Wescott, Bath.
> Secretary and Treasurer—Samuel L. Miller, Waldoboro.

The report was accepted and the nominations confirmed.

Report of Secretary and Treasurer read and approved.

A motion to present the colors to the State was not carried.

Voted, That the Executive Committee confer with Gen. Ames in regard to keeping the old battle flag in the possession of the association.

Voted, That the Secretary be instructed to have the historical address published in pamphlet form.

A contribution of $10.73 was taken for associational purposes.

Adjourned.

Thursday forenoon the Twentieth, numbering sixty men, under the command of Capt. R. B. Plummer, joined the parade and were much cheered as they bore their old battle flag along the route of the procession.

Thursday afternoon about forty members of the Twentieth, commanded by Capt. Plummer, participated in the sham fight.

Thursday evening a business meeting was held at regimental headquarters for the purpose of deciding upon a badge. At this meeting it was:

Voted, That the Executive Committee be authorized to procure badges, worth one dollar each, for the use of the association.

Voted, That the badges be procured in season for the next reunion.

Voted, That the next reunion of the Twentieth Maine be held with the general reunion of the soldiers and sailors of Maine.

After a general and affecting hand-shaking the veterans of the Twentieth regiment separated.

LETTER FROM GENERAL AMES

The President of the Twentieth Maine Regiment Association has received the following letter from General Ames, which will be readily understood:

NEW YORK, OCT. 3, 1881.

H.S. Melcher
President Twentieth Maine Volunteers Association
Portland, Maine

Dear Sir:—
Returning to the city after a long absence I find yours of the 10th ult.
Out of respect for the wishes of the Association I withdraw my request to have the colors delivered over to the State authorities. The further request that they may be used on occasions of parade and assembly I also acquiesce in. I will leave them with your association for the present, at least, knowing the respect and attention they will receive.

Yours truly,
A. Ames

Taken from the Maine Bugle, January, 1895;

The Twentieth Maine Volunteers observed the thirty-second anniversary of their muster into the service of the United States, August 29, 1862, at Cushing Island, 1894.

It was one of the most noble regiments which Maine furnished for the Northern armies, as soon as it landed in Maryland in the dark days of 1862, hurried to the front by forced marches in time to take part in the Battle of Antietam when General McClellan was commander-in-chief.

In, 1863, under command of the gallant General Chamberlain, the Twentieth Maine were the heroes of Little Round Top in the terrible three days' struggle between the Army of the Potomac and the Army of Northern Virginia,--which was the great pivotal battle of the war.

In 1865, at Appomatox, the division commanded by General Chamberlain, of which his old regiment, the Twentieth Maine, was a prominent part, had the distinguished honor of being selected by General Grant to receive the surrender of General Lee, and the principal army of the Southern Confederacy, which virtually closed the war.

The steamer Forest City which transported to the lovely Cushing's Island the first delegation of the veterans at 2:15 o'clock, floated from its bow and stern flag staffs the colors of the grand old fighting Fifth Corps,--the red Maltese cross upon a white ground work.

The survivors of the Twentieth Maine regiment who arrived by this boat, and others who had previously landed, were soon in comfortable quarters at the Ottawa house. After a comforting lunch, the party took a stroll about the island which in itself is well worth a visit. Dinner was served at 7 o'clock, after which the veterans, with ladies and other guests, assembled in the Music hall for the annual meeting.

Major Holman S. Melcher, president of the association, presided with his usual grace and dignity. "Joe" Tyler then stirred the souls of the veterans with the familiar call, "Dan, Dan, Dan, Butterfield!" President Melcher opened the meeting with brief but appropriate remarks, and called upon Comrade Theodore Gerrish, who invoked the divine blessing. The president stated that it was our pleasure to have present member of the Thirty-Sixth Massachusetts, which regiment went from Boston to Alexandria on the steamer Merrimac thirty-two years ago, and introduced Major H.S. Burrage, editor of Zion's Advocate, Portland. Major Burrage responded in a very happy manner.

He was followed by Captain George W. Verrill, of Portland, president of the Seventeenth Maine association, as a representative of the regiment which returned to Portland with the Twentieth at the close of the war. Captain Verrill's remarks were to the point and were received with applause. The bugle call was again sounded, followed by remarks from Captain [James C.] Rundlett introducing a rifle which had served on both sides during the war.

The secretary read letters from General Adelbert Ames and Major Joseph F. Land, and expressed General Ellis Spear's regrets that, being suddenly called to Washington, he was unable to be present.

Interesting and stirring speeches followed from George S. Rowell, of the Portland Advertiser, himself a veteran, General [Jonathan P.] Cilley, of the First Maine Cavalry, [Edward P.] Merrill, of the First Maine Cavalry, and others. Samuel L. Miller, secretary of the association, then read a poem written for the occasion by Mrs. Sarah A. Martin, of Foxcroft, state vice-president of the Woman's State Relief Corps of Maine. The poem was as follows:

To the Twentieth Maine on the thirty-second anniversary of "Muster-in":

There were grand, brave hearts in that distant time,
In the days of the old crusade,
Who marched 'neath the folds of the Maltese cross
To the tomb where the Lord was laid.
How they fought, how they fell, conquered and died,
In the land of the Saracen foe,
Has in story been told, in song been sung,
Since those days long ago.
But I sing to-night of a nobler band;
In our nation's struggle and pain
They fought not for fame, but for native land.
'Tis the brave old Twentieth Maine !
The years have gone by since you mustered in,--
You number them in thirty and two,
As you meet to-night 'neath the Maltese cross
And the folds of the "red, white, and blue."
You miss them to-night, those comrades of old,
Whose elbows touched elbow with you;
From Antietam to Appomattox they lie,--
The boys in the brave army blue.
Petersburg claims them, and Chancellorsville:
Five Forks holds its share of your loss;
At Laurel Hill, Weldon, and Peebles they rest,
Who fell 'neath the Red Maltese cross.
North Anna runs softly and murmurs its tale,
On her banks they are sleeping, I ween;
And for those who fell in the thick of the fight,
In the Wilderness blossoms more green.
Fredericksburg claims them, and lone Hatcher's Run,
Where they fell 'neath the leaden rain,
And Gettysburg's height is dotted with graves
Of the gallant old Twentieth Maine.
And, Ah, Little Round Top! There 'bove the clouds,
You fought in the light of the sun,
'Neath the stars and stripes and the Red Maltese cross,
And a glorious victory won.
When the battle of life is finished at length,
And ended each gain and each loss
May you conquer at last through the glorious Son,
In the hallowed sign of the cross.

The Twentieth Maine Association   281

The poem was received with applause.
The report of the secretary and treasurer was read and accepted. A contribution to replenish the treasury was taken. Amount of contribution, $21.33. On a motion of Comrade J.C. Rundlett a committee of three, J.C. Rundlett, E.S. Coan, and F.M. Rogers, were appointed to nominate a board of officers. The committee reported as follows:

For president, Holman S. Melcher, Portland; vice-president, Reuel Thomas, North Cambridge; secretary and treasurer, Samuel L. Miller, Waldoboro. The report was accepted and they were unanimously elected. The new vice-president being called upon responded with a very happy speech, in which he highly complemented the "girls" as he termed the ladies present. He was followed by Comrades E. S. Coan, O.P. Martin, J.E. DeWitt.

Voted, That a reunion of the association be held in 1895 at such time and place as the board of officers, who constitute the executive committee, may deem best. The meeting was then closed by singing America.

There was present:
H.S. and Mrs. Melcher, Portland; Charles Powers, North Leominster, Mass.; H.M. Adams, Hodgdon, Me.; Theodore and Mrs. Gerrish, Master George Gerrish, Portland; A.C. Muncy, Livermore Falls; J.C. and Mrs. Rundlett, Portland; James R. Martin, Foxcroft; O.P. Martin, Foxcroft; J.E. DeWitt, Natick, Mass.; Charles R. Shorey, Waterville; L.F. Farris, Lowell, Mass.; John S. Parker, St. Albans, Vt.; A.P. and Mrs. Bateman, Lowell, Mass.; E.S. Coan, Auburn; E.P. Merrill, Portland; Wm. H. Stahl, North Waldoboro; J.W. Morris, Westbrook; F.M. Rogers, Melrose, Mass.; J.H. and Mrs. Stanwood, Waldoboro; A.J. and Mrs. Tozier, Litchfield; Reuel and Mrs. Thomas, North Cambridge, Mass.; Geo. L. Witham, Southport; Sullivan Johnson, St. Albans; S.A. Bennett, Norway; W.H. True, Portland; A.O. Shaw, Portland; P.S.

and Mrs. Graham, Cumberland Mills; A.B. Latham, Auburn; F.L. Hunnewell, Portland; Chas. Cook, Portland; W.G. Robinson, Hyannis, Mass.; L.P. and Mrs. True, Yarmouth; S.L. and Mrs. Field, Portland; S.B. Libby, Durham; J.E. Bennett, Foxcroft; C.T. Buck, Snow Falls; Moses Verrill, Buckfield; P.M. Morgan, Gorham; Wm. K. Bickford, Norway; Joseph Tyler, Portland; A.E. McLaughlin, Roxbury, Mass.; S.L. Miller, Waldoboro; G.W. Bowman, Orleans, Mass.

TWENTIETH MAINE REUNION

The annual reunion of the Twentieth Maine Regiment, which occurred at the Portland Club house, Great Diamond Island, August 29, 1895, was a very enjoyable affair for the survivors of this famous regiment, who were so fortunate as to be present.

The time before dinner was spent on the spacious piazzas in renewing old acquaintances, and recalling the stirring events of their war experience.

At seven o'clock the company assembled in the dining room to the number of sixty-five, and were served with a bountiful dinner by the hostess. The room had been beautifully decorated with flowers, evergreen, Chinese lanterns, and red, white and blue streamers. At the head of the hall was hung a copy of the old division flag, bearing the red Maltese cross. The tables were also adorned with magnificent bouquets of choice roses, contributed by Comrade Ben. Gribben.

During the banquet the Club House orchestra furnished excellent music and at its conclusion, Major H. S. Melcher, President of the Twentieth Maine Association, welcomed the comrades to the reunion, and then introduced the old commander of the Twentieth, General Joshua L. Chamberlain, who was received with hearty applause. General Chamberlain made one his impressive speeches, in the course of which he said: "The great force which inspired the Northern Soldier was the elevating, and holy inspiration of the home which he had left behind him in the North. The home, with its attachments, its memories, and its loved ones, was the great force behind our armies. For after all, it was our homes for which were fighting. For it is the institutions for which we then fought that are building up the noble manhood and womanhood of today." General Chamberlain referred to an evening which he recently had with General Locke, who said: "That Twentieth Maine of yours was the best regiment I ever saw." General Chamberlain said he had hoped to bring Colonel Merriam with him, but the latter had been unable to remain so long in Maine.

General John Marshall Brown, the first adjutant of the regiment, was introduced next, and received with applause. Although he had not been with the regiment when it earned its great laurels, he said he had a great pride in the achievements of the regiment. This was a double anniversary, for on the day when this regiment was mustered in, thirty-three years ago, a great celebration was held at Popham, to observe the anniversary of the settlement of that spot by the English. He was on the train going to Popham, when be received a telegram signed "Chamberlain," informing him that he had been chosen adjutant. He left the train and returned to Portland. That telegram was now a cherished relic. Speeches followed from Major Fogler of Augusta, and others.

Letters were read from Captain Howard L. Prince (at which time his son, a stalwart young man, was introduced, and received a round of applause), Charles E. White, Charles H. Mero, Major J. F. Land, J. Wesley Gilman, Charles Powers, Arad Thompson, Merritt Stimson, E. C. Allen, George R. Rich, and a telegram from General Ellis Spear.

The following comrades were appointed committee on nominations: DeWitt, Stanwood, Wetherell.

The secretary reported names of comrades who had died since last meeting.

President Melcher referred to the matter of regimental history, and was followed by General Chamberlain, E. S. Wetherell, Geo. W. Reynolds, and A. E. Fernald.

Voted, To choose a committee of five, with power, to take into consideration the preparation of a regimental history.

Committee on nominations reported the following board of officers:

> President—Holman S. Melcher.
> Vice-President—George W. Reynolds.
> Secretary and Treasurer—Sam'l L. Miller.

Voted, To accept the report of the committee, and to authorize General Chamberlain to cast the vote of the association for the comrades nominated.

Remarks by Captain J. C. Rundlett.

Secretary Miller extended an invitation to the association, to hold its reunion in Waldoboro next year.

Voted, Unanimously, to accept the invitation.

Voted, That the thanks of the association be extended to Comrade Gribben for his generous contribution of flowers.

The president announced the following committee on history: J. L. Chamberlain, Ellis Spear, H. L. Prince, S. L. Miller, E. S. Wetherell.

REUNION OF VETERAN ASSOCIATIONS

On the morning of August 21, a body of veteran troops appeared on the outskirts of Waldoboro village, and, after some preliminary arrangements, marched into town and held complete control during the day and evening.

They were the surviving veterans of the Twentieth Maine Regiment, a regiment which fought from Antietam to Appomattox.

On the arrival of the 10:06 a.m. train, bringing General Chamberlain, General John Marshall Brown, and many other comrades and ladies, regimental line was formed by the association officers, who were mounted. The old battle flag was carried by brave old Sergeant Tozier, who bore it through the terrible struggle at Little Round Top. The colors were guarded by two files of men armed with Enfield rifles, and on either side marched Sergeant Wyman and Corporal DeWitt.

The following committee was appointed to nominate a board of officers: George W. Reynolds, J. F. Land, Reuel Thomas.

The committee reported the following nominations:

> President—H. S. Melcher, Portland.
> Vice President—T. S. Benson, Sidney.
> Secretary and Treasurer—S. L. Miller, Waldoboro

The report was adopted and the officers elected.

Being called, each officer briefly responded.

At this time Department Commander Carver was escorted to the platform and received with applause.

The following were nominated a Committee on Resolutions: Ellis Spear, John Marshall Brown, P. M. Folger, I. A. Macurda, C. M. Chase.

General Chamberlain, from the Committee on History, reported the progress that had been made to correct the list of men engaged in the Battle of Gettysburg.

Remarks by Major Fogler on the same subject.

Voted, That the work of the Committee on History be continued.

Letters were read from Comrades C. H. Mero, D. S. Baker, Charles G. Whittier, A. P. Daggett, E. Folsom, N. S. Clark, and Major William H. Hodgkins (Thirty-sixth Massachusetts Infantry).

The Twentieth Maine Association 287

Voted, That the secretary be requested to reply to letters read from comrades.

Comrades J. H. Stanwood and G. L. Witham were appointed a committee to take up a collection to defray running expenses of the association. The committee reported amount received, $26.21.

The president reported that among the deceased comrades were J. C. Rundlett, E. S. Coan, J. M. Kennedy, and Thomas D. Chamberlain. General Spear briefly addressed the comrades on the character and war record of Kennedy, Rundlett, and Chamberlain; and Major Land paid tribute to the memory of E. S. Coan.

Voted, That the matter of next reunion be left with the Executive Committee.

Previous to adjournment, the names of all present were given to the secretary. The result was as follows:

Field and Staff.—J. L. Chamberlain, J. M. Brown.

Company A.—G. W. Reynolds, S. L. Miller, T. S. Benson, J. W. Morris, William M. Elwell, Samuel Longley, Ira R. Sylvester, Ambrose Hoch, Gideon Hoch.

Company B.—J. F. Clifford.

Company C.—J. H. Stanwood, C. T. Buck, A. B. Latham.

Company D.—None present.

Company E.—William K. Bickford, O. F. Mank, S. Cummings, E. A. Leach, C.E. Bickmore, Barden Turner, William H. Stahl, Raymond Hoffses, Selden Hunt, J. M. Shuman, Elbridge Bryant, Timothy Brown, E. S. Wetherell, William D. McKim, William H. Levensaler, E. S. Levensaler, Chandler Bracket, C. G. Stewart, S. L. Messer, O. G. Miller, E. A. Humphrey, Thomas C. Little, Thomas R. Hogue, Robert Creamer, Porter Richmond, Edward K. Chapman.

Company F.—H. S. Melcher, Silas S. Meserve, A. M. Stone, J. E. DeWitt.

Company G. —Ellis Spear, E. Hodgkins, J. J. a. Hoffses, J. M. Bateman, Benjamin Fairbrother, Alvin Butler, S. T. Lowell, I. A. Macurda, A. S. Hiscock, J. A. Nash, Moody Barnes, James Brann, Israel K. Hearin, A. P. Bateman, Alden Miller, Jr., A. Moody, Cyrus Osborn, William Rankin, A. Cunningham, R. N. Bailey.

Company H.—J. F. Land, A. C. Munsey.

Company I.—P. M. Folger, Reuel Thomas, Aaron Andrews, Daniel J. Andrews, Alwood Andrews, Eli Bickmore, J. L. Bradford, W. B. Bradford, C. A. Copeland, G. H. Dow, Eben Elwell, Lewis Hall, Oliver Hower, Sylvanus Hyler, E. B. Kelleran, J. M. Leighton, Edward Light, O. T. mann, J. d. Morse, Theodore Roosen, J. B. Wescott, W. F. Wight, G. W. Witham, Oscar Thomas, C. A. Jones, A. J. Tozier, Emerson Creighton, J. D. Creighton, Frank Geyer.

Company K.—Charles M. Chase, S. M. Wyman, Joel S. Hart, Edwin Keating.

It is possible some who were in town are omitted from this list, as all were not present at roll-call. Companies E, G, and I had the largest numbers, Company I leading with twenty-nine present.

Many of the comrades brought their wives.

During the afternoon an open-air concert was given by the band, and carriages were provided for the lady visitors to ride about town.

Major-General Butterfield arrived from New York on the 4:32 train.

At 5:30 a large crowd assembled to witness the "dress parade" on Miller's lawn. General Chamberlain assumed command, with General Brown as adjutant, Major Melcher as sergeant-major, and Lieutenant Miller as drum-major. The drum corps was composed of local talent and did remarkably well. The parade was hardly up to those conducted by Colonel Ames, but was very interesting to the veterans as well as to spectators.

At 7:30 line was formed and the regiment marched down Main street to the music of the band to Clark's hall. During the march a beautiful display of fireworks was given.

Clark's hall was packed. The exercises opened with a selection by the band—"Sheridan's Ride"—and continued as follows:

Prayer	Comrade T. R. Hogue.
Address of Welcome	S. L. Miller.
Response	President Melcher.

Remarks .... General Chamberlain.
Recitation .... Mrs. Maude Gay.
Reading letter from General Fitz John Porter.
Remarks .... Major Land.
Remarks .... General Spear.
Remarks .... Department Commander Carver.

Selection by the band.

The following resolution was presented by General Spear:

Resolved, That the thanks of this association are due and heartily given to our comrades of Company E and to the citizens of Waldoboro, for the generous entertainment they have given us on this occasion of pleasant gathering of the Twentieth Maine association. The day, this beautiful village, and their kind hospitality have made this a day long to be remembered. We carry with us a pleasant remembrance of their generous entertainment.

Adopted by a standing vote.

The day was perfect and the visitors all expressed themselves as highly pleased with Waldoboro and the hospitality shown them. It is considered one of the best reunions the regiment had held.

There were present during the day five comrades who wore stars during the war. They were Generals Daniel Butterfield, J. L. Chamberlain, Ellis Spear, John Marshall Brown, and William G. LeDuc of Minnesota. General Butterfield commanded the Fifth Corps at the Battle of Fredericksburg and was chief-of-staff of the Army of the Potomac during the Chancellorsville and Gettysburg campaigns. General Chamberlain was terribly wounded while leading a brigade in front of Petersburg, and was promoted to brigadier-general on the spot by General Grant. He commanded the troops which received the surrender of Lee, and was four times elected governor of Maine. General Spear, besides his war record, had held the position of commissioner of patents at Washington. General Brown was the first adjutant of the Twentieth, promoted to assistant adjutant-general, and colonel of the Thirty-second Maine. General LeDuc was a famous quartermaster-general during the war, and was commissioner of agriculture under President Hayes. It was undoubtedly the most distinguished party ever in Waldoboro at one time.

Holman S. Melcher circa 1895.

Taken from the Daily Eastern Argus, Monday, June 27, 1905.

OBITUARY

Ex-Mayor Holman S. Melcher died at his home on Pine Street at an early hour yesterday morning, after a short illness from two serious attacks of the grippe, which he had last winter and which left him in a greatly enfeebled condition from which he was unable to rally.

Major Melcher has long been identified with the business interests of the city, and has taken a prominent part in its public affairs.

A veteran of the Twentieth Maine regiment, he participated in many of the severest battles of the war, including Antietam, Shepardstown Ford, Fredericksburg, Aldie, Gettysburg, Rappahannock Station, Mine Run, the Wilderness, Spottsylvania, Hatcher's Run, Five Forks, and Appomattox.

In the history of the Maine troops at Gettysburg, entitled "Maine at Gettysburg," Major Holman S. Melcher is spoken of as the hero of Little Round Top, and in the elaborate account of the three days' fighting, the detailed story of the brilliant work of his company and regiment is fully set out.

Major Melcher was member of the Bosworth Post G.A.R., of which he has been a past commander and a trustee. He was president of the Twentieth Maine Regimental association, registrar of the military order of the Loyal Legion, is a life member of the Ancient Landmark lodge of Masons, a member of the Young Men's Christian Association and the Free Street Baptist church.

As a business man Major Melcher has been successful. He conducted business under the firm name H.S. Melcher & Co., until Jan. 1, 1896, when H.S. Melcher company was organized with Major Melcher as president. While his large business demanded close attention, he was officially connected with several financial institutions and has always been interested in public affairs. In 1880 and '81 he was elected to the city council and the following two years was elected to the board of aldermen.

He served two terms as mayor of this city, being first elected in 1889 and re-elected in 1890.

Major Melcher was married to Alice Hart, and a daughter, Georgina Hill Melcher, is the only child of this marriage.

LAST HONORS

Funeral Services for Hon. Holman S. Melcher.

The funeral of the late ex-Mayor was held yesterday afternoon. Prayers were held at the house at 1:30 p.m. and there were services at the Free Street Baptist church at 2 o'clock. About 100 members of the Bosworth Post, No. 2, G.A.R., members of the Loyal Legion and members of the Wholesale Grocers' Association all occupied seats in the church which were reserved for them. Other societies to which he belonged were well represented and there was a large attendance of friends.

The State Street choir rendered several selections and the eulogies were by Rev. Dr. J.K. Wilson, and Dr. Henry S. Burrage, both of whom spoke feelingly of their long acquaintance with Major Melcher and many of his estimable qualities.

Interment was at Evergreen.

APPENDIX I

The Spear-Chamberlain Controversy

*Forty-four years after the Battle of Gettysburg, the life-long friendship between Ellis Spear and Joshua Chamberlain became strained and irreconcilable. Not much is known of the controversy and the exact cause remains a mystery. What is known is that in 1907, after the publication of the book, **Deeds of Valor**, in which the Medal of Honor recipients recorded their heroic deeds on the battlefield, Ellis Spear took issue with Chamberlain's version of the action on Little Round Top. Of the many accounts written by Chamberlain, this was his most egotistical, and to Spear, the most insulting. After its publication, Spear, for the rest of his life, denounced Chamberlain's "fabric of lies."*

*The following account by Gen. Joshua Lawrence Chamberlain appeared in the book **Deeds of Valor, or How American Heroes won the Medal of Honor**. Edited by W.F. Beyer and O.F. Keydel, Perrien-Keydel Co., Detroit MI., 1907.*

A Bayonet Charge the Last Hope

Never had a bayonet charge more effective results than had that of the Twentith Maine Volunteers, on the slope of Little Round Top, at Gettysburg, July 2, 1863. It not only saved the position of the Union troops, but compelled General Lee to change his whole plan of attack. The incident is thus described by Colonel Joshua L. Chamberlain, commanding the Twentith Maine:

"My regiment held the extreme left of the Union lines, at Gettysburg. The enemy was shelling the whole crest heavily, and moving a large force to seize this commanding height, while we were rushing up to get the position ourselves. We had scarcely got our troops into something like a line among the rocks of the southern slope, when the enemy's assault struck us. It was a hard hand to hand fight, swaying back and forth under successive charges and counter-charges, for an hour. I had been obliged to throw back my left wing at a right-angle or more in order to hold the ground at all.

"As it was a sort of echelon attack, the enemy was constantly coming up on my left, and outflanking me. The losses in my regiment were very heavy. In the center of the apex of the angle, made by throwing back the left wing, the colorguard was shot away, the color-company and that next to it lost nearly half their number, and more than a third of the regiment was disabled. We had, in the lull of the fight, thrown together a low line of loose rocks that were scattered about the ground, and the men were taking such shelter as they could behind these, though they could do this only by lying down and firing over them. This helped us but little; it served chiefly to mark the line we were bound to maintain.

"At last I saw a heavy force that had just come up over the opposite slopes of Great Round Top, coming to envelop our left. They were close to us, advancing rapidly, and firing as they came. We had expended our last round of cartridges, and had been gathering what we could from the cartridge-boxes of the dead and dying, friend and foe. We met this fresh force with these cartridges, but at the critical moment, when the enemy were within fifty feet of us, our fire fell to nothing. Every round was gone.

"Knowing the supreme importance of holding this ground, which covered the flank of Hazlett's Battery on the summit and gave a clear enfilading and rear fire upon the whole force holding Little Round Top, I saw no other way to save it, or even ourselves, but to charge with the bayonet. The on-coming force evidently outnumbered us three or four to one, but it was the last resort.

"Giving the order to charge, I placed myself beside the colors at the apex of our formation, sent word to the senior officer on my left to make a right wheel of the charge and endeavor to catch the enemy somewhat in flank on the right. Then we sprang down the rocky slope into the presence of the astonished foe. I came directly upon an officer commanding the center of the opposing line. He attempted to fire a pistol in my face, but my sabre point was at his throat, and instantly he turned the butt of his pistol and the hilt of his sword, and surrendered. His whole line began to throw down their arms likewise. My officers were also in the line with the bayonets.

"This charge was successful beyond all my hopes. We not only cleared our own front, but, by the right wheel, cleared the front of the entire brigade on our right, and also the whole ground between Little and Great Round Top. We took twice as many prisoners as we had men in our ranks, and found 150 of the enemy's dead in our front. These were of the Fifteenth, Forty-seventh and Fourth Alabama, and the Fifth Texas regiments.

"The result of this movement, beyond question, was the saving of Hazlett's Battery, and, in fact, Round Top itself, to our troops. It now appears that it also changed Lee's plans for his attack of the next day which had been intended to be a crushing blow on our left again, but was abandoned for Pickett's charge on the center. The honors belong to my regiment."

Appendix I 297

*In 1916, Oliver W. Norton, author of **The Attack and Defence of Little Round Top**, wrote to Ellis Spear inquiring about Gen. Chamberlain's **Passing of the Armies**. The embittered Spear then launched a personal tirade against his former commander.*

                                                St. Petersburg, Florida
Mr. Oliver W. Norton   January 18, 1916.
813 Masonic Temple,
Chicago, Ill.
My dear Comrade:

    Your esteemed favor of the 12th inst. was forwarded from Washington and is received. I have the book but left it in Washington. It was published by his son, or rather the publication was procured by his son, a young man without knowledge or discretion in the matter. I have not read it through; like yourself, I was disgusted though not unprepared. And I may as well make a clean breast of it. I knew Chamberlain in college in '54 to '58. He had the same infirmity then, notoriously of inability to tell the truth always.

    So far as I have read, "The Passing of the Armies" is a tissue of lies. He was not wounded on the Quaker road. I know that absolutely, as I was with him part of the time and not far off any time. His coat was torn by a bullet. Of his wound at Petersburg I know, as I went back to the Hospital after dark and was with him. He was in charge of our regimental surgeon and was sitting up, but making some fuss. He was wounded in the penis. Of course I made no examination but the surgeon explained the wound to me. It was a painful wound of course, as a catheter had to be introduced to carry urine past the wound. That was the only time he was touched by iron or lead. He artfully made much out of that wound, and by adroit and persistent lecturing and writing after the war. His literary ability was of a high order, and he always had a gracious manner, but was absolutely unable to tell the truth and was of inordinate vanity. As far as he could, he robbed Vincent. Did I ever tell you the true story of the 20th Maine at Gettysburg? I wrote it for the National Tribune two or three years ago.

I think I once called your attention to an article published by Chamberlain in the Cosmopolitan Magazine. I wrote comments upon it, but not for publication. I sent it to Ames and one other friend, Col. Alexander has read it. I will write to my office to mail it to you. I wish you could see the article itself, but I have lost my copy, and probably it is out of print.

I have suffered much from sciatica and came here for the winter trying to get well.

With kindest regards, I am sincerely
Your friend and comrade,
Ellis Spear

O.W. Norton
813 Masonic Temple
Chicago, Ill.

St. Petersburg, Florida
February, 1, 1916

Dear Companion,

I appreciate highly your letter of the 28th ult. I was reluctant to put in print my comments on Chamberlain's "Story." He left a sister who was a friend of my first wife, and a son, and the criticism took a personal tinge beyond the control of my pen. I never had any but kindly feelings, but saw so much of the egotism, which you rightly call "colossal," that I could not write otherwise. He had figured in Maine as the Hero of Little Round Top. Some years ago I was at commencement, (I am an Overseer at Bowdoin) and as I sat in a path near some students who passed, one of them remarked, "There goes the man who took Little Round Top." He also heard the remark, and without turning his head he replied in a loud voice, "Yes, I took it and I held it." It seemed almost impossible, but that is a sample. Knowing so well the facts, it seemed to me like robbing the dead. Of course he should of said, "No, that honor belongs to Strong Vincent." But as a matter of fact, he was himself the author of all these stories.

Your suggestion that I write comments on Chamberlain's book, appeals to me. Gen. Ames has urged me to do the same thing. I will endeavor to find the book. I fear I left it at my house, now shut up. I have time here, but no resource of reference and shall have to write from memory, and with care to make the matter as impersonal as possible. But, as you say, we owe it to posterity that the truth be given. It is also due to our dead comrades. I will let you see the manuscript.

Very cordially, your companion,
Ellis Spear

Soon after, Spear began to write his memoirs, detailing his wartime experiences.

Ellis Spear died on April 3, 1916, without seeing his memoirs published.

This letter was written to eleven year old Mildred P. Grant, by her step-grandfather, Gen. Ellis Spear, on March 14, 1910. (Spear had married Capt. Samuel Keene's widow). The little Miss Grant asked Gen. Spear if he had been in the battle of Gettysburg and would he tell her all about it. In her later years, she would remember that the General had a very dry wit, as seen by this letter.

Dear Mildred-

    I was much surprised to learn, from your letter, that you were not at the battle of Gettysburg. So many people were there that I do not fully understand how you missed it. It is not unreasonable, therefore, that you should wish to know something about it. I fear you will never know all about it. Nobody does, and nobody ever did or ever will. It was a very mixed up and extensive affair.

    As you will infer, from what I have said, I did not see the whole of the battle, I saw enough, and was quite satisfied with that. Nor did I hear anybody complain of lack. There was enough to go around.

    (Then) indeed there began a fuss and a mess. Such a noise you could not hear any particular bang, smoke & yelling, and the smell of gun powder and the air was very unhealthy. And it soon became very serious, for the men were dropping, but most in your grandfather Keene's company, which was in the center and carried the colors excepting the color bearer himself, and picked up a gun (for the color bearer does not carry a gun) but this was dropped by one of the men who fell. He was resting the color staff on the ground, with his left arm around the flag, and was loading and firing as if he were doing it all, and I noticed that he was chewing a piece of cartridge paper, torn from a bullet. The soldiers in those times used paper cartridges, and tore them open with their teeth. But, after a while it became very tiresome and monotonous to stand there and be fired at, and we fixed bayonets, and made a rush for the enemy. Just then they all seemed to remember something they had left at

Appendix I 301

home, and they ran like mad intending to go in the direction of home and their mothers. But in their haste, and unfamiliarity with the country, a great many, two or three hundred, ran into a worm fence lane. A worm fence is not made of worms, but I cannot now delay to describe it, particularly as the Rebs are in the lane, and may get out & escape. You can, at your leisure look that matter up in the Encyclopedia, while I attend to the Confederates. In fact they did try to get out, some of them, and these got upon the fence and, painful as the necessity was, we were obliged to shoot them. I mean those who were trying to scale the fence & escape without asking leave. The rest, who dropped their guns & showed signs of repentance, we magnanimously spared, and accepted their apologies. A great many deeds of valor were performed, but in the excitement of the time and the unavoidable mental occupation & close attention to the business, they were not noticed; but many have been invented since, after much reflection and in an amplified form. It is much easier to tell about a battle than to fight it, and safer, especially after a lapse of 47 years, and the witnesses have become few and scattered.

Later when we had gathered in the prisoners we followed those of the enemy who had retreated up the hill, and captured more of them on the other side, then without supper or bed we lay down in the woods and slept. And as it is late, and this letter is already too long, I think it better to do the same thing. Another day, and in another volume I may tell you about the general plan of the battle though that would be rather dull.

                              In the meantime I am
                              your loving,
                              grandpa

The following article by Holman Melcher, was read before the Maine Commandery of the Loyal Legion on February 12, 1902.

Lincoln and the Commanding Officers of the Army of the Potomac.

When Abraham Lincoln was inaugurated President of the United States in March, 1861, he found affairs in a disturbed and alarming condition. Treason was rampant, the departments were honeycombed with disloyalty, with traitors and secession spies everywhere. Prominent officials had for months been preparing for the disruption of the government, and had scattered the little bands of troops constituting the small regular army to distant places in the states and territories; while the navy—such as it was at the time—was assigned to remote stations of foreign countries. The Secretary of War had been for months quietly but persistently transferring ordnance, arms and ammunition to arsenals in the southern states.

While Mr. Lincoln, by every word and act, tried to conciliate the secessionists, his advances were scorned, and he soon saw that nothing but strong and heroic measures would prevail to save even a few of the forts along the southern seacoast from falling under their complete control. Even officers of highest rank in the army could not be depended on as truly loyal to the service and the flag they had taken their solemn oath faithfully and loyally to support.

This was most forcibly illustrated in the case of Robert E. Lee, one of the most prominent and able officers in the United States Army, a favorite of General Scott, who had at once, in his own mind selected him as the most capable and promising officer in the service to become the principal commander in the field. But the treason of Major-General Twiggs, commanding the department of Texas, Brigadier-General Joseph E. Johnston, chief quartermaster, and Samuel Cooper, adjutant-general of the army, had caused

Mr. Lincoln to distrust every officer of southern birth. He therefore requested F. P. Blair, Senior, an intimate friend, to ascertain Lee's feelings and intentions. April 18, Mr. Blair invited Lee to an interview. In this interview he positively affirmed that secession was anarchy.

In a letter to his son, only a few weeks before this, Lee wrote "Secession is nothing but revolution. The framers of our Constitution never exhausted so much labor, wisdom and forbearance in its formation, and surrounded it with so many guards and securities, if it was intended to be broken by any member of the confederacy at will. It was intended for perpetual union, so expressed in the preamble, and for the establishment of a government. . . . . . It is idle to talk of secession. Anarchy would have been established, and not a government, by Washington, Jefferson, Madison and the other patriots of the Revolution." From this interview he called on General Scott. It is morally certain that Scott, also a Virginian, gave Lee a lesson in patriotism, but he caught no generous emulation from the voice and example of his great chief. Yet after writing and saying all this only a few weeks and days before, on the twentieth of April, Lee wrote to General Scott, his old commander: "General: Since my interview with you on the eighteenth instant, I have felt that I ought not longer to retain my commission in the army. I therefore tender my resignation, which I request you will recommend for acceptance. It would have been presented at once but for the struggle it has cost me to separate myself from a service to which I have devoted all the best years of my life and all the ability I possessed. Save in defence of my native state I never again desire to draw the sword."

Lee was at this time, in military phrase, "on leave of absence," and, without waiting to hear whether his resignation had been accepted, he was appointed by

Governor Letcher and practically mustered, April 23, chief in command of the Virginia state forces, with all his military obligation to the United States intact and uncanceled, thus rendering himself guilty of desertion and treason. No danger whatever menaced his native state. The President had positively disclaimed any intention of invading it.

In contrast to this story of treason is the loyal and patriotic conduct of General Scott. Called on by a distinguished gentleman appointed by the Virginia convention to tender him the command of the forces of Virginia, General Scott listened to the proposition, but promptly replied: "I have served my country under the flag of the Union for more than fifty years, and, as God permits me to live, I will defend that flag with my sword even if my own native state assails it."

Although advanced in years, General Scott applied himself to mustering the forces necessary for the defense of the Capital, and the organization into an effective army of volunteers who so promptly and heroically responded to the call of the President when Sumter was fired on; and he was the man of all others at that time to whom Mr. Lincoln turned for the creating of the force that he saw must be the power to uphold the government and save the Union.

Mr. Lincoln had done everything in his power to avert a resort to arms. From the time he first opened his lips as President of the United States, he had breathed none but pacific words. The great act of the conspirators in the bombardment of Fort Sumter brought upon the heads of the secessionists the full responsibility for the beginning of the war and the train of horrors that followed it. The fall of Sumter was the resurrection of patriotism. The North needed just this. Such an unusual burst of patriotism at this insult to the national flag had never been witnessed. There was no lack of strong and patriotic men to maintain the honor of the flag, but generals to organize and properly mold this mass into an effective fighting machine were the great need of the time; and well may the President have sought the interest and anxiety for men to do this service, since he recognized that in them must be trust for the organizing and handling of the great power that must now be resorted to in order to save the government. His deep interest and concern in military affairs never waned during the four years the war continued.

Mr. Lincoln had had some experience in military matters in the Black Hawk War as a captain of infantry, but no theoretical military training; yet throughout the War of the Rebellion, every movement of the great armies was followed by him as carefully and intelligently as though he was the commanding general, rather than the Commander-in-Chief by virtue of being President; and he came to be recognized by the most vigorous and best trained intellects as "the ablest strategist of the war."

From the very beginning it was evident that the Army of the Potomac was to bear the brunt of the war, and hence it was important that it should be most efficiently commanded. As this was the army in which I served during the three years of my service, of which I knew most, and in which I was most deeply interested, I shall limit myself to this army in this necessarily brief paper.

On account of his age, his military training, and the successes he had achieved in his West Virginia campaign, General George B. McClellan was ordered to Washington, where he arrived on the twenty-sixth of July and assumed command of the army the next day. This army was being speedily formed by regiments arriving on an average of one each day, made up of the very best material the North had to give. On the twenty-seventh day of October, three months after General McClellan assumed command, he reported the strength of his army as one hundred and sixty-eight thousand, three hundred and eighteen men, well officered, well clothed, armed with the best and most improved weapons of the time, and fully inspired with the patriotic impulses to save the country and maintain the honor of the flag.

This was the magnificent weapon put in the hand of General McClellan, the beautiful and highly tempered Damascus blade with which to strike the blow for the destruction of secession; yet he allowed the Confederates to blockade the Potomac by building batteries along its shore below Washington, to occupy numerous heights in sight of the Capitol, and let all the fine days of the autumn go by without striking a blow, notwithstanding the outspoken demand of the whole North for something to be done, and the persistent urging of the government.

To the urgent demand, almost orders of the President, he said: "I intend to be careful and do as well as possible. Don't let them hurry me is all I ask".

The fine weather of the fall was not improved, and the winter passed without any general movement of the Army of the Potomac. The patience of the President was exhausted, and, being convinced that nothing would be done unless he intervened by a positive command, he issued January 27, 1862, General Order No. 1. He wrote it without consultation with any one, and read it to the members of his cabinet, not for their sanction, but for their information.

The order directed that the twenty-second day of February, 1862, be the day for a general movement of the land and naval forces of the United States against the insurgent forces; that General McClellan, commanding the Army of the Potomac, form an expedition to seize the railroad south of Manassas Junction. Had McClellan obeyed this order of the President, it is known he could have won a great victory at little cost and captured the immense accumulation of provisions and stores at Manassas.

On receiving this order General McClellan began to file objections, and insisted that he be permitted to transfer the Army of the Potomac to a new base of operations from Urbana on the Rappahannock or to the Peninsula. As this was against the judgement of Mr. Lincoln, it was a question of the utmost gravity whether he should force the general in command to follow a plan of campaign not approved by him. It would certainly have been a serious measure to have removed General McClellan from command of the Army at that time. As it was, Mr. Lincoln gave his consent to the Peninsula plan, which resulted at length in terrible disaster to the cause of the Union. Mr. Lincoln, however, did not give his consent until he had gone over the whole plan of the campaign with General McClellan, trying to induce him to adopt the direct movement against the enemy at Manassas; but failing in this, he made the condition that a force should be left sufficient to make Washington safe against any sudden attack of the enemy.

A council of war was held at Fairfax Court House, March 3, 1862, to settle the question of how large a force should be left to cover Washington. This council consisted of Generals McDowell, Sumner, Heintzelman and Keyes, the commanders of the four corps of the army. It was urged that Washington would be secure if the forts on the right bank of the Potomac were garrisoned with eight thousand men and those on the left bank with four thousand men, while the covering force in front of the Virginia line should consist of twenty-five thousand men. This view was endorsed by McDowell, Keyes and Heintzelman. Sumner insisted on forty thousand.

This was satisfactory to the President, but the day after General McClellan sailed for Fortress Monroe, Mr. Lincoln was astonished to hear from General Wadsworth, the military governor of the district of Washington, that General McClellan had left only nineteen thousand men for garrison and defense and orders to detach eight regiments of this force. He also reported that "his command was entirely inadequate to the important duty to which it was assigned." As General Wadsworth was a man of the highest intelligence, courage and calm judgment, the President was greatly concerned by this emphatic statement made by General Wadsworth. They fully confirmed this report, and the President on receiving their opinion directed that McDowell's Corps should not be sent to the Peninsula until further orders. McClellan's greatest grievance was the retention of McDowell's Corps, and his clamor in regard to it was loud and long.

On the ninth of April Mr. Lincoln wrote to General McClellan in answer to his complaints with as much kindness and consideration as a father would use toward a petulant child: "Your dispatches complaining that you are not properly sustained, while they do not offend me, pain me very much. Blenker's Division was withdrawn before you left here, and you know the pressure under which I did it and as I thought acquiesced in it. After you left I ascertained that less than twenty thousand organized men without a single field battery were all you designed to be left for the defense of Washington and Manassas Junction, and a part of this even was to go to General Hooker's old position. My explicit order that Washington should, by the judgement of all the commanders of the army corps, be left entirely secure, had been neglected. It was precisely this that drove me to detain McDowell."

Franklin's Division of McDowell's Corps was sent to him on April 10, and this he did not have disembarked for ten days after its arrival. McCall's magnificent division of this corps was sent to him before the middle of June.

The correspondence between the President and General McClellan during the Peninsula Campaign would be interesting, as showing the peculiar make-up of the commanding general, were there time to review it.

As soon as he had his army ashore at Fortress Monroe, General McClellan began to call for reinforcements and continued this in the most persistent, and at times insulting manner, in intimating that the authorities at Washington sought the destruction of his army in order that his reputation might be ruined.

The President was always patient and kindly in his communications with McClellan. In a reply to his demand for reinforcement of a division the last of June when in front of Richmond, he wrote: "Your dispatch of yesterday suggest the probability of your being overwhelmed by two hundred thousand, and talking of where the responsibility will belong, pains me very much. I give you all I can, and act on the presumption that you will do best you can with what you have, while you continue, ungenerously I think, to assume that I could give you more if I would. I have omitted and I shall omit no opportunity to send you reinforcements whenever I possibly can."

After his retreat to Harrison's Landing, giving up his magnificent chance to make a hero of himself and immortalize his army at Malvern Hill, General McClellan continued his correspondence with the government, giving full expression to recrimination and querulousness. He writes: "I have no faith in the administration. I am tired of serving fools. I begin to believe they want this army to be destroyed. I am satisfied that the dolts in Washington are bent on my destruction."

After the disaster connected with the second Bull Run battle, Pope's scattered army came under the command of General McClellan as well as the Army of the Potomac. The positive and oft-repeated order of the President to General McClellan was: "You must find and hurt the enemy now." He hurried forward the new regiments as fast as they arrived in Washington, and spared no effort to give McClellan an army with which he might "hurt the enemy."

One day, Mr. Lincoln, exasperated at the discrepancy between the aggregate of troops he had sent to the front and the number McClellan reported as having received, exclaimed in one of his grotesque similes: "Sending men to that army is like shoveling fleas across a barnyard; not half of them get there."

The result of the battle of Antietam was a great disappointment to the President. While thankful that Lee had been driven back across the Potomac, he felt that the results were not commensurate with the efforts made and the resources employed.

Becoming impatient at the inaction of the army after that battle, Mr. Lincoln made a visit to McClellan's camp on October 2, to see if by a personal interview he could not inspire him to a sense of the necessity of action. He reviewed that great army as it was drawn up across the hills along the Maryland shore of the Potomac, and, as far as he could see, it was a mighty force, fully armed and equipped, ready for any work that could be asked of it.

It was the first time I had seen Mr. Lincoln, and you may be sure I looked at him with eager interest as he rode directly across the front of my regiment as we were drawn up in line with the Fifth Corps.

During all his visit he urged, with as much energy as was consistent with is habitual courtesy, the necessity of an immediate employment of this force. He went back to Washington taking little comfort from his visit. After a few days of painful deliberation, no movement of the army taking place, he sent the following positive instructions:

Washington, D.C., October 6, 1862.
Major-General McClellan:

I am instructed to telegraph you as follows: The President directs that you cross the Potomac and give battle to the enemy or drive him south. Your army must move now while the roads are good. If you cross the river between the enemy and Washington and cover the latter by your operation you can be reinforced by thirty thousand men. If you move up the Valley of the Shenandoah not more than twelve thousand or fifteen thousand can be sent to you.

The President advised the interior line between Washington and the enemy but does not order it.

He is very desirous that your army move as soon as possible. You will immediately report what line you will adopt and when you intend to cross the river; also to what point the reinforcements are to be sent. It is necessary that the plan of your operations be positively determined on before orders are given for building bridges and repairing railroads.

I am directed to add that the Secretary of War and the General-in-Chief fully concur with the President in these instructions.

H.W. Halleck,
General-in-Chief.

Notwithstanding this positive order, followed by many dispatches of the same character, it was not until the first of November that McClellan got his army across the Potomac (without opposition of any importance whatever) and slowly distributed it along the eastern slope of the Blue Ridge under the vigilant but now distrustful eye of the President. Before the close of October he had begun to think McClellan had not desire to defeat the enemy and in his own mind he had set the limit of his tolerance, viz: that if McClellan should permit Lee to cross the Blue Ridge and place himself between Richmond and the Army of the Potomac he would remove him from command.

When, therefore, it was reported in Washington that Lee was at Culpepper Court House the President sent an order, dated November 5, to McClellan which reached him at Rectortown on the seventh, directing him to turn over the command of the Army of the Potomac to General Burnside. General McClellan's remark on receiving this order was, "Alas, my poor country!" He took credit to himself in after years for not heading a mutiny of the troops at this time.

Thus ended the military career of George Brinton McClellan. General Buckingham was the messenger that brought the orders changing the commanders of the Army of the Potomac. Burnside was surprised, and as he says "shocked at the news." He said he was not competent to command such an army, and only after long and earnest urging by General Buckingham and his own staff did he accept. It can be safely said that from the hour when he accepted the command to the hour when he laid it down in discouragement and despair, he did not see a single happy day.

General Burnside moved promptly in pursuit of the enemy, but the disaster at Fredericksburg, followed by the famous Mud March in January, completely ruined his usefulness as commander of the army, and the President, without asking the advice of any one, removed Burnside at his own request, placing him in command of the Department of the Ohio, and appointed General Joseph Hooker to the command of the Army of the Potomac.

Public opinion greatly approved this act of Mr. Lincoln. On the day that Mr. Lincoln appointed General Hooker commander of the army, he wrote him a letter, which was so remarkable for its frankness and its magnanimity, that it distinctly deserves to be given in full. "I have placed you at the head of the Army of the Potomac. Of course I have done this upon what appear to me to be sufficient reasons, and yet I think it best for you to know that there are some things in regard to which I am not quite satisfied with you. I believe you to be a brave and skillful soldier, which of course I like. I also believe you do not mix politics with your profession, in which you are right. You have confidence in yourself, which is a valuable, if not an indispensable, quality. You are ambitious, which within reasonable bounds does good rather than harm. But I think that during General Burnside's command of the army you have taken council of your ambition and thwarted him as much as you could, in which you did a great wrong to the country and to a most meritorious and honorable brother officer. I have heard, in such a way as to believe it, of your recently saying that both the army and the government needed a dictator. Of course it was not for this, but in spite of it, that I have given you the command. Only those generals who gain successes can set up as dictators. What I now ask of you is a military success and I will risk the dictatorship. The government will support you to the utmost of its ability, which is no more nor no less than it has done and will do for all commanders. I much fear that the spirit which you have aided to infuse into the army of criticizing their commander and withholding confidence from him, will now turn upon you. I shall assist you as far as I can to put it down. Neither you nor Napoleon were he alive again could get good out of an army while such a spirit prevails in it. And now beware of rashness. Beware of rashness, but with energy and sleepless vigilance go forward and give us victories."

This letter made a deep impression upon the general. He was chagrined at its severe chiding, but was touched by its tone of mingled authority and kindness. To a friend he said: "He talks like a father. I shall not answer this letter until I have won him a great victory."

He immediately went about his work in the most faithful and efficient manner. In the early part of April he was able to say that under his command he had a "living" army and one well worthy of the Republic, "the finest army on the planet." It numbered one hundred and thirty thousand effective men for service and with it he should have won a glorious victory at Chancellorsville the first days of May; and he would, had it not been for his over confidence of success. Before Hooker had recovered from the effect of Chancellorsville sufficiently to resume the offensive, Lee started on his great northern campaign that resulted in the decisive battle of Gettysburg.

When Hooker became fully satisfied of the intent and extent of this movement, he submitted to the government his plan of attacking the rear of Lee's army at Fredericksburg. The President replied to his dispatch within an hour of its receipt. "The enemy would fight," said the President, "in entrenchments and have you at a disadvantage and so man for man worst you at that point, while his main force would in some way be getting an advantage of you northward. In one word, I would not take any risk of being entangled upon the river like an ox jumped half over a fence and liable to be torn by dogs in front and rear without a fair chance to gore one way or kick the other."

General Hooker, being convinced by the information obtained by the affair at Brandy Station that the Confederate army was well on its march north, submitted to the President the plan he had conceived to march directly on Richmond. There is something in this proposition which stirs the blood of any soldier who reflects upon the exciting possibilities it contains. If it had been attempted and succeeded, a world of blood and treasure would have been saved, Hooker would have gained one of the greatest names of modern times, and Lee's career would have ended in disaster mingled with ridicule.

But the suggestion was too extravagant and hazardous to commend itself to the calm judgment of the President. He answered without a moment's delay, "Lee's army and not Richmond is your sure objective point. Fret him and fret him. If the head of Lee's army is at Martinsburg and the tail of it on the plank road between Fredericksburg and Chancellorsville, the animal must be very slim somewhere. Could you not break him?"

General Hooker's action was never more intelligent and energetic than during this campaign. He made no mistakes and he omitted nothing that could properly be done. When, however, he demanded the abandonment of Harper's Ferry, and that General French's command be assigned to the Army of the Potomac and this was refused by the authorities at Washington, he requested to be relieved from the command of the army, which was promptly granted and General George G. Meade, commanding the Fifth Corps, was appointed in his place.

It was a tremendous responsibility that came to General Meade, but he assumed it like the noble soldier that he was. In reply to the order appointing him to the command of the army, he said, "As a soldier I obey it and to the utmost of my ability will execute it."

To the army he said, "It is with diffidence that I relieve in the command of this army an eminent and accomplished soldier whose name must ever appear conspicuous in the history of its achievements, but I rely upon the hearty support of my companions in arms to assist me in the discharge of the duties of the important trust which has been confided to me."

With but one day's halt from this change of commanders the army resumed its march northward June 29, and falling upon Lee's army at Gettysburg fought that great battle on the first, second and third of July. The news of this victory was received at Washington with great rejoicing. The President accompanied his generous words of praise and congratulations to the general with strict injunctions to give Lee no rest or respite. The pursuit of Lee's retreating army was prompt and persistent, but when overtaken it was found strongly posted at Williamsport, unable to cross the Potomac on account of its flooded condition from recent heavy rains.

The Army of the Potomac had lost so heavily at Gettysburg, and General Meade had been so short a time in command, that he did not feel like assuming the responsibility of ordering an assault on the enemy's entrenched position. So he called a council of war consisting of his corps commanders, who advised against an assault. To this decision the President made a vehement reply. "You are strong enough to attack and defeat the enemy before he can effect a crossing. Act upon your own judgment, and make your generals execute your orders. Call no councils of war. It is proverbial that councils of war never fight. Do not let the enemy escape."

The next morning, however, it was found that the enemy

had escaped across the Potomac during the night. When the President heard of Lee's escape he suffered one of the deepest and bitterest disappointments of the war. He said, "We had them in our grasp. We had only to stretch forth our hands and they were ours, and nothing I could say or do could make the army move."

To General Meade he wrote: "I do not believe you appreciate the magnitude of the misfortune involved in Lee's escape. He was within your easy grasp, and to have closed upon him would, in connection with our other late successes, have ended the war. As it is the war will be prolonged indefinitely. Your golden opportunity is gone, and I am distressed immensely because of it."

In February, 1864, Congress passed the bill reviving the grade of lieutenant-general in the army. The President immediately upon signing it nominated for the position Major-General Ulysses S. Grant. The Senate promptly confirmed the nomination and General Grant was directed to report in person to the War Department as "early as practicable, considering the condition of his command."

He started the next day, reached Washington on the eighth of March and met the President for the first time. Mr. Lincoln had followed his career in the western armies with admiration and had written him many letters of commendation. When others had slandered and traduced him and asserted that he was addicted to hard drinking, he replied: "If I knew what brand of whiskey he drinks, I would serve a barrel or so to some other generals." When, therefore, the way was opened by Congress he did not hesitate to appoint General Grant to the highest position in the military service. He received him cordially and said: "General Grant, the nation's appreciation of what you have done, and its reliance upon you for what remains to do in the existing great struggle, are now, with this commission constituting you lieutenant-general in the army of the United States. With this high honor devolves upon you, also, a corresponding responsibility. As the country herein trusts you, so under God it will sustain you. I scarcely need to add that with what I here speak for the nation goes my own hearty personal concurrence." With extreme embarrassment, General Grant replied, but what he said could hardly have been improved: "Mr. President, I accept this commission with gratitude for the high honor conferred. With the aid of the noble armies that have fought on so many fields for our common country, it will by my earnest endeavor not to disappoint your expectations. I feel the full weight of the responsibility now devolving on me, and I know if they are met, it will be due to those armies and above all to the favor of the Providence which leads both armies and men."

The next day Grant visited General Meade at the headquarters of the Army of the Potomac at Brandy Station. The manner in which General Meade received him impressed Grant most favorably. General Meade explained to him that the work of the Army of the Potomac was of such vast importance that no person should stand in way of the one he wanted to command, and that, if Grant preferred some one else in command, he would serve to the best of his ability in any position to which he might be assigned.

Grant assured him he had not thought of making any change. When he had looked over the situation he decided that here was where he should be, and until the surrender of Lee's army at Appomattox he made his own headquarters with the Army of the Potomac, and is therefore classed as a commander of that army in this paper.

The confidence which the President had in Grant is best shown in the following correspondence. Just before the great campaign of 1864 opened, the President wrote to him: "Not expecting to see you again before the spring campaign opens, I wish to express in this way my entire satisfaction in what you have done so far as I understand it. The particulars of your campaign I neither know nor seek to know. You are vigilant and self-reliant and pleased with this I wish not to obtrude any constraints or restraints upon you. . . . . . If there is anything wanting which is within my power to give do not fail to let me know it; and now, with a brave army and a just cause, may God sustain you."

General Grant was touched with the generous feeling of the President's letter and answered next day: "Your very kind letter of yesterday is just received. The confidence you express for the future and the satisfaction with the past in my military administration is acknowledged with pride. It will be my earnest endeavor that you and the country shall not be disappointed . . . . since the promotion which placed me in command of all the armies and in view of the great responsibilities and importance of success, I have been astonished at the readiness with which everything asked has been yielded without even an explanation being asked. Should my success be less than I desire and expect, the least I can say is the fault is not with you."

What a change had come to the Army of the Potomac. The tone of this letter was an augury of ultimate victory. This confidence of the President in the Lieutenant-General continued to the end. During all that terrible carnage in the Wilderness, at Spotsylvania and Cold Harbor, the President recognized in General Grant a commander of ability and determination "to fight it out on that line if it takes all summer;" and he gave him his full confidence, his hearty support and all the troops that could be gathered for reinforcements.

Just before the beginning of the final campaign in 1865, Mr. Lincoln went to City Point to be near the scene of action. Hither also came General Sherman, whose army was now at Goldsboro, N.C., having accomplished that memorable march from "Atlanta to the sea," from Savannah north through the Carolinas, and was now within supporting distance from the Army of the Potomac; while the impetuous Sheridan with his dashing cavalry had swept up the Shenandoah Valley like a whirlwind, destroying the last remnants of Jubal Early's command, breaking through the Blue Ridge at Waynesboro, marching across the state of Virginia to the White House on the Pamunky, thence across the Peninsula without opposition of importance, and crossing the James River was bivouacked with the Army of the Potomac, ready to co-operate with it in the last great struggle of the war.

The circle of the hunt was completed. It only remained for the quiet hunter, sitting in his log house at City Point, to sound the "*Laissez aller*," when the work would be speedily finished.

When General Grant, with his staff, left City Point for the front on the twenty-ninth of March, the President shook him heartily by the hand, saying, "Good-by, gentlemen, God bless you all and remember your success is mine."

For three long anxious days the President waited at City Point for news from the front, but when it came it was good news indeed. At 7.45 o'clock on the evening of April 1, General Grant telegraphed him from his headquarters at Dabney's Mills: "Sheridan with his cavalry and the Fifth Corps has evidently had a big fight this evening. The distance he is off is so great, however, that I shall not probably be able to report the result for an hour or two."

When later in the evening General Porter of General

Grant's staff came riding in from the field at Five Forks, bringing the glorious news of that battle, General Grant calmly listened to his impassioned report and then sent to the President such news as he had never received from this army during the four long weary years of the war, news to warm his patriotic heart at last before it was chilled forever: "I have just heard from Sheridan. He has carried everything before him. He has captured three brigades of infantry, two batteries, and a wagon train and is now following up his success."

The President recognized this great victory at Five Forks as the "beginning of the end," as everything had been staked on this battle by the commanders of both the Union and Confederate forces. General Grant at once ordered an assault along the whole line for the earliest daylight the next morning, which resulted in the fall of Petersburg and Richmond that had been so heroically defended all these years.

At 4.40 o'clock on the afternoon of April 2, in response to an invitation from General Grant to come to the front, Mr. Lincoln telegraphed from City Point: "Allow me to tender you, and all with you, the nations's grateful thanks for this additional and magnificent success. At your suggestion I think I will meet you tomorrow."

At daylight on the morning of April 3, the corps and divisions of the army under Grant entered into hot pursuit of the fleeing Confederates, but he tarried in Petersburg, seated on the piazza of an abandoned mansion of the fallen city, awaiting the coming of the President. When he arrived he seized General Grant's hand as he stepped forward to greet him, and stood shaking it for some time as he poured out his thanks and congratulations with all the fervor of a heart that seemed overflowing with its fullness of joy. The scene was singularly affecting and one never to be forgotten. Mr. Lincoln said: "Do you know, General, that I have had sort of a sneaking idea for several days that you intended to do something like this?"

From this brief interview General Grant rode to the front to lead the army to its complete and final victory at Appomattox a few days later. At 4.30 P.M., April 9, General Grant telegraphed to Washington as follows:

Headquarters, Appomattox C.H., Va.
4.30 P.M., April 9, 1865.

Honorable E. M. Stanton
    Secretary of War.

General Lee surrendered the Army of Northern Virginia this afternoon on terms proposed by myself. The accompanying correspondence will show the conditions fully.

U.S. Grant,
Lieutenant-General.

That evening General Griffin, commanding the Fifth Corps, on whose staff I was serving as *aide-de-camp*, invited his staff to ride with him to General Grant's headquarters. We found the general sitting in front of his tent apparently admiring the beauty of the sunset. He arose to receive our salutations and congratulations and then said: "Gentlemen, this has been a good day's work. When Johnston learns of Lee's surrender he will surrender his army to General Sherman; then the war will be over and you can return to your homes."

Two months later the victorious and rejoicing Army of the Potomac and Sherman's glorious Army of the West were encamped side by side on Arlington Heights opposite

Washington, having marched by the way of Petersburg and Richmond and the many battlefields of northern Virginia, waiting their turn to be "mustered out" to return to their homes and their friends, and to the grateful people of the North, to receive the hearty welcome due the heroes of the great struggle.

Mr. Lincoln had made no mistake in appointing General Grant the chief in command and in resting his confidence with him. After times will wonder not at the few and unimportant mistakes Mr. Lincoln made, but at the intuitive knowledge of his duties as commander-in-chief of the national forces engaged in the most extensive, complex and difficult war of modern times.

General W.F. Smith says: "I have long held to the opinion that at the close of the war Mr. Lincoln was the superior of his generals in his comprehension of the strategic movements and the proper method of following up victories to their legitimate conclusions."

General W. T. Sherman repeatedly expressed his "admiration and surprise at the remarkable correctness of Mr. Lincoln's military views" as shown in the correspondence with his generals.

Picture Credits

Cover: Abbott Spear; pages 4, 6, 14, 15, United States Army Military History Institute; page 16, Bowdoin College; page 24, U.S.A.M.H.I.; page 43, From Deeds of Valor; page 47, U.S.A.M.H.I.; page 49, Gettysburg National Military Park; page 58, U.S.A.M.H.I.; page 60, From the National Tribune; page 74, G.N.M.P.; pages 81, 85, U.S.A.M.H.I.; page 86, Maine Historical Society; page 91, G.N.M.P.; pages 135, 182, 193, 199, 209, 214, 216, 229, 233, U.S.A.M.H.I.; page 240, Maine State Archives; page 242, Henry Deeks; page 244, Library of Congress; **Photo Gallery**: page 2, Abbott Spear; page 4, Maine Hist. Society; page 5, Bedford Hayes; page 6, Pejepscot Hist. Society; page 7, Library of Congress; pages 8, 9, 10, Maine Hist. Society; page 11, Bedford Hayes; page 12, U.S.A.M.H.I.; pages 13, 14, 15, 16, 17, 18, 19, 20, 21, Maine Hist. Society; page 22, U.S.A.M.H.I.; page 23, Bedford Hayes; page 24, Abbott Spear; pages 25, 26, Maine Hist. Society.

SELECTED BIBLIOGRAPHY

MANUSCRIPTS & ARTICLES

Augusta, Maine
  Maine State Archives
    Miscellaneous correspondence
    Photographic Collection
Bangor, Maine
  Bangor Public Library
    Reunions of the 20th Maine Assoc. 1881.
Brunswick, Maine
  Hawthorne-Longfellow Library, Special Collections
    Elisha S. Coan Papers
    Nathaniel Melcher Papers
  Pejepscot Historical Society
    John C. Chamberlain Diary
    Joshua Lawrence Chamberlain Collection
    Alice R. Trulock Collection
Cambridge, Massachusetts
  Arthur and Elizabeth Schlesinger Library, Radcliffe College, Harvard University
    Chamberlain-Adams Family Correspondence
Carlisle, Pennsylvania
  U.S. Army Military History Institute
    Manuscript Collection
    Photographic Collection
Concord, New Hampshire
  New Hampshire Historical Society
    John B. Bachelder Papers
Gettysburg, Pennsylvania
  Gettysburg National Military Park
    William C. Oates Correspondence Scrapbook
    Photographic Collection
    Ellis Spear Unpublished Memoir
    G. K. Warren Survey 1868-1869

New York, New York
   New York Public Library, Special Collections
      The Century Collection
Portland, Maine
   Maine Historical Society
      Holman S. Melcher Collection
   Portland Library
      Portland Press Newspaper
Washington, D.C.
     Library of Congress
       Joshua L. Chamberlain Collection
       National Tribune Microfilm
     National Archives
        Fifth Corps Records
        Holman S. Melcher Pension & Service Records
        Twentieth Maine Records

BOOKS

Alleman, Tillie Pierce. *At Gettysburg or What a Girl Saw and Heard of the Battle.* New York, 1889.

Beyer, W. F. *Deeds of Valor from Records in the Archives of the United States Government.* Detroit, Michigan, 1907.

Chamberlain, Joshua Lawrence. *The Passing of the Armies.* Dayton, 1981.

Gerrish, Theodore. *Army Life: A Private's Reminiscences of the War.* Introduction by Hon. Josiah H. Drummond. Portland, 1882.

Long, E.B. *The Civil War Day by Day.* New York, 1971.

Maine Adjutant General. *Annual Reports, 1861-65.* Augusta, 1862-65.

Maine at Gettysburg: Report of the Maine Commissioners, Prepared by the Executive Committee. Portland, 1898.

Oates, William C. *The War between the Union and the Confederacy and Its Lost Opportunities.* New York, 1896.

Pfanz, Harry W. *Gettysburg, The Second Day.* Chapel Hill. 1987.

Powell, William H. *History of the Fifth Army Corps (Army of the Potomac) A Record of Operations during the Civil War in the United States of America, 1861-1865.* New York, 1896.

Pullen, John J. *The Twentieth Maine: A Volunteer Regiment in the Civil War.* Philadelphia, 1957.

Ripley, William. *Vermont Riflemen in the War for the Union.* Rutland, 1883.

Trulock, Alice R. *In the Hands of Providence: Joshua Lawrence Chamberlain and the American Civil War.* Chapel Hill, 1992.

U.S. Army. Adjutant General's Office. *Proceedings, Findings, and Opinions of the Court of Inquiry in the Case of Gouverneur K. Warren.* 3 pts. Washington, D.C. 1883.

Wallace, Willard M. *Soul of the Lion: A Biography of General Joshua Lawrence Chamberlain.* New York, 1960.

Warner, Ezra J. *Generals in Blue.* Baton Rouge, 1977.

Whitman, E.S. and True, C.H. *Maine in the War for the Union.* Lewiston, 1865.

Index

Alabama infantry regiments, 44, 51-58, 94, 102-104, 110-117, 131-134, 140, 143.
Aldie, Va., 33-35, 105, 174, 257.
Alleman, Tillie Pierce, 142.
Amelia Court House, Va., 215.
Ames, Adelbert, 13, 14, 23, 27, 31, 62, 79, 105, 251, 254, 256, 277, 279, 289, 298, 299.
Antietam, battle of, 5, 105, 106, 145, 174, 252, 254, 273, 280.
Appomattox Court House, Va., 217-219, 223, 250, 273, 278, 280, 322.
Bartlett, Joseph J., 172, 216, 239, 263.
Bowdoin College, 251, 299.
Boydon Plank Road, 272.
Burkeville, Va., 220, 222, 223.
Burnside, Ambrose E., 3, 4, 17, 23, 255, 312, 313.
Butterfield, Daniel, 4, 119, 246, 249, 279, 289.
Camp Mason, 2, 251, 252.
Chamberlain, Joshua Lawrence, 5, 13, 23, 35, 37-48, 68, 69, 77, 78, 82-84, 86, 88, 100, 108, 119-128, 133, 139, 140, 143, 149, 163, 188, 190, 210, 240, 241, 246, 248, 258, 259, 260, 274, 278, 287, 289, 294-299.
Chamberlain, Thomas Davee, 189, 236.
Chancellorsville, battle of, 25-27, 105, 151, 256.
City Point, Va., 187, 192, 205, 206, 227, 320.
Coan, Elisha S., 82-84, 112, 249, 281, 287.
Crawford, Samuel W., 195, 205, 219.
Donnell, William E., 162, 163, 241, 268.
Falmouth, Va., 17, 19, 22, 230.
Five Forks, battle of, 211, 212, 223, 272, 280.
Fort Stedman, 208.
Frederick, Md., 3-5, 253.
Fredericksburg, first battle of, 10-16, 105, 174, 230, 255.

Index

Fredericksburg, second battle of, 25-28, 256.
Gerrish, Theodore, 64-72, 88, 90, 131.
Gettysburg, battle of, 36-144, 163, 174, 248, 257, 258, 259, 274, 280, 286, 294-296, 316.
Gilmore, Charles D., 13, 190, 191, 243, 271.
Gordon, John B., 218, 220, 223.
Grant, Ulysses S., 158, 217, 218, 269, 278, 291, 317-323.
Griffin, Charles, 170, 214, 223, 232, 235, 263, 267, 322.
Halleck, Henry W. 154, 229.
Hanover, Pa., 76.
Hatcher's Run, battle of, 186, 195, 196, 205, 207.
Hooker, Joseph, 17, 22, 26, 27, 30, 313-315.
Howard, Oliver O., 27, 28, 145.
Jerusalem Plank Road, 184, 271.
Keene, Samuel F., 24, 83, 112, 145, 162, 170, 269, 300.
Laurel Hill, battle of, 178, 266, 280.
Law, Evander M., 45, 50, 52-54, 101, 102, 104.
Lee, Fitzhugh, 218, 223.
Lee, Robert E., , 51, 64, 144, 158, 200, 217-219, 260, 278, 291, 302-304, 314-317, 322.
Libby Prison, 227, 229.
Lincoln, Abraham, 221, 222, 224, 302-323.
Little Round Top, 36-144, 163, 174, 248, 258, 259, 274, 280, 294, 295, 296.
Livermore, William T., 76-81, 112.
Locke, Frederick T., 189, 205.
Longstreet, James, 51, 64, 102, 105, 144, 217-219.
McClellan, George B., 17, 250, 278, 305-312.
McLaws, Lafayette, 51, 52.
Maine infantry regiments: 2d, 28; 6th, 25, 26, 154, 155, 166; 16th, 193; 19th, 194; 20th, 1-49, 59-62, 64-72, 74-146, 149-156, 158-181, 186, 188, 191, 208, 226, 231, 236-238, 245-301.
Malbon, Joseph H., 185, 193, 204, 209, 238.

Meade, George G., 96, 97, 196, 205, 206, 215, 229, 239, 315-317.
Medal of Honor, 294-296.
Melcher, Holman S., 2, 5, 7, 8, 14, 16, 18, 22, 25, 27, 29, 31, 33, 35, 36, 37, 69, 83, 84, 88-90, 103, 115, 122, 132-135, 139, 143, 144, 146, 150, 155, 156, 158, 162, 164, 166, 168-180, 181, 185, 186, 204, 213, 218, 237, 245, 247, 248, 249, 266, 275, 277, 279, 281, 288, 289, 291-293.
Melcher, Nathaniel, 2, 3, 5, 10, 17, 22, 25, 27, 29, 32, 33, 144, 148, 151, 154, 159, 162, 164, 166, 180, 183, 184, 188, 194, 195, 199, 212, 217, 228, 231, 236, 239, 241, 243.
Military Order of the Loyal Legion, 168, 292.
Mine Run, 151-154, 174, 262.
Morrell, William W., 178, 181, 266.
Morrill, Walter G., 39, 42, 48, 49, 59, 66, 77, 80, 83, 101, 117, 133, 143, 156, 236, 265, 273.
Morse, Hiram, 181.
New York, N.Y., 146, 243.
New York Herald, 20, 218-220.
Norton, Oliver W., 297-299.
Oates, William C., 50-61, 104, 107, 109, 110, 113, 116-118, 133, 143.
Petersburg, Va., 184, 208, 211, 212, 227, 250, 269, 291, 321.
Porter, Fitz John, 5, 253, 290.
Portland, Me., 5, 155, 234, 236, 243, 247, 248, 273, 279, 281, 292, 293.
Rappahannock Station, Va., 148, 151, 154, 155, 159, 162, 164, 178, 262, 263.
Richmond, Va., 44, 185, 227-230.
Shaw, Abner O., 191, 281.
Sheridan, Philip H., 210-212, 223, 234, 289, 320.
Sickles, Daniel E., 65.
South Mountain, 4, 6, 145.

Spear, Ellis, 59-62, 92, 107, 114, 115, 139, 142, 189, 226, 236, 264, 270-272, 275, 287-289, 294, 297-301.
Spottsylvania Court House, Va., battle of, 266, 267.
Sykes, George, 99, 109, 145, 253.
Tozier, Andrew J., 112, 247, 249.
Vincent, Strong, 32, 39, 44, 59, 100, 103, 124, 126, 127, 132, 256, 298, 299.
Warren, Gouverneur K., 59, 98, 99, 126, 163, 169, 182, 186, 187, 195-197, 200, 203, 206, 210, 223, 227, 261, 263.
Washington, D.C., 2, 3, 28, 180, 181, 190, 228, 231-234, 238, 273.
Wilderness, battle of, 158, 168-181, 264.